STUDYING POETRY

STEPHEN MATTERSON

Senior Lecturer in American Literature,
Trinity College Dublin

and

DARRYL JONES

Lecturer in English, Trinity College Dublin

A member of the Hodder Headline Group
LONDON
Copublished in the United States of America by
Oxford University Press Inc., New York

First published in Great Britain in 2000 by
Arnold, a member of the Hodder Headline Group,
338 Euston Road, London NW1 3BH

http://www.arnoldpublishers.com

Co-published in the United States of America by
Oxford University Press Inc.,
198 Madison Avenue, New York, NY10016

British Library Cataloguing in Publication Data
A catalogue record for this book is available from the British Library

Library of Congress Cataloging-in-Publication Data
A catalog record for this book is available from the Library of Congress

ISBN 0 340 75941 0 (hb)
ISBN 0 340 75942 9 (pb)

1 2 3 4 5 6 7 8 9 10

Production Editor: Rada Radojicic
Production Controller: Iain McWilliams
Cover Design: Terry Griffiths

Typeset in 10 on 12 pt Sabon by Cambrian Typesetters, Frimley, Surrey
Printed and bound in Great Britain by MPG Books, Bodmin, Cornwall

What do you think about this book? Or any other Arnold title?
Please send your comments to feedback.arnold@hodder.co.uk

Contents

Acknowledgements

Grateful acknowledgement is made to copyright holders for permission to quote the following: 'Let's Hear it for Goliath' from *Out of Wales: Fifty Poems 1973–1983*, by Jon Dressel, reprinted by permission of Alun Books; 'Annus Mirabilis' from *High Windows*, by Philip Larkin, quoted with permission from Faber and Faber Ltd; 'If I Could Tell You' from *Collected Poems* by W. H. Auden, quoted with permission from Faber and Faber Ltd; 'Records' from *The Dolphin* by Robert Lowell, quoted with permission from Faber and Faber Ltd.

We would like to thank a number of people for their (sometimes unwitting) contributions to this book; in particular, Terence Brown, John Coggrave, Patrick Crotty, Bob Jones, Dewi and Yvonne Jones, Stuart Murray, John Nash, Amanda Piesse, Brin Price, Ian Campbell Ross, Madeleine Ruth, Elena Seymenliyska, Christina Wipf-Perry and, collectively, the students who have participated in our course 'Poetry: Form, Language, Interpretation' since it began in 1995.

Since this book is very much a joint venture, a note on our method of collaborating is appropriate. Each chapter was written by only one of us, but before the first draft was produced we worked closely together to determine the scope of each chapter, and afterwards worked to try and make chapters fairly consistent in terms of style and tone. Stephen Matterson is primarily responsible for the Introduction, Chapters 4, 5, 6 and 9 and the final section of 8, and Darryl Jones for Chapters 1, 2, 3, 7 and 8. It is likely the reader will perceive the different authorship because of the range of poems that we tend to draw on for examples and the way our different literary and theoretical interests are engaged, but, to adapt Mark Twain's 'Explanatory' to *The Adventures of Huckleberry Finn*, we did not want readers to suppose that the authors were trying to sound alike and not succeeding.

Darryl Jones would like to dedicate his share of the book to Margaret Robson and Miss Morgan Elizabeth Hannah Jones, age 4, with love.

Introduction

When readers first opened *The Oxford Book of Modern Verse 1892–1935* edited by W. B. Yeats, they were probably surprised to find that the first piece in it was by Walter Pater.

MONA LISA

She is older than the rocks among which she sits;
Like the Vampire,
She has been dead many times,
And learned the secrets of the grave;
And has been a diver in deep seas,
And keeps their fallen day about her;
And trafficked for strange webs with Eastern merchants;
And, as Leda,
Was the mother of Helen of Troy,
And, as St Anne,
Was the mother of Mary;
And all this has been to her but as the sound of lyres and flutes,
And lives
Only in the delicacy
With which it has moulded the changing lineaments,
And tinged the eyelids and the hands.

Yeats had taken one prose sentence from Pater's essay 'Leonardo Da Vinci' and arranged it as though it had been written as a poem. Pater's words were certainly very well known; however surprised readers of Yeats's anthology may have been to find them arranged as a poem, they probably knew the words themselves – in fact, they had already appeared in Arthur Quiller-Couch's *Oxford Book of English Prose* (1925). There, they are printed thus:

She is older than the rocks among which she sits; like the vampire, she has been dead many times, and learned the secrets of the grave; and has been a diver in deep seas, and keeps their fallen day about her; and trafficked for strange webs with Eastern merchants; and, as Leda, was the mother of Helen of Troy, and, as Saint Anne, the mother of Mary; and all this has been to her but as the sound of lyres and flutes, and lives only in the delicacy with which it has moulded the changing lineaments, and tinged the eyelids and the hands.

While he has capitalized 'vampire' and abbreviated 'Saint', the only actual word change that Yeats made was to add the word 'was' to begin the line 'Was the mother of Mary'. By way of introduction to *Studying Poetry* it is worth briefly considering both the mechanics and the implications of what Yeats did. The mechanics involve the formal elements of poetry, which are the chief concern of the first third of this book. The implications include issues of readership, authorship, interpretation, historical context, and the very ontology of the poem (that is, its particular way of being), which are discussed in the second and third sections of this study.

In terms of the poem's mechanics, we would need to consider the formal properties that Yeats has either added or emphasized, properties that may be said traditionally to distinguish prose from poetry. How has Yeats made a piece of prose into a poem? There are at least five ways in which he has done this or, to put it in a slightly but fundamentally different way, he has given the reader at least five cues to read this piece as a poem and not as prose. Firstly, the piece is here placed in an anthology of poetry. Secondly, he has given it a title. Thirdly, he has made the piece appear as if it were a self-contained unit rather than an extract from something longer – it is the length we might expect a lyric poem to be. Fourthly, he has arranged the lines so that a parallelism of form and structure is apparent. Fifthly, he has broken up the continuous prose into shorter lines and, at the same time, has capitalized the first letter of each line.

Some of these points may seem so obvious as to be redundant. Or again, to put it differently, they may seem so obvious that they are rarely commented on. The fifth point, that Yeats has varied the lengths of the lines, may seem the most observable difference between the piece as a poem and the piece as prose, but we should not neglect the other, perhaps more subtle cues: more subtle because we may take them more for granted and not stop to question them. When he changed the lines into shorter ones, Yeats also brought out (or did he create?) the rhythm inherent in the language, and he also made prominent a feature which is actually one of the basic elements we associate with a poem: some sort of formal repetition or parallelism. Thus there are nine lines which begin with the word 'And', two with 'She' and two with 'Was'. Yeats, then, did not just print the sentence as prose and ask us to give attention to it as if it were a poem. He formal-ized or made more apparent some of the patterns that the sentence already possessed, and he invited us to read it as a poem by encoding a series of elements that the reader expects in poetry. When it appears in the poem the reader may notice that line 4, 'And learned the secrets of the grave' is a regular iambic tetrameter, while it is unlikely that this would be apparent when the line appears as prose. There is also a powerful rhythmic effect due to the 15 monosyllabic words of line 12; again, an effect that would probably go unnoticed in prose.

What about some of the broader implications of what Yeats has done? Yeats's 'Mona Lisa' can be classified as a particular type of poem, the 'found' poem, where a piece of writing not intended as a poem is presented as if it were one. Many of the implications that arise from this poem, then, also grow out of found poetry. Some of them involve authorship, or readership, or the status of poetry as knowledge. For instance, who is the author of this poem? Is it Pater, because he is the acknowledged author of the words themselves? Is it Yeats? He made the prose into a poem, and if it is to be considered a poem, then it is surely his. Was Yeats being generous in attributing this poem to Walter Pater rather than to himself? Was he being appropriately cautious in respect of the legal issue of copyright? Can we do to a piece of prose what Yeats did and call it a poem? Would anyone believe us if we did? Who is the reader? Yeats has invited us to read these words as a poem rather than as prose and in so doing has constructed a different kind of reader. After all, readers opening a book titled *The Oxford Book of Modern Verse* expect to find poems in it, not prose. We are different readers of these words as a poem than we were when we read them as prose. We give each word more weight, more study than we did; we hear the rhythms of the words differently, we find the words more memorable and more resonant. Certainly if we consider poetry as language charged with an excess of meaning, or, as Ezra Pound saw it, as language at its most concentrated, then this poem fits the definition. But the words themselves have not substantially changed: what has changed is the kind of attention we give to them. To extend the question of authorship, could we even say that with Yeats's mediation, it is we, the readers, who make this poem? That is, in giving the words a kind of attention appropriate to reading poetry, are we in fact makers of the poem?

There are a lot of questions being asked here, there are many more that could be, and it is the purpose of this book, if not precisely to answer them, then at least to alert readers to the existence of the questions and some of the answers that have been given to them. That is, one of the aims of this book is to help readers become selfconscious about the act of reading poetry. At this point, some outline of how this book came into being might be helpful in elucidating its scope and its aims.

This book has its roots in a course called 'Poetry: Form, Language, Interpretation' taken by first-year undergraduates in English Studies at Trinity College, the University of Dublin. When the English Studies curriculum was extensively revised in the early to mid-1990s, the School Committee decided that a one-term (nine-week) course devoted to poetry would be desirable. It recognized that some students often had difficulties in approaching poetry and were often hesitant about how to read, understand, evaluate and write critically about it. 'Poetry: Form, Language, Interpretation' was devoted to the genre, and not to a particular period or theme or poetic movement, nor to practical criticism exercises. It was about how the genre had developed and changed, and what were considered its distinguishing characteristics.

The course had two principal aims. The first was to foster the development of the students' knowledge and critical vocabulary relating to poetry. Thus we wanted students to be familiar with the patterns of poetry and with the technical terms involved with them. We wanted students to know the difference (or at least know that there was one and know that it mattered) between a sestina and a villanelle, between iamb and dactyl, and between a metaphor and a symbol. The second aim was to help the students become selfconscious readers of poetry.

The first aim could be fulfilled in a relatively straightforward way (in spite of the perceived challenge of making metrics interesting). First-year students are used to being taught, used to being told things and learning them. (It is a truth universally acknowledged that one of the challenges of teaching first-year university students in the humanities is to rid them of the idea that they are passive receivers of information.) The second aim, of developing selfconsciousness, was much less straightforward. The problem, and naturally this was why this aim was built into the course, was not that the students knew nothing about poetry but rather that in a relatively unselfconscious way they held a set of preconceptions and assumptions about it. The way that poetry had usually been mediated to them in the classroom mainly had to do with the author, the historical context, the poetic language. Usually the teaching method reinforced seldom-examined assumptions about the presence of the author, the importance of sincerity, the belief that the poem was a paraphrasable unit of knowledge. Generally, since students had had little opportunity to reflect on the assumptions they brought to poetry, they tended not to see these even as assumptions but as *the* ways of seeing poetry.

As we taught the students in the first years of the course, which started in 1995, we could see that they were fairly comfortable with poems which did not challenge their assumptions. (Teaching was by a weekly lecture with related small-group tutorials.) But when given, say, a poem that seemed to have no 'content' or no discernible 'message', such as a concrete poem or a language poem or a number poem or even a found poem, the general reaction was to dismiss it as at worst a silly or irritating waste of time and at best an interesting experiment which we could enjoy before turning back to real poetry. Dispiriting as such reactions could be, the situation was ameliorated considerably during the academic year as the students themselves became more sophisticated. Since this also relates to a distinguishing feature of *Studying Poetry*, it also needs some explanation.

The revised English Studies syllabus which saw the introduction of 'Poetry: Form, Language, Interpretation' also saw the initiation of a compulsory first-year course, 'Critical and Cultural Theory', running for the academic year and introducing the students to theoretical concepts and movements. From the first, 'Poetry: Form, Language, Interpretation' was developed to be closely related to 'Critical and Cultural Theory' in the belief that the overlap would be beneficial to the students in both courses. Ideally, the student would be learning about, say, New Criticism in one class while in another being invited to reflect on how New Critical practice endorsed a certain kind of poem. Accordingly, the second and third parts of *Studying Poetry* incorporate some specific aspects of critical theoretical movements: broadly, at least, from New Criticism to deconstruction. The book is not intended to be a primer of critical theory. We look at New Criticism, Formalism, Reception Theory, aspects of structuralism and post-structuralism and New Historicism, and the book constantly returns to the theoretical claims made for poetry by Romanticism and Modernism. This is because these have been more influential than other theories in defining the terms in which poetry has been studied. While other theoretical movements such as feminism, post-colonialism or psychoanalysis receive less attention here, at the same time we emphasize that the study of poetry cannot be divorced from an awareness of theoretical positions taken with regard to literature.

We hope that after taking our 'Poetry: Form, Language, Interpretation' course, students will have developed an awareness of poetry as a distinct genre, will be confident in using the critical vocabulary pertaining to poetry, will feel more assured about reading and evaluating poems, will be open to the varieties of poetry, responsive to the nuances of the language that poets use, alert to the broader implications of studying poetry, and will have become imaginative and sensitive readers. While this list stops just short of wishing them also to be better citizens and kind to animals, it may sound idealistic, nevertheless it is what we would also hope for the readers of *Studying Poetry*.

PART

I

FORM AND MEANING

|1|

Poem and form

It ain't what you do, it's the way that you do it.
That's what gets results.

Bananarama[1]

The meaning of form

It is impossible to discuss poetry, or even to understand it, without some knowledge of poetic form. Form is, or should be, the starting-point of any analysis of poetry, because its form distinguishes poetry from other kinds of writing or communication. Whilst students are occasionally even now required to memorize and have a basic working knowledge of metrical forms – the iamb, dactyl or spondee – and are certainly required to recognize the basic specific forms of poetry – a sonnet, blank verse, an ode, free verse – nevertheless, the *meaning* of poetic form, *why* a poem looks the way it does, and what significance this might have for the poem, may not be subjects frequently addressed in the classroom or seminar. Poetic form is sometimes considered an abstruse subject, difficult to understand; in extreme cases it may be considered a distraction, an unnecessary complexity, a barrier between reader and text, or else as an index of a kind of old-fashioned education, drilling students in Latin grammar or the mysteries of Renaissance prosody – perhaps seen as an irrelevance to many contemporary readers or students.

The *content* of poetry (what is often mistakenly called its *meaning*), conversely, is often thought of as easy to understand, and therefore as sufficient in itself, all we need to know about a poem: poetry *is* its content. This is an inherently reductive view, which can lead to meaningless generalizations of what poems are 'about', ignoring what they are, or what they do. For example, one might say that William Shakespeare's Sonnet 18 ('Shall I compare thee to a summer's day?') is 'about' love, John Donne's Divine

Meditation 'Death be not proud' is 'about' death, William Wordsworth's 'Tintern Abbey' ('Lines Composed a Few Miles Above Tintern Abbey on Revisiting the Banks of the Wye During a Tour. July 13, 1798', to give it its full, unwieldy title) is 'about' nature, and so on. Now, none of these statements is *wrong*, and not to recognize these thematic concerns would risk serious misreadings; nevertheless, by themselves they are inadequate as responses to the complex verbal artefacts they describe. It could fairly be argued, though, that the 'meanings' we have just offered of these poems are travesties ('subjects', perhaps, rather than 'meanings'). *Of course* there is more to them than that; but even expanded to considerable length, these kinds of content-based analyses can leave much to be desired. This is 'Death be not proud' in full:

> Death be not proud, though some have called thee
> Mighty and dreadful, for, thou art not so,
> For, those, whom thou think'st, thou dost overthrow,
> Die not, poor death, nor yet cans't thou kill me;
> From rest and sleep, which but thy pictures be,
> Much pleasure, then from thee, much more must flow,
> And soonest our best men with thee do go,
> Rest of their bones, and soul's delivery.
> Thou art slave to fate, chance, kings and desperate men,
> And dost with poison, war, and sickness dwell,
> And poppy, or charms can make us sleep as well,
> And better than thy stroke; why swell'st thou then?
> One short sleep past, we wake eternally,
> And death shall be no more. Death, thou shalt die.[2]

Read purely for its content, the poem is clearly a refutation of death's power: 'Death' here is personified as an individual with whom the speaker of the poem is in debate. Death is overcome, at least for the duration of the poem, initially through the force of logic, albeit the superficially plausible, playfully false logic, or sophistry, for which Donne is celebrated. Given that 'rest and sleep', diluted forms of death (its 'pictures' – 'emblems' or 'types' of death: Donne is drawing here on the Renaissance critical theory of typology, in which meanings are understood as 'types' of a pre-existing pattern, usually religious),[3] give 'Much pleasure, then from thee, much more must flow'. This is a kind of rhetorical argument known as *a fortiori* – 'If X is so, then how much more must Y be so' – an argument returned to and expanded upon in lines 11–12, where death's power is rhetorically imaged as *inferior* to opiates ('poppy') or 'charms'. Death, far from being all-powerful, is a 'slave', its strike governed by the dictates or whims of 'fate, chance, kings and desperate men'; far, too, from being 'mighty and dreadful', death is degraded, even seedy, dwelling with 'poison, war and sickness'. The closing couplet, returning at first to the death–sleep metaphor which the poem has established, clinches its argument, as we knew it would (because of the assumptions, as readers, that we tend to make about the world-view of Renaissance poetry), by recourse to the resurrection of the body in the afterlife, which, in a logical paradox transcended by religious faith, turns death's power back upon itself: 'Death, thou shalt die'.

This is what the poem is 'about' – in effect, we have paraphrased its meaning here. Nothing in the reading we have offered is 'wrong', but as a reading it is inadequate as it fails to account for why 'Death be not proud' is a *poem* – while accounting for what it is 'about', it does not account for what it is. This reading, in other words, could just as easily be an account of a rhetorical argument in prose. On a broad thematic level, this type of reading also makes it difficult to distinguish between different kinds of poem: there are many poems about the triumph of death through the resurrection of the body – for example Gerard Manley Hopkins' 'That nature is a Heraclitean fire', a poem about which a purely content-based analysis has very little to say beyond commonplace banalities; or Dylan Thomas's 'And death shall have no dominion':

> And death shall have no dominion.
> Dead men naked they shall be one
> With the man in the wind and the west moon; . . .
> Though they sink through the sea they shall rise again;
> Though lovers be lost love shall not;
> And death shall have no dominion.[4]

On a thematic level, the level of content, 'Death be not proud' and 'And death shall have no dominion' seem very similar: both refutations of death's permanence through recourse to the resurrection of the body. Conceivably, a reasonably effective student essay of the 'compare and contrast' variety could be produced by yoking them together. But such a reading would further have to account for the fact that they are, clearly, very different poems. The logic of Donne's rhetoric is fairly easily abstractable from its poetic context and can be paraphrased for a 'meaning' – this is one of the reasons why Donne, and Metaphysical poetry in general, has traditionally been a favourite target for 'practical criticism' exercises, where a single poem is given, often without a poet's name appended, to a class for study (this is a technique for the study of poetry which we will look at more closely in Chapter 4).

'And death shall have no dominion', however, like much of Thomas's earlier poetry, seems to resist any attempts at paraphrase – what, exactly, could 'the man in the wind and the west moon' mean? Is it a metaphor, or a symbol? If so, for what? Try to isolate the poem from its own linguistic frame, try to study it in any terms other than those of poetic form, as a poem about itself, or about poetry, or the production of poetic language, and the poem falls apart, leaving us only with vague statements about rebirth. Nor should this necessarily be seen as a fault in the Thomas poem – if anything, 'And death shall have no dominion' is the 'purer' poetic artefact, a poem which resists discussion except on its own terms. Certainly, as the word 'pure' here implies, it is a poem far more in keeping with the ideas of one poetic theory, 'la poésie pure' – 'pure poetry' – developed by the French symbolist poets in the late nineteenth century (Mallarmé, Baudelaire and others). Influenced by the poetic theories and practice of Edgar Allan Poe, these poets believed that poetry should come as close as possible to music, and should be as far as possible devoid of an extractable semantic meaning, reliant on sound alone, an idea which Ezra Pound also endorsed: 'poetry begins to atrophy when it gets too far from music'.[5]

Any parallel reading of these two poems would also have to take account of the great historical gap between them: Donne is a Renaissance poet, a contemporary of Shakespeare, writing on the cusp of the sixteenth and seventeenth centuries; Dylan Thomas is a twentieth-century Modernist. In spite of Pound's famous dictum that 'Literature is news that STAYS news',[6] recent critical theories, as Chapter 7 will show, have cast serious doubt on the 'transhistorical' or 'universal' qualities traditionally understood as a given quality of literary value. Given that the two poems are separated by over 300 years, and given the very different attitudes to religion, death, and for that matter poetry, of the ages in which they were produced, do these poems *really* have that much in common beyond a common, generalized thematic concern? This kind of universalizing attitude to poetry also runs the risk of turning it into no more than a handy compendium of insights into 'the human condition', essentially indistinguishable from philosophy or theology, albeit more memorably phrased: like many grand soundbites on the provenance of poetry, Alexander Pope's celebrated axiom, 'What oft was *Thought*, but ne'er so well *Exprest*', is a sonorous half-truth.[7]

Samuel Taylor Coleridge, in his *Biographia Literaria* (1817), a hugely influential though characteristically eccentric work of poetics which draws heavily on the ideas of German Romantic philosophy, understood the creative process, and its product, poetry, as 'organic', like a living thing made of interdependent parts.[8] This idea was further developed in this century by the New Critics, whose work will be discussed in Chapter 4, who argued that the relationship between a poem's form and content is itself organic, that each is contingent upon the other, and that one cannot be dissociated from, or discussed without, the other: they exist dialectically.

The most extreme implication of this kind of thinking is that form *is* content. Indeed, according to the critical theory known as Formalism, literature is nothing *but* its form, as it is only this which distinguishes it from other kinds of communication. In the famous words of the linguist Roman Jakobson, literature is 'organized violence committed on everyday speech'![9] Poetry, as the most selfconsciously artificial deployment of language, is thus the most 'literary' of forms. A similar theory was offered by Ezra Pound, who wrote that 'Great literature is simply language charged with meaning to the utmost possible degree', and that poetry is 'the most concentrated form of verbal expression'.[10] According to Pound, then, poetry is *condensed* language, language 'charged' with a surplus of meaning, a super-abundance of meaning, language which does not simply denote its object. Similarly, poetic language is characterized for the poet and critic William Empson by *ambiguity*, by its ability to contain a multiplicity of meanings.[11] Crucial to all these ideas is a heavy reliance on *metaphor* as a defining characteristic of poetry, an idea which will be the subject of Chapter 3. A dialectical theory of metaphor, and one which can easily be applied to form/content, was offered by I. A. Richards, who reintroduced the concepts of 'tenor' (what is meant) and 'vehicle' (what is said) – which had been included in Dr Johnson's *Dictionary* in the eighteenth century – as the combinatory elements of metaphor.[12] One could think of a poem as a whole as being indissolubly made up of its tenor (content) and its vehicle (form). One of the clearest accounts of Formalist 'literariness' is this one, by Terry Eagleton:

> If you approach me at a bus stop and murmur 'Thou still unravished bride of quietness', then I am instantly aware that I am in the presence of the literary. I know this because the texture, rhythm and resonance of your words are in excess of their abstractable meaning – or, as the linguists might more technically put it, there is a disproportion between the signifiers and the signifieds. Your language draws attention to itself, flaunts its material being, as statements like 'Don't you know that the drivers are on strike?' do not.[13]

As we noted, content-based analyses of poetry are based on the idea of paraphrase. Cleanth Brooks, a leading light amongst the New Critics, whose theories remain dominant in the teaching of poetry, at least in schools, wrote of 'The Heresy of Paraphrase'. The implication here is that to paraphrase is to commit an effective act of blasphemy, or of violation, upon the poem, a removal from it of all that is poetic.[14] It is true that paraphrasing is, at best, reductionist, when, as the examples of poetic theory we have referred to above all argue, poetry, if anything, exhibits a refusal to have its meaning reduced to one thing.

To paraphrase poetry is to perform an act of translation, from one medium (poetry) into another (prose). In his *Defence of Poetry*, Shelley wrote of 'the vanity of translation. It were as wise to cast a violet into a crucible that you might discover the formal principle of its colour and odour, as seek to transfuse from one language to another the creations of a poet.'[15] As a warning against the problems and the inadequacy of translation, consider the following stanzas:

1
With his fiftieth birthday behind him, a man sees with fair clarity
The people and surroundings that made him what he is,
And the steel ropes that tether me strongest to these things
In a village of the South, are the graves in two cemeteries.

2
Reaching fifty, a man has time to recognize
His ordinary humanity, the common echoes
In his own voice. And I think with compassion
Of the graves of friends who died . . .[16]

Looking at these two excerpts, we might be struck by their similarity, both of theme – meditations on age and on belonging, reflections on the passing of friends, both common enough poetic themes – and, more strongly, by the close similarities of diction here, especially in the first lines: 'With his fiftieth birthday behind him, a man sees . . .'; 'Reaching fifty, a man has . . .' Is there enough here for us to make explicit connections between the two? Is one influenced by the other? Is one a direct response to the other? If so, which one? Or, can we argue for a shared 'intertextuality' here? – that both poems resemble each other in their partaking of common poetic tropes, that they resemble each other so closely because they are the same kind of poem, and thus tend to adopt the same kinds of language, a shared vocabulary? Or might readers agree on their similarity because, as readers of poetry, they are attuned to every nuance of language (reading, in fact, precisely for nuances of language) and are thus on the lookout for patterns and connections; might we, as readers, recognize the similarities because we belong to a shared 'interpretive community', and thus share common expectations in reading?

But, then again, we might attend to the poems' manifest differences, the ways in which they are not the same. The first poem deals in particulars and specifics – 'the people and surroundings that made him what he is', 'steel ropes', 'a village in the South', 'graves in two cemeteries'; we might want to say that its language and metre are rawer, harsher, grimmer. The second poem deal in universals – 'ordinary humanity', 'common echoes'; its rhythm is more modulated, one might say more elegant or even 'poetic'; its tone more wistful. Thus, the differences might strike us as much as the similarities, though they may not be as immediate. This exercise, then, would be another response to those kinds of exam questions that begin 'Compare and contrast . . .'.

So far, so good. However, to what extent might our attitude to the poems be different when we discover that they are in fact both translations, and translations of the *same* poem? The poem is 'Y Meirwon' ('The Dead'), by the Welsh-language poet Gwenallt; the translations are by Tony Conran and Leslie Norris respectively, both substantial (English-language) poets in their own right. Yet they are obviously very different poems: as with the 'Mona Lisa' excerpt from the Introduction, these examples raise issues of authorship and authority – are they, in fact, the 'same' poem, in spite of their verbal, tonal and syntactic differences, or are they 'different' poems, written by Conran and Norris rather than Gwenallt? A reader could go further and ask whether the poems might not, in fact, be incomparable? Do the differences in form and style here make for *entirely* different poems, irrespective of their common origin? Language, as contemporary theorists argue, is inherently slippery or unstable, never saying precisely what we intend it to mean (our signifiers tend to float free from our signifieds). Translation, be it from one language to another, or from one medium to another within the same language, is fraught with perils. As with the above examples, it can be fruitful for analysis, but requires caution.

Awareness of form, then, is absolutely crucial if we are to be able to talk about poetry at all, for without this awareness we cannot even account for our recognition that poetry *is* poetry, rather than prose. Beyond this first stage comes the recognition that poetic forms are not neutral entities, each carrying the same value, and hence meaning, as the other. Rather, they can be said to contain their own ideologies, and poetry is often the site of ideological struggle or hidden premises. (As is criticism: the New Critical valorization of the lyric as the dominant poetic form is due in part to the fact that the lyric, which can relatively easily be understood as a free-standing verbal object, is teachable in class in a way that, say, the epic or narrative poem is not.) Crudely put, different poetic forms mean different things, irrespective of the specifics of individual poems. On a simple level, a reader should instantly know, before a word of the poetry is read or understood, that an ode to Queen Elizabeth II and a limerick about Queen Elizabeth II presuppose radically different attitudes to their subject. The former suggests a serious, celebratory formality and ostentation, the latter jocularity or even hostility; an elegy written about the Queen presupposes that she is dead (or, in the hands of a republican, it might presuppose satire).

Sometimes form and content can be in direct conflict. In 1984, Bruce Springsteen released the song 'Born in the USA', a bitter account, realized through the story of a Vietnam veteran, of the state in which America, under the current Reagan administration, found itself: 'Born down in a dead man's town / First kick I took was when I hit the ground' is the song's opening couplet; its chorus, the obsessively repeated 'BORN in the USA!', was surely intended as a sardonic comment (though, as a later chapter will show, issues of intentionality are notoriously tricky).[17] Springsteen's liberal political stance was a matter of public record, as was his antipathy towards president Ronald Reagan: in 1982, in the middle of Reagan's first presidential term, Springsteen released *Nebraska*, a depressing collection which included several Murder Ballads,[18] recorded acoustically, in stark contrast to the usual, joyous E-Street Band arrangements of Springsteen's songs. In 1984, Reagan was up for re-election, and on the campaign trail in Springsteen's home state of New Jersey he gave a speech which included the following remarks:

America's future rests in a thousand dreams inside your hearts. It rests in the message of hope in the songs of a man so many young Americans admire: New Jersey's Bruce Springsteen. And helping you make those dreams come true is what this job of mine is all about.[19]

It is fair to say that much of the song's popularity in the middle 1980s, when Springsteen really became a major popular figure, stemmed from an ostensible misreading of its lyrics: 'BORN in the USA!' was taken as a statement of patriotism, and the song soon became an occasion for flag-waving and even jingoism: 'Clearly the key to the enormous explosion in Bruce's popularity is the misunderstanding [of the song 'Born in the USA']. He is a tribute to the fact that people hear what they want', the music critic Greil Marcus wrote.[20]

But did the song's audience really 'hear what they want[ed]'? Partly, but it seems also that their response was governed by the dictates of the song's form. It is an anthem, and thus traditionally a vehicle for patriotic assertion, a patriotism given further credence by Springsteen's own semiotics, the iconography of the *Born in the USA* album sleeve: Levi's, baseball cap, Stars and Stripes. The song's emotions, anger and bitterness, were transformed into aggressive national pride; the song's content – its lyric – was overwhelmed and even reversed by its anthemic form.[21] Springsteen seems himself to have realized this, and has latterly taken to performing the song as a downbeat, muted acoustic blues number, a form far more congruent with its lyrical content.

One can talk of poetry as deploying an 'appropriate' or 'significant' form,[22] a form which comments upon, endorses, heightens, undermines or otherwise exists in a dynamic tension with its content. William Blake's poems from the *Songs of Innocence and Experience* are often read and studied, but what is less often understood is the significance of the formal source upon which Blake draws, Isaac Watts's collection *Divine Songs for Children* (1715). Throughout the eighteenth century, this volume was used as a didactic tool to inculcate into children the ethics of dissenting Christianity (that is, those forms of Protestantism which refused to accept the authority of the established church). Blake, himself from a dissenting home, knew the volume well, and uses it as the formal basis for his own *Songs*. Nor was Blake alone in drawing on Watts for formal inspiration: Lewis Carroll's rhyme 'How doth the little crocodile' in *Alice in Wonderland* is an overt parody of Watts's 'Against Idleness and Mischief', which opens 'How doth the little busy bee'.[23] Parody can frequently be understood as an interpretation of the original, which draws out, by using the same form, absurdities or pomposities inherent in its original – it can thus be a form of correction.

Watts's *Songs*, like many of Blake's, use a standard song metre of iambic tetrameters (eight-syllable lines with stresses on alternating syllables), or alternating tetrameters and iambic trimeters (six-syllable lines), with an abab or abcb rhyme scheme – a 'simple' form intended to be put to music for mnemonic purposes. (Blake himself frequently composed his poetry whilst singing; as, later, did Yeats.) What is notable about Watts's songs is the dissonance between the simple, childlike form and the astonishing violence of the rhetoric and imagery marshalled here for the education of children (who are, it seems, to be terrified into religious belief): Watts consistently images forth a vengeful, Old Testament God with a particular taste for dismembering children. The songs are typically constructed around moral homilies or lessons, such as 'Against Scoffing and Calling Names':

> Our tongues were made to bless the Lord,
> And not speak ill of men;
> When others give a railing word
> We must not rail again.
>
> Cross words and angry names require
> To be chastis'd at school;
> And he's in danger of hell-fire
> That calls his brother Fool.
>
> But lips that dare be so profane
> To mock and jeer and scoff,
> At holy things or holy men,
> The Lord shall cut them off.
>
> When children in their wanton play
> Serv'd old Elisha so,
> And bid the prophet go his way,
> 'Go up, thou bald head, go.'
>
> God quickly stopped their wicked breath,
> And sent two raging bears,
> That tore them limb from limb to death,
> With blood and groans and tears.
>
> Great God! How terrible art thou
> To sinners, e'er so young!
> Grant me thy grace, and teach me how
> To tame and rule my tongue.[24]

Violence against children is also consistently imaged forth in Blake's songs, with their cast of chimney-sweepers, slaves and orphans. But Blake, recognizing the dissonance of form and content, turns this into an ideological statement or weapon – the 'innocence' of the form comments upon the institutionalized brutality (by church, state, parents, employers) of children which the poems describe. In 'A Little Boy Lost', a free-thinking child is tortured by a priest:

> The weeping child could not be heard;
> The weeping parents wept in vain –
> They stripped him to his little shirt
> And bound him in an iron chain,
>
> And burned him in a holy place,
> Where many had been burned before.

> The weeping parents wept in vain –
> Are such things done on Albion's shore?[25]

Even more explicitly, Blake's *Songs* can turn Watts's homilies on their heads
by deploying not only the same form and imagery, but the same diction.
Where Watts had written in 'Praise for the Gospel',

> Lord, I ascribe it to thy grace,
> And not to chance as others do,
> That I was born of Christian race,
> And not a heathen or a Jew.[26]

Blake writes in 'The Divine Image',

> And all must love the human form
> In heathen, Turk or Jew.
> Where mercy, love and pity dwell
> There God is dwelling too.[27]

Thus, there are multiple dialectics operating in the *Songs of Innocence and
Experience*, between the two halves of the collection itself, 'Songs of
Innocence' and 'Songs of Experience' (conceived of as 'Showing the Two
Contrary States of the Human Soul'), between Blake's *Songs* and their
source, Watts's *Songs*, and, perhaps most strikingly, within individual
poems themselves, between simple, childlike form and brutal content.

Poetic forms can be used as means of stressing rather than undermining
content. Given that forms carry their own ideologies, it follows that certain
forms will be more appropriate, or more enriching, than others for certain
subjects. As with the examples given above from Springsteen and Blake, this
is often contingent upon historical and generic knowledge, a knowledge of
the history and past meaning of form, and a knowledge of the significance
of poetic tradition, which is to be the subject of Chapter 3. In that chapter,
we will examine why, when Tony Harrison came to write *v.* (1985), his
great 'state of the nation' poem on unemployment, class, alienation and
urban despair in the 1980s England of Margaret Thatcher, he chose to use
the form and metre of Thomas Gray's 'Elegy Written in a Country
Churchyard', long considered one of the defining poems of 'Englishness'.
This, too, would be an example of the kind of tension or conflict that the
choice of a given form can create, in a manner analogous to Blake and
Watts.

Chapter 3 will also look at how, when Milton came to write an elegy for
his friend Edward King, *Lycidas* (1638), the form provided a necessary
distancing effect, or objectivity, allowing emotion – in this instance,
personal grief – to be channelled into a public or commemorative form.
This kind of distancing or objectivity – this kind of *formality* – is a puzzle
to many modern readers: is poetry not supposed to be *about* emotion and
self-expression? This preconception, as several later chapters will argue, is

emphatically a post-Romantic one. Romantic poetry, with its emphasis on the creation of a poetic self as the fit – in extreme cases, the only – subject for poetry, and with its total renegotiation of the significance of the figure of the poet, has also largely succeeded in renegotiating many readers' perceptions of what poetry is, or should be (in saying this, it is worth suggesting that Wordsworth, more responsible than anyone for these rene-gotiations, may now be the most influential single figure in English poetic history). But, though many (most?) readers tend emphatically now to be post-Romantic, that is not to say that emotion and self-expression are the only criteria by which poetry can be judged. Catherine Phil MacCarthy's 1998 collection, *The Blue Globe*, is for the most part an excellent example of this kind of post-Romantic poetry, almost entirely personal and charac-terized by an almost total absence of external referent – full of unidentified, unidentifiable 'he's, 'she's, 'you's, 'we's, and, of course, 'I's; it is also, like much contemporary poetry, characteristically written in a spare *vers libre*:

> In the school holidays
> you wrote to me. Described
> the amber and purple of sunset
> as if I were there with you.[28]

One poem, however, stands out stylistically – 'Lucy's Song' is a strictly formalized villanelle, which opens:

> Uncover my bones, long dead and clean,
> The moon of my skull that gleams in the mire,
> Hold me to your breast, carry me unseen.[29]

A villanelle is a 19-line poem consisting of five tercets (three-line stanzas) with a closing quatrain (four lines). The first and third lines of the opening stanza are alternated as refrains in the final lines of stanzas 2–5, and form the closing couplet of the quatrain; the second lines of every stanza rhyme with each other, and the opening line of the quatrain rhymes with both refrains. (See Chapter 4 for an extended reading of a villanelle.) It is, in other words, a highly stylized, artificial form, entirely out of keeping with the rest of *The Blue Globe*. However, 'Lucy's Song' carries the following dedication: 'For Lucy Partington, murdered in 1973, aged twenty-one years'. Lucy Partington was one of the victims of the serial-killers Fred and Rosemary West, and the poem is written for and about her, and in her persona. There is a strong sense in which subject-matter this sensitive *requires* the formal pressure MacCarthy applies here, requires something more public, more commemorative than her usual form allows – and the villanelle, furthermore, is a form which has become associated with death, meditations on mortality, grief. In writing 'Lucy's Song' as a villanelle, then, MacCarthy places her subject within a tradition of public mourning as well as personal emotion, fittingly, as in the mid-1990s when the Wests' unbear-able crimes were discovered, Lucy Partington and all the other victims *were* the subjects of public mourning, as well as private grief. Here, poetic form is used to objectify otherwise unbearably personal material – a distancing device.

Of course, not even all canonical Romantic poetry conforms to the kinds of post-Romantic readerly expectations we described: it too can be formalized by tradition and ideology, as we saw with Blake's *Songs*. Shelley's 'The Mask of Anarchy' (1819), written on the occasion of the Peterloo Massacre when government troops charged on a mass demonstration calling for political enfranchisement, killing and wounding many, is unproblematically considered a major document in Romantic poetry. The poem's form is the ballad, essentially a popular narrative song characterized by uncomplicated verse-structure and diction and intended to be put to music – here, Shelley uses a four-beat line (usually seven or eight syllables) assembled into quatrains of rhyming couplets, aabb; the poem's famous, ringing refrain adds a fifth line to rhyme with the second couplet:

> Rise like lions after slumber
> In unvanquishable number,
> Shake your chains to earth like dew
> Which in sleep had fallen on you –
> Ye are many, they are few.[30]

As traditionally a popular and even an oral form, a form available more than most to the working class, many of whom were illiterate, the ballad was frequently used as a vehicle for the articulation of political radicalism or mass dissent – for the articulation of a popular working-class consciousness overlooked by high-cultural 'literature'. (Even today, there is an uncomfortable class snobbery revealed in the fact that ballads are relatively infrequently studied in schools or universities; often they are considered crude folk documents or doggerel whose standards do not conform to those expected of 'great literature'. Such assumptions should be made only *after* we have asked who precisely is setting these 'standards'.) In 'The Mask of Anarchy', Shelley, the Old Etonian, aligns himself with the People, both in his political sympathies and in his choice of a form indissociable from those sympathies. That is, although culturally and geographically removed from the events he describes (the poem's opening line is 'As I lay asleep in Italy'), Shelley is here producing the kind of poem that working-class witnesses to the Massacre might themselves have produced.

Furthermore, 'The Mask of Anarchy' is an allegory, whose second stanza opens with the line 'I met Murder on the way' and proceeds to image forth other allegorical figures: Fraud, Anarchy, Hope. Allegory, in which abstractions are personified as individuals, has also traditionally been a device for the articulation of radicalism: in William Langland's medieval dream-poem *The Vision of Piers Plowman* (written between the Statute of Labourers in 1351 and the Peasant's Revolt in 1381, a time of popular dissatisfaction with the establishment, the poem contains many attacks on corruption within the Church),[31] in John Bunyan's *The Pilgrim's Progress* (written while Bunyan was in prison for his beliefs), through to Orwell's *Animal Farm*. This is partly because the personification of abstractions allowed for the wide dissemination of complex ideas in an understandable form (hence the massive popularity of *The Pilgrim's Progress* throughout the eighteenth and nineteenth centuries). But it is also because allegory carries an interpretive doubleness; it is a form made of encoded meanings, useful in times when a writer could face imprisonment or even death for unpopular beliefs. Orwell, in writing *Animal Farm* as an allegory of Stalinist Russia through the vehicle of pigs and other animals, was unlikely to face trouble from the post-war British government under which he wrote; the allegorical form does however mimic the kinds of techniques which Russian writers might have deployed in their own writings. Thus, again, in his choice of the allegory, Shelley is deploying a form appropriate for his content.

Prosody: metrics – scansion – rhythm – rhyme

This book is not intended as a guidebook on metrics, or to the specifics of poetic forms: readers wishing for detailed taxonomies should consult one of the several excellent dictionaries or encyclopedias of terms available, or specialist studies such as Paul Fussell's *Poetic Meter and Poetic Form* and Philip Hobsbaum's *Metre, Rhythm and Verse Form*.[32] Nevertheless, we feel that it is important here to offer a brief account of the most significant terms for the study of poetry (with the proviso that whole books – at times, whole careers – have been dedicated to each of the subjects with which we deal). Thus, where succeeding chapters will close with readings of specific poems in the light of the ideas and theories which those chapters have discussed, this one closes with an introductory overview.

Prosody (which actually has nothing to do with prose) is the theory or study of specifically poetic devices – versification, metre, rhythm, scansion and rhyme. A line of poetry is usually subdivisible into metrical units, known as feet: units of stress or beat. Thus, for example, the opening lines of Milton's *Paradise Lost*:

> Of man's first disobedience, and the fruit
> Of that forbidden tree, whose mortal taste[33]

can be divided up as follows:

> Of man's / first dis / obed / ience and / the fruit
> Of that / forbid / den tree / whose mor / tal taste

Note here that the division into feet does not necessarily respect the integrity of individual words but rather of phonemes – units of sound – or syllables. This line, subdivisible into five metrical feet, is the pentameter (from the Greek 'penta' + 'meter', 'a measure of five'). Note also that both these lines contain a *caesura*, a break or pause in the line, usually at or near its centre:

> Of man's first disobedience // and the fruit
> Of that forbidden tree, // whose mortal taste

These lines also use *enjambment*, the running-on of a poetic unit of signification from one line to the next: 'and the fruit / Of that forbidden tree' is one phrase, and thus the lines might be divided into three phrases, roughly consistent with breath-pauses: 'Of man's first disobedience / and the fruit Of that forbidden tree / whose mortal taste'.

Metrics is the specific study of poetic metre; *scansion* the annotation of metre. Metre is usually annotated by dividing the metrical feet into 'stressed' (given the symbol (') or 'unstressed' (∪) syllables depending on the weight given by the voice in pronunciation. The iambic metre – an unstressed syllable followed by a stressed one (∪'), was, until the twentieth century, by far the dominant one in English poetry: the dominant metre (albeit with frequent deviations) of Chaucer's *Canterbury Tales*, Shakespeare's plays and sonnets, the poetry of John Dryden and Alexander Pope, of Wordsworth's *The Prelude*, Coleridge's *The Rime of the Ancient Mariner*, and of much of the poetry of Browning, Tennyson, Yeats, Frost and Larkin. Thus, scanning Milton's lines, we see that they are written in iambic pentameters:

> ∪   '   ∪   '   ∪'   ∪   '   ∪   '
> Of man's / first dis / obed / ience and / the fruit
>
> ∪   ' ∪'   ∪   '   ∪   '   ∪   '
> Of that / forbid / den tree, / whose mor / tal taste

Scansion of this sort, however, can often force a rhythm upon a line, and does not take account of the metrical flexibility of much poetry. We noted that the iambic pentameter is the metre of Shakespeare's sonnets; strictly, this is not always the case. This, for example, is perhaps the most famous opening couplet of any Shakespeare sonnet:

> Shall I compare thee to a summer's day?
> Thou art more lovely and more temperate[34]

Scanned as iambic pentameters, it looks like this:

> ∪ ' ∪ '   ∪' ∪'   ∪   '
> Shall I / compare / thee to / a sum / mer's day?
> ∪   '   ∪   '   ∪'   ∪   '   ∪'
> Thou art / more love / ly and / more tem / perate

But does this actually tally with the way we would read the poem? Surely, in the first line, the greatest stress of all should be placed on the opening interrogative ('*Shall* I compare thee to a summer's day?'); surely, also, the force of the meaning in the second line requires that we stress the two 'mores' ('Thou art *more* lovely and *more* temperate') – yet none of these words is stressed according to the metrics of the iambic pentameter. Here, what's abstrusely called the Trager-Smith method of notating stress is a useful alternative:[35] according to this method, the stress given each syllable in a line is numbered from 1 to 4, with 1 being the strongest, 4 the weakest. In Trager-Smith notation, the lines would be scanned as follows, much more in keeping with their stress patterns:

<pre>
 1   2 3   2   2 2 4 2   4   2
Shall I compare thee to a summer's day?
</pre>

<pre>
  2   2   1   2   4 3   1   2   4 2
Thou art more lovely and more temperate
</pre>

It is sometimes thought that the iambic line (specifically, the iambic pentameter) reached its technical peak in the so-called 'heroic couplet' of the Augustan poets of the late seventeenth to mid-eighteenth centuries, notably Dryden, Pope, Swift and Johnson. This, for example, is the opening passage from Johnson's 'The Vanity of Human Wishes':

> Let Observation, with extensive view,
> Survey mankind, from China to Peru;
> Remark each anxious toil, each eager strife,
> And watch the busy scenes of crowded life;
> Then say how hope and fear, desire and hate
> O'erspread with snares the clouded maze of fate,
> Where wavering man, betrayed by venturous pride
> To tread the weary paths without a guide,
> As treacherous phantoms in the mist delude,
> Shuns fancied ills, or chases airy good;
> How rarely Reason guides the stubborn choice,
> Rules the bold hand, or prompts the suppliant voice[36]

The heroic couplet is a rhyming couplet in iambic pentameters. More than this, however, the couplets form self-contained and internally balanced units within the poem: rarely does enjambment occur across couplets. Furthermore, the poem makes heavy and clever use of the caesura, often balancing a line across it, offering a sense of repetition ('parallelism') or symmetry: 'Remark each anxious toil, / each eager strife'; 'Shuns fancied ills, / or chases airy good'; 'Rules the bold hand, / or prompts the suppliant voice'. Again, one might see an ideological imperative behind this: the Augustan poets (a term coined by Oliver Goldsmith) looked back to the Latin poets in the age of the emperor Augustus (Virgil, Horace, Ovid) as having achieved an incomparable artistic mastery, which they themselves wished to emulate (hence they are often called 'neo-Classical'). Thus we might think of their poetics as traditionalist or conservative. This poetics

also bespeaks a world-view, or at least an ideal view of society: the stabil-
ity, balance, symmetry and harmony of their poetry images forth a society
which itself partakes of these qualities – a social view characterized by
stability and harmony, which we might call High Toryism. (Though it has
to be said that not all poetry in heroic couplets is conservative – Tony
Harrison's 'A Kumquat for John Keats' is a good counter-example to the
argument we have just offered.)

Other metrical forms are rarer than the iamb, at least as the bases for
entire poems, let alone the entire *oeuvres* of poets. Edgar Allan Poe, whose
poetics we alluded to earlier, is one of the relatively few habitually non-
iambic metrical poets in English, and as such found himself derided by
Ralph Waldo Emerson as 'the jingle man'. It is true that the musicality of
Poe's poetry (and Poe may well have been a better theorist of poetry than
he was a poet) can sound jarring, twee, or in extreme cases risible, as in
'The Bells':

> In a happy Runic rhyme,
> To the rolling of the bells –
> Of the bells, bells, bells, –
> To the tolling of the bells,
> Of the bells, bells, bells, bells,
> Bells, bells, bells,
> To the moaning and the groaning of the bells.[37]

(A poem only Quasimodo could love.)

A trochee is an iamb in reverse: a stressed syllable followed by an
unstressed one ($'\cup$), as in Blake's 'The Tyger':

$$' \quad \cup \quad ' \cup \quad \quad ' \quad \cup \quad \quad '$$
$$\text{Tyger, / tyger, / burning bright}$$

$$' \quad \quad \cup \quad ' \quad \cup \quad ' \quad \cup \quad \quad '$$
$$\text{In the / forests / of the night}[38]$$

Note that the third and final foot in the trimeter has an extra stressed sylla-
ble ($'\cup'$), thus making it technically a cretic (sometimes called an amphi-
macer). Frequently, non-iambic metres such as these, and the dactyl ($'\cup\cup$),
spondee ($''$) or anapaest ($\cup\cup'$), do not make up the entire metre of a poem,
but can be found interspersed, as in 'The Tyger', and in the opening line of
Robert Service's 'The Shooting of Dan McGrew':

$$\cup \quad ' \quad \quad \cup \cup \quad ' \quad \quad \cup \quad \quad ' \quad \cup\cup' \quad \cup \quad \cup \quad '$$
$$\text{A bunch / of the boys / were whoop / ing it up // in the Mal /}$$
$$\cup \quad ' \quad \cup '$$
$$\text{amute / saloon}[39]$$

The line alternates iambs and anapaests, a pattern recurring with variations
throughout the poem. Metrics at this level can become extremely complex,

and dull – it is usually enough to know that a metrical line is *not* iambic, and to be able to ask why that might be so, though at the same time a recognition of metrical qualities does give an increased appreciation of the skill of the poet, a reminder that poetry is a craft.

The non-rhyming iambic pentameters Milton uses in *Paradise Lost* are called 'blank verse' – 'blank' because they have been thought of as being as near as one can get to a neutral or natural metre – a normal, or even normative metre. The dominance of the iambic line in general has been put down to the idea that it is the metre which most closely corresponds to the rhythms of spoken English. Certainly, it is fairly easy to speak in iambic pentameters during normal conversation (a bit like this phrase being written now), albeit that doing so habitually does sound very weird.

However, the notion that the iamb most closely corresponds to the rhythms of spoken English seems at variance with the fact that much poetry written for, or created by, the voice (oral and ballad poetry) tends not to be iambic at all. Often it tends to conform to no consistent metre, but rather to a rhythm – to the number of beats rather than the number of syllables per line (often notated with a circle above the beat in a line). Thus, although we noted that 'The Shooting of Dan McGrew' is (largely) written in a combination of iambs and anapaests, it is actually much simpler (and more accurate) to scan it as alternating four-beat and three-beat rhythms within a line, with the caesura operating as a line-break:

>   o   o   o   o
>
> A bunch of the boys were whooping it up //
>   o   o   o
>
> in the Malamute saloon

This alternating four-beat / three-beat rhythm is one of the most common ballad and song rhythms (the other being four-four, the rhythm of 'The Mask of Anarchy', Longfellow's *Hiawatha* and 'Born in the USA') and is the rhythm of Edward Lear's 'The Owl and the Pussy-Cat':

>   o   o   o   o
>
> The Owl and the Pussy-cat went to sea
>   o   o   o
>
> In a beautiful pea-green boat,
>   o   o   o   o
>
> They took some honey, and plenty of money,
>   o   o   o
>
> Wrapped up in a five-pound note.[40]

And also of Isaac Watts's 'Against Scoffing and Calling Names':

>   o   o   o   o
>
> Our tongues were made to bless the Lord,

```
    o        o        o
```
And not speak ill of men;
```
    o        o      o          o
```
When others give a railing word
```
    o              o      o
```
We must not rail again.

Vers libre – free verse – is poetry without a regular or strictly defined metre. This is predominantly a twentieth-century form, particularly associated with Modernist poets (notably those from America: Pound, William Carlos Williams, H. D., Marianne Moore, some T. S. Eliot) and with contemporary neo-Romantic 'confessional' poetry. T. S. Eliot, in his essay 'Reflections on *Vers Libre*' (1917), dismissed the form as a 'preposterous fiction' which had simply been made the excuse for the production of too much bad poetry (in and of itself, a fair judgement):

> *Vers libre* does not exist . . . If *vers libre* is a genuine verse-form it will have a positive definition. And I can define it only in negatives: (1) absence of pattern, (2) absence of rhyme, (3) absence of metre.[41]

While it is true that, as Eliot suggests later in his essay, any verbal utterance can be scanned, and thus an absolute freedom from metrics of the kind claimed for *vers libre* is technically impossible, nevertheless few commentators today would agree with Eliot's hard-line stance.

In his 1842 essay 'The Poet', the American transcendentalist man of letters Ralph Waldo Emerson called for a new and distinctively American poetics, one commensurate with the scope of the land and its guiding, self-fashioning ideology: 'America is a poem in our eyes; its ample geography dazzles the imagination, and it will not wait long for metres.'[42] Indeed, there was not long to wait: in 1855 Walt Whitman published the first, anonymous, edition of *Leaves of Grass*, a selfconsciously mythopoeic document of American self-fashioning with a poetics to match, as, famously, in this excerpt from 'Song of Myself':

> If I worship one thing more than another it shall be the spread
>   of my own body, or any part of it,
> Translucent mould of me it shall be you!
> Shaded ledges and rests it shall be you!
> Firm masculine colter it shall be you!
> Whatever goes to the tilth of me it shall be you!
> You my rich blood! your milky stream pale strippings of my life!
> . . . You sweaty brooks and dews it shall be you!
> Winds whose soft-tickling genitals rub against me it shall be
>   you!
> Broad muscular fields, branches of live oak, loving lounger in
>   my winding paths, it shall be you!
> Hands I have taken, face I have kiss'd, mortal I have ever
>   touch'd, it shall be you[43]

This, rather self-evidently, is the 'long line', which soon became identified as the American metre for which Emerson had called. Again, there is clearly a connection between form and ideology here, a secession from what may be thought of as the colonizing presence of the 'English' iambic pentameter: 'to break the pentameter, that was the first heave', Ezra Pound wrote in his Canto LXXXI.[44] Poe, we remember, had also tried to deviate from the iamb, whilst remaining within standard metrical structures, and it was for this reason that Pound yoked together Poe and Whitman as the definitional American poets: 'Poe is a good enough poet, and after Whitman the best America has produced (probably?).'[45]

Whitman's poetics in this section of 'Song of Myself' (section 24) is based on *parallelism*, in which the structuring principle of verse is not metre or even, more loosely, rhythm, but repetition – here, the repetition of the phrase 'it shall be you!' Parallelism is the structuring principle of much Hebrew (biblical) poetry, and is often used by poets for its incantatory effect. The chant, with its mesmeric, trancelike quality is often used as the cornerstone of those ideas of poetry as 'bardic' or 'shamanic', capable of inducing in its readers or hearers some kind of divine or quasi-supernatural experience (and concomitantly in those theories which tend to view poets themselves as divine or quasi-supernatural figures), as notably expressed in Robert Graves's mystico-Celtic *The White Goddess* or the poetic theories of Allen Ginsberg, himself a major modern exponent of parallelism and the long line.[46]

Another obvious characteristic of *vers libre* is that it dispenses with rhyme. In poetry's oral roots, rhyme served a mnemonic as well as an aesthetic function. That is, it was an aid to memory, helping the speaker to remember what came next, because what came next sounded like what he or she had just said. Rhyme has traditionally been a major defining characteristic of poetry: along with metre, rhythm and parallelism, one of the form's structuring principles. However, poetry whose *sole* defining characteristic as poetry is that it rhymes can often be *doggerel*: poetry in name only, as in the following example:

> It must have been an awful sight,
> To witness in the dusky moonlight,
> While the Storm Fiend did laugh, and angry did bray,
> Along the Railway Bridge of the Silv'ry Tay.
> Oh! Ill-fated Bridge of the Silv'ry Tay,
> I must now conclude my lay
> By telling the world fearlessly without the least dismay,
> That your central girders would not have given way,
> At least many sensible men do say,
> Had they been supported on each side with buttresses,
> At least many sensible men confesses,
> For the stronger we our houses do build,
> The less chance we have of being killed.[47]

This is the final stanza of 'The Tay Bridge Disaster' by William McGonagall, a nineteenth-century Scottish poet who specialized in grand public elegies on the occasion of national disasters. McGonagall is also generally recognized (and rather beloved) as the worst poet in the English language. Formally, this is obviously poetry – it is recognizably divided into lines; its final couplet achieves (rather in the manner of one of Shakespeare's sonnets) an aphoristic closure; there is a spot of imagery here – an allegory, in fact ('the Storm Fiend'); and, most obviously, it rhymes (in a different context, in the hands of a Byron or a Bob Dylan, 'buttresses' / 'confesses' might even be though of as an ingenious rhyme). However, any reader that thinks that this is aesthetically good, as opposed to unintentionally hilarious, poetry is probably beyond the help of the authors of this study.

Rhyme can be imaginative, can produce meaning. Whole poems, indeed, can be distinguished by the unusual, daring, or downright bad rhyme – in his poem 'Sunny Prestatyn', Philip Larkin produces the following toe-curler:

> *Come To Sunny Prestatyn*
> Laughed the girl on the poster, . . .
> Behind her, a hunk of coast, a
> Hotel with palms

'Poster' / 'coast a': this is obviously a deliberate poetic joke on Larkin's part, playing with our conventions and expectations that poetry should rhyme, and offering an excruciating rhyme in what is an excruciating poem.

It is, indeed, for comedy that rhyme can be most effective. Byron is perhaps the most notable exponent of the outrageous comic rhyme – he could, it seems, rhyme anything with anything (though some words, such as 'the', 'months' and 'orange', are said to be unrhymable – or at least impossible to produce full rhymes for, though 'orange' and 'strange' are half-rhymes). Byron's comic epic, *Don Juan*, is a sustained exercise in proving this: even the title contains a rhyming joke: 'Juan' is pronounced 'Ju-an' merely for the expediency of a rhyme in the opening stanza – 'Juan' / 'true one' – and thereafter always pronounced in this way; similarly, Juan's hometown of Cadiz is deliberately (and again, thereafter, consistently) mispronounced to bend it into a rhyme with 'ladies'.

These flamboyant rhymes are more than exercises in poetic dexterity (though they are that too). Rhyme can be used to produce, or undercut, meaning:

> 'Tis pity learned virgins ever wed
> With persons of no sort of education,
> Or gentlemen, who, though well-born and bred,
> Grow tired of scientific conversation.
> I don't choose to say much upon this head,
> I'm a plain man and in a single station,

> But – oh ye lords of ladies intellectual!
> Inform us truly, have they not henpecked you all?[48]

In the closing couplet, 'henpecked you all' is used to undermine through ridicule the idea of being 'intellectual' – you cannot be an 'intellectual' if you are made to rhyme with 'henpecked you all', and the intellect here becomes a conduit for a (devastatingly clever) stupid rhyme. Byron's rhyme-games continue throughout the poem: 'Agamemnon'/ 'condemn none' (a deflationary rhyme whose target is classical heroism); 'mathematical' / 'attic all' (which works in the same way as the earlier 'intellectual' rhyme); 'potatoes' / 'apparatus' (my own personal favourite); 'evil is' / 'syphilis'; and so on. Byron, it seems, is deliberately setting himself poetic challenges, setting himself (near-) impossible multisyllabic rhymes which he then gets away with. This is, in other words, an exercise in poetic pyrotechnics.

Some poetry uses the *half-rhyme*. Half-rhymes usually employ assonance (the repetition of vowel sounds) or consonance (repetition of consonants), and can be put to good effect, as, famously, in Wilfred Owen's 'Strange Meeting':

> I am the enemy you killed, my friend.
> I knew you in this dark: for so you frowned
> Yesterday through me as you jabbed and killed.
> I parried; but my hands were loath and cold.[49]

All the line-endings of 'Strange Meeting' are half-rhymes. Given that rhyme usually produces a harmonious effect, then this produces a jarring absence of harmony, wholly congruent with its subject, war and death.

If the Whitmanesque long line can be said to typify an expansive poetics, much *vers libre* works in the opposite way, by reducing or contracting standard metrical lines, often into brief semantic units. William Carlos Williams famously compared a poem to a machine:

> To make two bald statements: There's nothing sentimental about a machine, and: A poem is a small (or large) machine made of words. When I say there's nothing sentimental about a poem I mean that there can be no part, as in any other machine, that is redundant.[50]

As if literalizing Wordsworth's suspicion, articulated in the 'Preface' to the *Lyrical Ballads* (1800, 1802), of needless, ostentatious 'poetic diction' for its own sake,[51] not to mention Pound's later ideas of poetry as 'condensed' language, this kind of *vers libre* tends to be spare, even stark in its diction, but also its rhythms. This, for instance, is the opening stanza of 'Sea Rose' by H. D. (Hilda Doolittle):

> Rose, harsh rose,
> marred and with stint of petals,
> meager flower, thin
> sparse of leaf [52]

Poetry of this kind – anti-aesthetic, radically anti-Romantic – often deals in concrete things, rather than the kinds of emotion or abstraction with which Romantic poetry is frequently concerned. Here, all expression (and rhythmic quality) is pared down to a minimum, leaving only a series of images – which is why such poetry is called 'Imagist'. Following the ideas of the philosopher T. E. Hulme, who believed that the language of poetry should be a 'visual concrete one . . . Images in verse are not mere decoration, but the very essence of an intuitive language',[53] such poetry takes as its structuring principle not rhythm or metre or parallelism, but the image – and this is to be the subject of the next chapter.

Endnotes

1 Fun Boy Three and Bananarama, 'It Ain't What You Do It's The Way That You Do It', Chrysalis CHS 2570 (1982). Original words by Cy Oliver and Trummy Young.

2 John Donne, *The Complete English Poems*, ed. A. J. Smith (Harmondsworth, 1971), p. 313.

3 For a lucid discussion of Renaissance typology, see the chapter entitled 'Biblical Exegesis and Typology' in Isabel Rivers, *Classical and Christian Ideas in English Renaissance Poetry* (London, 1979), pp. 148–57. There are works of modern typology, for example A. C. Charity, *Events and their Afterlife: The Dialectics of Christian Typology in Dante and the Bible* (Cambridge, 1966).

4 Dylan Thomas, *Collected Poems 1934–52* (London, 1952), p. 62.

5 Ezra Pound, *ABC of Reading* (London, 1991), p. 14.

6 Pound, *ABC of Reading*, p. 29. For Poe's poetics, see his essay 'The Poetic Principle', in *Essays and Reviews* (New York, 1984), pp. 71–94. For 'Pure Poetry', see *The New Princeton Encyclopedia of Poetry and Poetics*, ed. Alex Preminger and T. V. F. Brogan (Princeton, N.J., 1993), pp. 1007–8.

7 Alexander Pope, 'An Essay on Criticism', in *The Poems of Alexander Pope*, ed. John Butt (London, 1963), p. 153. This is actually Pope's definition of '*True Wit*', a cornerstone of Pope's poetics; it is frequently, as here, taken as a comment on poetry in general.

8 Samuel Taylor Coleridge, *Biographia Literaria* (London, 1949), Chapter 14, and *passim*. For discussions of 'organicism' and poetics, see *New Princeton Encyclopedia*, pp. 868–69; M. H. Abrams, *The Mirror and the Lamp: Romantic Theory and the Critical Tradition* (Oxford, 1971), pp. 156–225; Tom Furniss and Michael Bath, *Reading Poetry: An Introduction* (Brighton, 1996), pp. 55–56.

9 Quoted in Terry Eagleton, *Literary Theory: An Introduction* (Oxford, 1983), p. 2.

10 Pound, *ABC of Reading*, p. 36.

11 See William Empson, *Seven Types of Ambiguity* (London, 1991).

12 I. A. Richards, *The Philosophy of Rhetoric* (Oxford, 1936), pp. 99–109 and *passim*.

13 Eagleton, *Literary Theory*, p. 2. It has to be said, though, that a reader might reasonably respond to Eagleton: If someone walked up to *me* at a bus stop and murmured 'Thou still unravished bride of quietness', I would know instantly that I was in the presence of a lunatic.

14 See Cleanth Brooks, 'The Heresy of Paraphrase', in *The Well-Wrought Urn* (London, 1968).

15 Percy Bysshe Shelley, *A Defence of Poetry*, in *Romanticism: An Anthology*, ed. Duncan Wu (Oxford, 1994), p. 959.

16 These two poems are put together, though in a very different context and for very different ends (an analysis of cultural aesthetics) in M. Wynn Thomas, *Internal Difference: Twentieth-Century Writing in Wales* (Cardiff, 1992), p. 46.

17 Bruce Springsteen, 'Born in the USA', from *Born in the USA* (Columbia Records, 1984).

18 The Murder Ballad is a folk form with its American origin in country and blues music, usually told from a perspective of sympathy towards a killer, and often used as a vehicle to comment on the social conditions which drove the subject to murder: poverty, unemployment and racial oppression, leading to rage and jealousy. 'Stagger Lee', 'Tom Dooley' and 'Hey Joe' are all examples of the form.

19 Quoted in Mikal Gilmore, 'Bruce Springsteen's America', in *Night Beat: A Shadow History of Rock and Roll* (London, 1998), p. 216.

20 Quoted in Gilmore, 'Bruce Springsteen's America', p. 215.

21 A similar argument to the one used here is offered by Simon Frith, *Performing Rites: On the Value of Popular Music* (Cambridge, Mass, 1998), pp. 165–66.

22 For a discussion of 'significant form', see Furniss and Bath, *Reading Poetry*, pp. 52–75.

23 Lewis Carroll, *The Annotated Alice*, ed. Martin Gardner (Harmondsworth, 1965), pp. 38–9.

24 Isaac Watts, *Divine Songs Attempted in Easy Language for the Use of Children*, ed. J. H. P. Pafford (Oxford, 1971), pp. 174–5.

25 William Blake, *The Complete Poems*, second edition, ed. W. H. Stevenson (London and New York, 1989), pp. 217–18.

26 Watts, *Divine Songs*, p. 157.

27 Blake, *Complete Poems*, p. 70.

28 Catherine Phil MacCarthy, 'Under My Skin', in *The Blue Globe* (Belfast, 1998), p. 9.

29 MacCarthy, *The Blue Globe*, p. 40.

30 Shelley, 'The Mask of Anarchy', in *Romanticism: An Anthology*, p. 947.

31 The dating and manuscript history of *Piers Plowman* is notoriously complex: four versions of the poem exist in four extant manuscripts, known as the A-, B-, C- and Z-texts (the Z-text antedates the A-text, though its existence was discovered much later). See William Langland, *The Vision of Piers Plowman: A Complete Edition of the B-Text*, ed. A. V. C. Schmidt (London, 1978), pp. xi–xvi.

32 See 'Further reading' for details of these texts.

33 John Milton, *Paradise Lost*, Book I, in *The Complete Poems*, ed. Gordon Campbell (London, 1980), p. 159. For simplicity, the spelling has been modernized here.

34 *Norton Anthology of Poetry*, p. 235.

35 For Trager-Smith notation, see *New Princeton Encyclopedia*, p. 1008.

36 *Norton Anthology of Poetry*, p. 597.

37 Edgar Allan Poe, *Poetry and Tales* (New York, 1984), p. 95.

38 Blake, *Complete Poems*, p. 214.

39 Robert Service, 'The Shooting of Dan McGrew', in *The Rattle Bag*, ed. Seamus Heaney and Ted Hughes (London, 1982), p. 381.

40 *Norton Anthology of Poetry*, p. 942.

41 T. S. Eliot, 'Reflections on *Vers Libre*', in *Selected Prose*, ed. John Hayward (Harmondsworth, 1953), pp. 86, 87–8.

42 Ralph Waldo Emerson, 'The Poet', in *Selected Poetry and Prose* (New York, 1969), p. 138.

43 *Norton Anthology of Poetry*, p. 964.

44 Pound, *The Cantos of Ezra Pound* (London, 1960), p. 553.

45 Pound, letter to Harriet Monroe, 31 January, 1915, in *Selected Letters 1907–1941*, ed. D. D. Paige (London, 1950), p. 50. The parenthetical '(probably?)' here presumably alludes again to the idea that Poe was a much better poet in theory than in practice: Pound's letter continues, 'He is a damn bad model and is certainly not to be set up as a model to any one who writes in English.' Poe did, however, turn out to be a very *good* model for many who wrote in French.

46 See Robert Graves, *The White Goddess* (London, 1961); Ann Waldman and Marilyn Webb, eds, *Talking Poetics from Naropa Institute: annals of the Jack Kerouac School of Disembodied Poetics*, introduction by Allen Ginsberg, 2 vols (London, 1978).

47 William McGonagall, *Poetic Gems* (London, 1989), p. 47.

48 George Gordon, Lord Byron, *Don Juan* (Harmondsworth, 1977), Canto I, Verse 22, p. 51.

49 *Norton Anthology of Poetry*, pp. 1279–80.

50 William Carlos Williams, *The Collected Poems of William Carlos Williams*, vol. 2 (London, 1991), p. 54.

51 William Wordworth, 'Preface', in William Wordsworth and Samuel Taylor Coleridge, *Lyrical Ballads*, ed. R. L. Brett and Alun R. Jones (London, 1991), pp. 252–3. Wordsworth's particular target here is the poetry of Thomas Gray.

52 *Norton Anthology of Poetry*, p. 1202.

53 T. E. Hulme, 'Romanticism and Classicism', quoted in *New Princeton Encyclopedia*, p. 574.

|2|

Poem and communication

Poetry is a special way of thinking: it is, precisely, a way of thinking in images.

Victor Shklovsky[1]

At the end of the last chapter, we noted how Imagist poetry used the image as a structuring principle. Technically, Imagism was a poetic movement that lasted only from about 1912 to 1917, though its influence was felt throughout the twentieth century. *Imagery*, however, has traditionally been a staple of poetics: sharing an etymological root with the verb 'to imitate', the image can be understood as an alternative model to standard verbal representation. If metre and rhythm can be understood as the points at which language comes closest to music (as Poe, the theorists of 'pure poetry' and Pound suggested), then imagery might broadly be understood as those points at which language comes closest to the visual arts ('image' also shares an etymological root with 'icon' and 'idol').[2] With its ability to concentrate multiple meanings in one semantic unit, imagery is language at or near its most 'charged' state: as we noted in the previous chapter, many of the most influential poetic theories of this century, from Pound to the Formalists to Richards to Empson, are largely predicated on the centrality of the image to poetic discourse. Types of imagery include the metaphor, the simile, the conceit, the symbol, metonymy and synecdoche, though owing to the complexity of the subject, which often calls for fine distinctions of meaning, many or all of these terms are sometimes subsumed into an all-encompassing category of 'metaphor' (for example, by Paul Ricoeur in his book *The Rule of Metaphor*).[3] Certainly, many of the linguistic and literary theories applied to metaphor apply equally to any image, and to a certain extent we shall be eliding their definitions when speaking theoretically here. These are sometimes called figurative language or figures of speech – meaning that they are not to be taken literally, but rather that their meaning is contingent upon interpretation – and they are to be the subjects of this chapter.

A metaphor, as most people were taught in school, is a linguistic device which substitutes one thing for another, representing something in terms of something else, thus producing new meanings or enabling readers to see one or both things in a new light. In Greek airports, a baggage trolley is called a *metaphora* – a metaphor.[4] Again, this makes an etymologically useful point, as metaphor in its Greek origin literally means 'transference', a method of getting (literally, in the original, carrying) meaning from one place or form to another – this is why one half of I. A. Richards' dialectic of metaphor is called the vehicle: it carries meaning. Indeed, the baggage trolley is here a useful metaphor for explaining and understanding the meaning of the word 'metaphor'! As with this 'metaphor-metaphor', metaphor often involves the transportation or carrying over of abstractions or difficult intellectual concepts into easier or more vivid concrete forms – a kind of reification, turning ideas into things.

Metaphor is habitual in language – many metaphors are now simply accepted as normal usage, and these are sometimes referred to as 'dead metaphors', metaphors we no longer recognize as such, whose vehicle has become lost: 'all at sea' (we are confused, not in the Atlantic Ocean with lots of other people); 'bugger off!' (an exhortation to go away, not to sodomize); 'the march of time' (time, like progress, does not have feet – therefore it cannot stand still either); 'the bottom line' (the final prognosis, not an actual line at the bottom of something – see also 'to draw the line'); 'over the moon' (delighted, not in a spaceship); 'fancy footwork' (behaviour meant to dazzle, sometimes in order to conceal something, not an Ali Shuffle); 'I don't get it' ('I don't understand', but literally something like 'the vehicle carrying your meaning has not arrived'). 'I don't get it' is an example of a common kind of metaphor for the conveying of information, called a 'conduit metaphor', in which abstractions of information or ideas are described in concrete or spatial terms ('the conveying of information' is another), as explained by the cognitive scientist Steven Pinker in his book *The Language Instinct*:

> Most of our everyday expressions about language use a 'conduit' metaphor that captures the parsing process. In this metaphor, ideas are objects, sentences are containers, and communication is sending. We 'gather' our ideas to 'put' them 'into' words, and if our verbiage is not 'empty' or 'hollow', we might 'convey' or 'get' these ideas 'across' to a listener, who can 'unpack' our words to 'extract' their 'content'.[5]

To coin a phrase, then, metaphors are woven into the very fabric of language. (Perceptive readers will have noticed two dead metaphors in that last sentence: we do not go to the mint to get our phrases made; language does not literally have a fabric, just as your being does not literally have a core, the problem a root, the issue a nub, or the matter a heart.)

Some modern language-theory, particularly of the structuralist and post-structuralist kind, has gone even further, arguing that *all* language is inherently metaphorical or figurative. The linguist Ferdinand de Saussure, whose ideas were collected posthumously as the volume *Course in General Linguistics*, demonstrated that in linguistic communication, the 'sign' (what is understood) is made up of a combination of the 'signifier' (what is said) and the 'signified' (what is meant); furthermore, he noted, the relationship between signifier and signified is *arbitrary*:

> The bond between the signifier and the signified is arbitrary. Since I mean by the sign the whole that results from the associating of the signifier with the signified, I can simply say: *the linguistic sign is arbitrary*.
>
> The idea of 'sister' is not linked by any inner relationship to the succession of sounds $s - ö - r$ which serves as its signifier in French; that it could be represented equally by any other sequence is proved by differences among languages and by the very existence of different languages: the signified 'ox' has as its signifier $b - ö - f$ on one side of the border and $o - k - s$ (*Ochs*) on the other.[6]

There is, in other words (to cite the example that is always used in this context), nothing *inherently* 'doggy' about the word 'dog' – if there were, why would the French call it a 'chien', the Germans a 'Hund' or the Welsh a 'ci'? A consequence of this is, then, that *all* language operates figuratively, as a form of conduit metaphor, since there is no single, agreed 'reality' which the signs transparently denote (my dog may very well be different from yours: thus when I say to you 'I took the neighbour's dog for a walk yesterday', I may be meaning a poodle while you may be thinking a pit bull, not the same thing at all). As Paul de Man writes:

> [A] discrepancy exists in everyday language, in the impossibility of making the actual sign coincide with what it signifies. It is the distinctive privilege of language to be able to hide meaning behind a misleading sign, as when we all hide rage or hatred behind a smile. But it is the distinctive curse of all language, as soon as any kind of interpersonal relation is involved, that it is forced to act in this way. The simplest of wishes cannot express itself without hiding behind a screen of language that constitutes a world of intricate intersubjective relationships, all of them potentially inauthentic. In the everyday language of communication, there is no a priori privileged position of sign over meaning or meaning over sign; the act of interpretation will always again have to establish this relation for the particular case at hand. The interpretation of everyday language is a Sisyphean task, a task without end and without progress, for the other is always free to make what he wants differ from what he says he wants.[7]

This has led to some important claims made for the significance of metaphor to language – claims which have some bearing on poetics. Paul Ricoeur, in *The Rule of Metaphor*, suggests that meaning is created in language *through* metaphor: it is 'not a dying perception, but a language being reborn'.[8] This potential in metaphor to 'create language anew' has clear connections with (can be understood as an extension of) Pound's notions of poetry as 'charged' language, notions which, we noted, are heavily dependent on the provenance of the image in poetics. Thus, while for de Man 'dog' may be a dead metaphor, for Ricoeur 'bloody great huge slavering hell-hound' is not.

Consider this opening couplet of an e. e. cummings poem:

> the Cambridge ladies who live in furnished souls
> are unbeautiful and have comfortable minds[9]

This is a metaphor: rooms (or houses) are furnished, not souls. Cambridge is the location of Harvard University, and the poem attacks the complacency and pomposity of Harvard 'faculty wives', or of 'bluestocking' women students, and by extension of the University itself as a 'comfortable' place, one which dissociates itself from the concerns of 'the real world' outside the institution (and it is true that universities can tend to foster an introspective self-importance in their faculty, most of whom have known nothing else for all their adult lives – have indeed never in *all* their lives been outside education); it is by further extension an attack on the American class system (and this in a country which purports not to have one), as Harvard has traditionally been one of the establishments for educating the American élite (that is, the children of the wealthy): the metaphor operates as an attack on *privilege*. 'Furnished rooms' are rooms rented with furniture already in place – you don't have to buy your own; the force of the metaphor, then, is that the 'souls' and 'minds' of 'the Cambridge women' come ready furnished, full of received ideas without the necessity of learning or discovering anything for themselves ('finding out the hard way', as another, dead, conduit metaphor has it), leading to a 'comfortable' complacency and self-satisfaction.

Furthermore, academics often did live in furnished college accommodation (some still do) on campuses. Thus, a reality is carried over here, by use of metaphor, into a moral critique, spatially: residence in college rooms signifies an inability to perceive (the importance of) a world beyond the confines of Harvard Yard, which in turn signifies the blinkered self-importance of an academic and, by extension, cultural and political establishment. 'the Cambridge ladies who live in furnished souls' was written in 1923, and by this time the notion of the 'furnished room' had a provenance within Modernism, as a recurring image in the poetry of T. S. Eliot:

> One thinks of all the hands
> That are raising dingy shades
> In a thousand furnished rooms.[10]

Here the 'furnished rooms' are 'dingy', they signify the seediness or sordidness with which many Modernists like Eliot (motivated as they frequently were by far-right political ideologies) associated the working class or 'masses'.[11] (Eliot's earlier poetry is full of rooms of this sort, registered with an emetic disgust: the 'restless nights in one-night cheap hotels' of 'The Love Song of J. Alfred Prufrock'; 'Gerontion', set entirely in a seedy boarding-house; the sexual encounter between typist and clerk in *The Waste Land* in her room hung with underwear; and many other examples.) Thus, cummings' metaphor performs another act of transference, turning Eliot's metaphor of condemnation of the working class into a condemnation of a cultural élite – precisely the élite to which Eliot himself belonged: thus, this metaphor could be read as a critique of T. S. Eliot's own poetry, or of Eliot himself.

As we noted earlier, metaphors and other images require interpretation. As they analyse highly condensed language, the interpretations, 'unpacking' the meanings, are by definition going to be longer (often, as above, consid-erably longer) than the metaphors themselves. We might think of images, then, as 'overdetermined', containing 'too much' meaning – a superabun-dance of meaning, to use a phrase from the previous chapter. This kind of overdetermination can lead to the frequently made accusation of 'reading too much into' a poem, of discovering in a poem meanings that 'just aren't there'. This is an issue with which we will deal in Chapter 6, but, to antic-ipate the conclusion of that chapter, it is better to read 'too much' into a poem than nothing at all (or, as Bob Dylan put it in another context, 'better use your sense / Take what you can gather from coincidence').[12]

Mixed metaphors are metaphors which employ two or more vehicles for only one tenor, or which yoke together apparently disparate metaphors in one semantic unit: 'you'll have to butter your own nest' (a conflation of 'butter your own bread' and 'feather your own nest', both metaphors for self-reliance); 'it was a sticky wicket, but against the odds she pulled out all the stops' (the vehicles here are cricket, gambling and organ-playing). Mixed metaphors are usually thought of as grammatically infelicitous, yet they can often produce startling or comic effects: the politician Ernest Bevin once remarked on the Council of Europe, 'If you open that Pandora's box, you never know what Trojan horses will jump out.'[13] This is an appropri-ation by a working-class Labour politician of the kinds of classical knowl-edge traditionally the preserve of the privately educated; furthermore, it is a conflation of two Greek myths which, in using them together in a mixed metaphor, questions their cultural validity – a bit like 'It's all Greek to me.' Mixed metaphors in poetry, then, need not be a mark of inadequacy. The opening couplet of Chidiock Tichborne's 'Tichborne's Elegy', subtitled 'Written with his own hand in the Tower before his execution' (1586) contains two of them:

> My prime of youth is but a frost of cares,
> My feast of joy is but a dish of pain.[14]

'Frost of cares' is itself a metaphor (frost does not have cares), but is used here not as a complete metaphor in itself but as the vehicle in a metaphor whose tenor is 'My prime of youth'; likewise 'dish of pain' / 'feast of joy' in the second line (albeit with a closer semantic link: 'dish' and 'feast' are cognates but 'prime' and 'frost' are not). As Chapter 5 will explain, the notion of 'sincerity' in poetry is a complex one: nevertheless, the historical fact of this poem (that it was written by a man on the verge of execution – and this is not a fact requiring research: it is written into the subtitle of the poem) surely ameliorates any grammatical qualms readers may have about mixing metaphors – the metaphor, in this poem, is used as the means of recreating, and understanding the meaning of, a brief life.

Some poetry is predicated entirely on the power of the image to 'create language anew', on its ability as a signifier to perform, in the terminology of the Formalist critic Victor Shklovsky, an act of 'defamiliarization' upon its signified, thus creating *reality* anew:

> Art exists that one may recover the sensation of life; it exists to make one feel things, to make the stone *stony*. The purpose of art is to impart the sensation of things as they are perceived and not as they are known. The technique of art is to make objects 'unfamiliar', to make forms difficult, to increase the difficulty and the length of perception because the process of perception is an aesthetic end in itself and must be prolonged. *Art is a way of experiencing the artfulness of an object; the object is not important.*[15]

(Our reading of the overdetermination of one metaphor in a cummings poem has already testified to the ability of the image 'to increase the difficulty and the length of perception'.) Some poetry sets out precisely to defamiliarize the familiar, reviving the dead metaphors that make language. Craig Raine's poem 'A Martian Sends a Postcard Home' could have been written deliberately as a practical adumbration of Shklovsky's theories:

> Caxtons are mechanical birds with many wings
> and some are treasured for their markings – . . .
>
> Model T is a room with the lock inside –
> a key is turned to free the world[16]

The unarticulated tenors in these stanzas are, respectively, books and cars (in case elucidation is required, William Caxton invented the printing-press in England, thus, effectively, books in English; the Ford Model T was the first successful mass-market automobile, bringing motoring and its concomitant freedom to the public). The poem sets out to view these commonplace objects as if they had no cultural or linguistic context, as if they had never been witnessed before (that is, through the eyes of a Martian), and does so through metaphors of resemblance: an open book does resemble a bird's spread wings. *Both* metaphors ultimately signify freedom – intellectual freedom in the case of the book ('free as a bird'); the freedom of mobility in the case of the car.

To return to the subject of dogs, this is part of the opening stanza of Francis Thompson's *The Hound of Heaven* (1893):

> I fled Him, down the nights and down the days;
> I fled Him, down the arches of the years;
> I fled Him, down the labyrinthine ways
> Of my own mind; and in the mist of tears
> I hid from Him, and under running laughter.[17]

The vehicle of this metaphor, articulated in the title but nowhere in the body of the poem's 182 lines, is of a foxhound or, more likely, a bloodhound, relentlessly pursuing the poem's narrator: wherever he flees, there is no escape. Its tenor is God ('Him'), or religious faith: the poem's title, 'The Hound of Heaven', overturns the more usual image of the 'hell-hound' (Cerberus, the Hound of the Baskervilles). A metaphor of this kind, extended across the whole span of a poem and governing its meaning, is sometimes referred to as a 'conceit'. A famous modern example of this is the predicating metaphor of Philip Larkin's poem, 'Toads':

> Why should I let the toad *work*
> Squat on my life?
> Can't I use my wit as a pitchfork
> To drive the brute off? . . .
>
> For something sufficiently toad-like
> Squats in me, too;
> Its hunkers are heavy as hard luck,
> And cold as snow[18]

Indeed, this predicating toad–work metaphor extends across the length of not one poem, but two: a later companion piece, 'Toads Revisited', returns to ('revisits') and further extends and develops the metaphor: 'What else can I answer', the poem closes,

> When the lights come on at four
> At the end of another year?
> Give me your arm, old toad;
> Help me down Cemetery Road.[19]

('Toads' and 'Toads Revisited', it should be noted, are also companion pieces in terms of form, or rather mirror-images: 'Toads' employs an alternating three-beat, two-beat rhythm, while 'Toads Revisited' is two-beat, three-beat.)

The conceit is a device most closely associated with seventeenth-century Metaphysical poetry: the poetry of Donne, Andrew Marvell, George Herbert, Henry Vaughan and others, so-called after a remark of Dryden's in his *Discourse Concerning the Original and Progress of Satire* (1692), where he argued that Donne 'affects the metaphysics . . . and perplexes the

minds of the fair sex with nice speculations of philosophy'.[20] The
Metaphysical poets were identified as a group by Dr Johnson (though,
historically, they were no such thing – but nor, for that matter, were the
Romantics), who described their poetry as that in which 'The most hetero-
geneous ideas are yoked by violence together.'[21] Metaphysical conceits are
generally characterized by their intellectual difficulty – or intellectual
gymnastics – deploying philosophical argument to unexpected ends (the
syllogism 'If . . . But . . . Therefore' in Marvell's 'To His Coy Mistress'; the
reductio ad absurdum in Donne's 'The Flea': both used to the same end –
to get a woman into bed) – taking rational premises to their logical, but
irrational, conclusions. The Metaphysical conceit can consequently be
formidably complex: Donne's 'A Nocturnal Upon S. Lucy's Day, being the
shortest day', interweaves and connects two apparently 'heterogeneous'
conceits. The first is introduced in the opening stanza:

> 'Tis the year's midnight, and it is the day's,
> Lucy's, who scarce seven hours herself unmasks,
> The sun is spent, and now his flasks
> Send forth light squibs, no constant rays;
> The world's whole sap is sunk:
> The general balm th' hydroptic earth hath drunk,
> Whither, as to the bed's-feet, life is shrunk,
> Dead and interred; yet all these seem to laugh,
> Compared with me, who am their epitaph.[22]

St Lucy's Day is 13 December, popularly considered the date of the shortest
day of the year or winter solstice, according to the old Julian Calendar, which
was used until Pope Gregory XII introduced the modern Gregorian Calendar
in 1582, and in doing so caused a loss of ten days – hence the shortest day is
now 21 December. Although the poem may have been written as late as
1627, Donne is still using the Julian Calendar here, as the new calendar was
not officially adopted in England until 1752. However, even when the
Gregorian Calendar was in official use, feast days and saints' days often
remained according to the Julian Calendar – much as, metric system notwith-
standing, many of us still measure in feet, miles, stones or pints (especially
pints). The condition of the poem's speaker, then, is metaphorically associ-
ated with midnight, darkness, blackness, and by an associative leap death,
emptiness and nothingness, deploying (as we saw Donne do in 'Death be not
proud') an *a fortiori* argument: 'yet all these seem to laugh, / Compared with
me, who am their epitaph'. 'Solstice-midnight-death-nothingness', then, is
the poem's first conceit; the second is introduced in the following stanza:

> Study me, then, you who shall lovers be
> At the next world, that is, at the next spring:
> For I am every dead thing,
> In whom love wrought new alchemy.

> For his art did express
> A quintessence even from nothingness,
> From dull privations, and lean emptiness
> He ruined me, and I am re-begot
> Of absence, darkness, death; things which are not.

The vehicle of this conceit is alchemy, the pseudo-science of creating gold from 'base metals' such as lead (that is, effectively, of creating something from nothing): to 'express / A quintessence' is an image from alchemy meaning to reduce, through chemical processes, a substance (lead) to what was believed to be its essence (gold). Where the winter solstice was an occasion for celebration – the days grow longer afterwards, the year renews itself, life is reborn – in both pagan and Christian religion (Christmas, falling around the solstice, is a Christianization of old seasonal fertility rituals), and thus an apposite tenor for the vehicle of alchemy (something is created from nothing, life from death), Donne's 'new alchemy' does the converse: from a *beginning* point of death and nothingness, established in the opening stanza, the speaker is reduced to the 'quintessence . . . [of] nothingness', and 're-begot' (reborn, like the year) as 'absence, darkness, death; things which are not'.

Whereas metaphor operates by transference, describing one thing in terms of another, simile (from the same root as 'similar') operates by comparison, by showing how one thing is *like* another ('like' or 'as' are usually the words which signal a simile): as Geoffrey Leech rather neatly puts it, 'Simile is an overt, and metaphor a covert comparison.'[23] Again, similes have entered normal usage, barely recognizable as figures of speech: 'as good as gold', 'as happy as Larry', 'as quiet as a mouse', 'as high as a kite', and so on – all 'dead similes'.

Like all images, similes are units of compressed or overdetermined meaning. Take 'I'm like a one-eyed cat peeping in a seafood store', from 'Shake, Rattle and Roll':[24] the simile signifies lasciviousness – the 'randy tomcat' – and monocularity here specifically signifies focus, the inability of the singer to remove his gaze from the object of his desire ('the seafood store' – itself in all probability a crude sexual metaphor). Sexuality, too, is the subject of what may well be the most famous simile of recent years, Madonna's 'You make me feel shiny and new // Like a virgin, touched for the very first time'.[25]

As with metaphors, similes can predicate – and thus make – whole poems: Shakespeare's 'Shall I compare thee to a summer's day?' is the opening of just such a poem-long simile (and, equally famously, his Sonnet 130's 'My mistress' eyes are nothing like the sun' is the beginning of a poem-long reverse-simile, in which the tenor is compared to what it is *not* like).[26] The opening stanza of Byron's 'She Walks in Beauty' also establishes its poem's governing extended simile:

> She walks in beauty, like the night
> Of cloudless climes and starry skies;

> And all that's best of dark and bright
> Meet in her aspect and her eyes:
> Thus mellowed to that tender light
> Which heaven to gaudy day denies.[27]

In *Paradise Lost*, Milton's characteristic image is what is called the 'epic simile', a simile of multiple comparison extended over many lines:

> Thus *Satan* talking to his nearest Mate
> With Head up-lift above the wave, and Eyes
> That sparkling blaz'd, his other Parts besides
> Prone on the flood, extended long and large
> Lay floating many a rood, in bulk as huge
> As whom the Fables name of monstrous size,
> *Titanian* or *Earth-born*, that warr'd on *Jove*,
> *Briarios* or *Typhon*, whom the Den
> By ancient *Tarsus* held, or that Sea-beast
> *Leviathan*, which God of all his works
> Created hugest that swim th' Ocean stream:
> Him haply slumbring on the *Norway* foam
> The pilot of some small night-foundered Skiff
> Deeming some Island, oft, as Sea-men tell,
> With fixed Anchor in his scaly rind
> Moors by his side under the Lee, while Night
> Invests the Sea, and wished Morn delays:
> So stretched out huge in Length the Arch-fiend lay
> Chain'd on the burning Lake[28]

This is not simply verbosity or exhaustiveness, or excess for its own sake; rather, the epic simile here and elsewhere in *Paradise Lost* is deeply bound up in Milton's cultural aesthetics. *Paradise Lost* is an epic, a form described by Pound as 'a poem including history'.[29] In the previous chapter, we noted how poetic forms are not neutral entities, but rather contain their own ideologies – this is radically the case with the epic: the historicity which Pound identified as contained within the epic is often put to directly political use, as part of a national or nationalist agenda of self-definition. (Epic often provides answers to such fundamental nationalist questions as 'who are we, as a people?', 'how did we come to be who we are?', 'what do we believe in?', 'who' – as the Klingons from *Star Trek*, epicists to the core, like to put it – 'are the enemies of our blood?': see, for example, Virgil's *Aeneid*, his epic poem of the foundation of Rome.) Furthermore, the epic had been theorized since Aristotle's *Poetics* as the most elevated, serious and important poetic form: to write an epic, then, constitutes an act of poetic self-aggrandizement. (As Wordsworth realized at the beginning of his own epic *The Prelude*, the highest poetic status requires an attempt at this highest poetic form: that poem, therefore, begins with Wordsworth trawling history for a suitably epic subject before deciding, in what must surely be the single most egomaniac gesture in literary history, to write an epic about himself.) Some literary historians have, indeed, tended to subdivide the epic into two classes on precisely the grounds of cultural aesthetics: the 'primary' epic (in essence, an oral national narrative: *The Odyssey*, *Gilgamesh*, *Beowulf*) and the 'secondary' epic ('literary', written by poets with a theorized knowledge of their form and its ideological significance: *The Aeneid*, *Paradise Lost*, *The Prelude*).[30] Thus, we note, the vehicles for comparison in Milton's epic simile are analogues to his own epic protagonist, Satan, from the classical tradition (Titans, giants; and from biblical epic Leviathan). In a kind of disguised typological master simile, Milton is here comparing *his own epic* to classical epic, valorizing his own work as fit epic material.

We noted earlier that metaphor can act as a form of reification, turning a concept into an object. Taken to its most extreme end, where language comes closest of all to visual representation, and especially when the vehicle is loaded with an emotional or spiritual significance, this reification makes a *symbol*. The commonest symbols carry a culturally validated, agreed-on meaning: the cross (Christianity – perhaps the commonest symbol of all); the dove (peace); the scales (justice); the Stars and Stripes (America: all flags, of course, are symbols – as well as displaying symbols); blue suede shoes (1950s teen rebellion: Elvis Presley throughout his career and continuing into his afterlife, is a powerful symbol).[31] In medieval romance, the Grail operates as a symbol for the loss of purity and the quest for rebirth (for fertility rites, originally) – a symbolism adopted in this century by T. S. Eliot in *The Waste Land*, who himself wrote under the influence of the French 'Symbolist' movement – Mallarmé, Baudelaire and, most notably for Eliot, Jules Laforgue.[32] In *Macbeth* or *Dracula*, blood operates as a symbol. English 'Country House' poems, such as Marvell's 'Upon Appleton House', or Ben Jonson's 'To Penshurst', figure the landed estate and estate management as symbolic of England, specifically of an idealized Englishness in which class relations operate on a familial basis (a society is transferred into a home), a social mechanics validated by the very bounty of the land:

> Thou hast thy ponds, that pay thee tribute fish,
> Fat aged carps that run into thy net,
> And pikes, now weary their own kind to eat, . . .
> Bright eels that emulate them, and leap on land
> Before the fisher, or into his hand.
> Then hath thy orchard fruit, thy garden flowers,
> Fresh as the air, and new as are the hours.
> The early cherry, with the later plum,
> Fig, grape, and quince, each in his time doth come;
> The blushing apricot and woolly peach
> Hang on thy walls, that every child may reach.

> And though thy walls be of the country stone,
> They're reared with no man's ruin, no man's groan[33]

This symbolism again bespeaks an ideology: a harmonious, familial model of England which is the essence of the kind of paternalist High Toryism most closely identified with the writings of Edmund Burke.

Because the symbol is an extreme form of linguistic representation, it can, where there is no agreed signification, become obscure or mystifying, apparently lacking in referent – a vehicle seemingly without a tenor. Readers generally seem able to tell that an image *is* symbolic, but sometimes have difficulty identifying the meaning of the symbol. Blake's 'The Sick Rose' contains such a symbol:

> O rose, thou art sick:
> The invisible worm
> That flies in the night,
> In the howling storm,
>
> Has found out thy bed
> Of crimson joy;
> And his dark secret love
> Does thy life destroy.[34]

Yes, this is symbolic – but of what? The poem has no external referent to guide readerly interpretation of the symbol, and thus it is fundamentally open-ended. Roses have traditionally symbolized love: is the poem a bitter comment on decaying and destroyed love, or on shattered ideals? Is it, indeed, a sexual poem: is the rose a vagina, and thus the poem about loss of virginity: 'Has found out thy bed / Of crimson joy'? Is the poem sexual, but about sexually transmitted disease: 'The invisible worm . . . / Does thy life destroy'? Conversely, the rose can also symbolize England (the Wars of the Roses; the England rugby team has a rose on its jersey): is the poem, then, a symbolic representation of 'something rotten' in England, a state-of-the-nation poem like so many others in its collection, *Songs of Experience*? This open-endedness means that there can be no one, definitive answer here.

At least with 'The Sick Rose' we can narrow down the symbol to a few potential, albeit conflicting, interpretations (most readers will recognize that it is not a poem about gardening). Some poetry resists even this measure of interpretive ease, offering an entirely personal, private symbolism. As T. S. Eliot noted, this is an inherent problem with the symbol, even for the poet:

> Why, for all of us, out of all that we have heard, seen, felt, in a lifetime, do certain images recur, charged with emotion, rather than others? The song of one bird, the leap of one fish, at a particular place and time, the scent of one flower, an old woman on a German mountain path, six

ruffians seen through an open window playing cards at night at a small
railway junction where there was a water-mill: such memories may have
symbolic value, but of what we cannot tell, for they come to represent
the depths of feeling into which we cannot peer.[35]

The 'six ruffians' here seem to come directly from Eliot's own poetic
symbolism, in 'The Journey of the Magi':

> Then we came to a tavern with vine-leaves over the lintel,
> Six hands at an open door dicing for pieces of silver,
> And feet kicking the empty wine-skins.[36]

(Eliot himself, when asked for the meaning of the line 'Lady, three white
leopards sat under a juniper tree' from 'Ash Wednesday', reputedly
responded, 'It means, "Lady, three white leopards sat under a juniper tree".')

W. B. Yeats is an example of a poet who frequently uses an entirely
private symbolism: the tower, the winding stair, the gyres, and, from 'Easter
1916', the stone:

> The long-legged moor-hens dive,
> The hens to the moor-cocks call;
> Minute by minute they live:
> The stone's in the midst of all.[37]

How can we interpret this symbol? According to Ernest Renan, the scholar
of Celticism whose works Yeats had studied, the Celts, as an 'ancient'
people, worshipped stones – a kind of religion called *chthonic*, of the earth.
Is this the significance of the stone here for Yeats – the primal symbol of
Celtic, and specifically for him Irish, belief? Perhaps, but according to
Terence Brown the stone has a different symbolic meaning here: Yeats's
private writings (memoirs, letters, journals) contain a recurring image of
women being turned into stone through their involvement in politics, at one
point imaging forth 'an hysterical woman, who will make unmeasured
accusations and believe impossible things, because of some logical deduc-
tion from a solitary thought which has turned her mind to stone'.[38] 'Easter
1916', commemorating the Easter Rising in Dublin, is partly written about
one woman, the Irish revolutionary Constance Markiewicz, and for
another, Yeats's beloved Maud Gonne; the poem partly conflates these two
figures. This reading would certainly make sense of the poem's other refer-
ence to the stone:

> Too long a sacrifice
> Can make a stone of the heart[39]

Used in this way, the stone is recognizably symbolic, a variant on 'having a
heart of stone', or 'getting blood out of a stone'. However, Yeats's usage is
far more specific, and there is nothing intrinsic to the poem, or in cultural
symbology at large, that might lead us to read the symbol in precisely the

way he meant it to be read: it remains a private symbolism, to be unearthed only through specialist biographical scholarship.

Symbolism is often articulated through the device of *metonymy*. If the metaphor operates through transference and the simile through comparison, then metonymy (and the closely related synecdoche) operates through substitution. In metonymy, an aspect of something is made to stand for (to act as substitute for) the whole: in 'traditional' gender stereotypes, beauty and virtue have stood as metonyms for 'woman', bravery and strength for 'man'. When we describe someone as 'heartless' (meaning callous), we are speaking metonymically, as we are when we refer to 'the crown', meaning the king or queen, or 'sources close to Number 10', meaning the 'sources close to the prime minister'. Amongst the most common metonyms is the soul, taken as an attribute of, and made to stand for, goodness or selfhood, as when someone is described as a 'kindly soul' or a 'brave soul', or as in this passage from T. S. Eliot's 'Preludes':

> His soul stretched tight across the skies
> That fade behind a city block,
> Or trampled by insistent feet
> At four and five and six o'clock[40]

Allegory, where characters exist as embodiments of their attributes, can therefore be seen as a form of metonymy: consider the Seven Deadly Sins – Sloth, Avarice, Gluttony, Wrath, Envy, Pride, Lust – or the Four Horsemen of the Apocalypse – Death, War, Famine and Pestilence. Metonymy, we noted, is sometimes used to articulate symbols, as in the following lines from '(I Can't Get No) Satisfaction':

> When I'm watching my TV
> And a man comes on and tells me
> How white my shirts can be:
> But he can't be a man, 'cause he doesn't smoke
> The same cigarettes as me[41]

Here, cigarettes are made to stand as an attribute of manliness (which, as any man who smokes will tell you, they are), and the right brand of cigarettes becomes a symbol for manliness. (These lines surely draw on the famous advertising figure of the 'Marlboro Man', a rugged cowboy, as well as alluding to slogans such as 'The Ultimate in Smoking Satisfaction': advertising, of course, is a powerfully symbolic medium.)

Like metonymy, the synecdoche operates through substitution, in this case the substitution of a part for the whole: when we say 'that's a nice set of wheels', meaning 'that's a nice car', or speak of 'sails' to signify ship, 'hearth' for home, or 'threads' for clothes, we are using synecdoches. Dylan Thomas's poem 'The hand that signed the paper' is a sustained exercise in poetic synecdoche – unusually, for Thomas, deployed for political comment. This is its opening stanza:

> The hand that signed the paper felled a city;
> Five sovereign fingers taxed the breath,
> Doubled the globe of dead and halved a country;
> These five kings did a king to death.[42]

The synecdoche here has the hand representing the whole body politic, symbolically itself an embodiment of ruthless, destructive power – that is, bombing campaigns. This hand–self synecdoche is the same as that famously used by Charles Dickens in *Hard Times* where the Coketown factory workers are habitually referred to as 'the hands' – a devastating synecdoche critiquing dehumanizing nineteenth-century industrial capitalism in which individuals are reduced to their hands, the only part of them which has any use value in the manufacturing process.

We shall end this chapter with an analysis of a sonnet by John Keats, one of the most densely metaphorical poets in the English language:

> Bright star! would I were steadfast as thou art –
> Not in lone splendour hung aloft the night
> And watching, with eternal lids apart,
> Like nature's patient, sleepless Eremite,
> The moving waters at their priestlike task
> Of pure ablution round earth's human shores,
> Or gazing on the new soft-fallen mask
> Of snow upon the mountains and the moors –
> No – yet still steadfast, still unchangeable,
> Pillowed upon my fair love's ripening breast,
> To feel forever its soft swell and fall,
> Awake forever in a sweet unrest,
> Still, still to hear her tender-taken breath,
> And so live ever – or else swoon to death.[43]

In common with most Romantic poets, Keats took his own vocation as a poet enormously seriously: his letters, which amount to a philosophical statement of aesthetics (that is, theories of beauty), testify to this. In a famous letter to his friend Benjamin Bailey, Keats wrote:

I am certain of nothing but the holiness of the Heart's affections and the truth of Imagination – What the imagination seizes as beauty must be truth – whether it existed before or not – for I have the same Idea of all our Passions as of Love they are all in their sublime, creative of essential Beauty – . . . The Imagination may be compared to Adam's dream, – he awoke and found it truth. I am the more zealous in this affair, because I have never yet been able to perceive how any thing can be known for truth by consequitive reasoning – and yet it must be – Can it be that even the greatest Philosopher ever arrived at his goal without putting aside numerous objections –

However it may be, O for a life of sensations rather than thoughts![44]

This insistence on the primacy of the imagination, on its creative power, makes Keats's aesthetics thoroughgoingly Romantic – an insistence, that is, on the individual creative agency and therefore on the central importance of the poet as creator (similar ideas can be found in Blake, in Coleridge and in Shelley). Similarly Romantic is the elevation of the 'sublime' – that which transcends reason: this kind of anti-rationalism can also be found in Wordsworth and especially in Blake. Thus, for Keats, the 'life of sensations rather than thoughts' is very much the life of the poet: he famously called this 'Negative Capability', a transcendental quality in poetry that cannot be accounted for rationally, 'when man is capable of being in uncertainties, Mysteries, doubts, without any irritable reaching after fact & reason'.[45]

The 'Bright Star' sonnet is a poem of 'Negative Capability', anti-rationalist in that its meaning *cannot* be reduced to any logical paraphrase: the poem does not, in the ordinary sense, 'mean' very much at all – but this was precisely Keats's point. In his aesthetics, Keats was fascinated by art and the capacity of art to survive (or transcend) life. His 'Ode on a Grecian Urn' ostensibly compares the transience of life with the permanence of art, albeit with ambivalence: the urn is described as a 'cold pastoral', beautiful but lifeless, having left behind 'all breathing human passions'. The poem ends with a famous aesthetic statement which reiterates the terms from his letter to Benjamin Bailey:

> 'Beauty is truth, truth beauty, – that is all
> Ye know on earth, and all ye need to know.'[46]

'Bright Star' is a Shakespearean sonnet (in more ways than one: Keats wrote the poem on the flyleaf of his edition of Shakespeare); furthermore, this *may* be the last poem he ever wrote – this is unclear, but commentators perhaps find it in keeping with Keats's Romantic poetic persona (live fast, die young, leave a good-looking corpse) that his last poetic words should be 'swoon to death'. The sonnet's octet (its first eight lines; the sestet is its concluding six) contains an intricate extended (and mixed) metaphor–simile combination: a star with eyes ('eternal lids', eyes which never close) is likened to 'Nature's patient, sleepless Eremite' (that is, hermit – a religious recluse: this is another metaphor – nature does not literally have hermits). The hermit star watches the waters, whose tides metaphorically perform the 'ablution' (ceremonial washing) of priests around the shores of the earth, which are metaphorically 'human', as are 'the mountains and the moors', which have upon them a 'mask / Of snow', and therefore metaphorically have faces (wear masks). But this dense and complex image is framed by words which deny its validity: 'Not in lone splendour ... No – yet still steadfast'. Thus this lengthy image, taking up more than half the poem, is revealed not to be an image at all, or to be the wrong image, *not* the image which governs the poem's meaning: it is an eight-line image giving an account of what the star is *not* like (not *un*like its Shakespearean precedent, 'My mistress' eyes are nothing like the sun').

So, how does the star resemble the speaker, or how does he wish it resembled him? In its unchangingness, he wants it metaphorically to represent himself lying with his love forever – yet even this is metaphorically represented: 'Pillowed upon my fair love's ripening breast'. This condenses two images: like the star whose constancy represents him, or whose constancy he wants to resemble, the speaker wants to lie forever on his love's breasts, which are themselves metaphorically represented simultaneously as pillows and as ripening fruit.

Are there too many metaphors here? This is a question which could also be asked of another of Keats's sonnets:

> When I have fears that I may cease to be
> Before my pen has gleaned my teeming brain,
> Before high-piled books, in charactery,
> Hold like rich garners the full-ripened grain;
> When I behold, upon the night's starred face,
> Huge cloudy symbols of a high romance,
> And think that I may never live to trace
> Their shadows, with the magic hand of chance;
> And when I feel, fair creature of an hour!
> That I shall never look upon thee more,
> Never have relish in the faery power
> Of unreflecting love! – then on the shore
> Of the wide world I stand alone, and think
> Till love and fame to nothingness do sink.[47]

This was Keats's first published attempt at a Shakespearean sonnet, and like some of Shakespeare's, this sonnet is divisible into four sections, distinguished here by changes in patterns of imagery: lines 1–4, 5–8, 9–12, 12–14. The first section contains an extended metaphor whose tenor is creativity (writing poetry) and whose vehicle is the harvest: the pen gleans (gathers corn or wheat from) the 'teeming brain'; books are garnered (stored) like ripening grain. The second section offers images within images: 'the night's starred face', a metaphor, is metaphorically represented as 'cloudy', and these clouds are themselves 'symbols of a high romance', whose 'shadows' the speaker wants to 'trace'. But this 'metaphor-metaphor-symbol' is itself a part of a greater double metaphor – symbols are poetic images, they do not cast 'shadows', and anyway tracing the shadows of these symbols is itself a metaphor, for writing poetry. As if this were not complicated enough, the writing of poetry is itself performed metaphorically, with 'the magic hand of chance'. This is another double metaphor: chance is an abstraction, it does not have hands; hands themselves are not 'magic', except metaphorically.

The harvest imagery of the first section of 'When I have fears' is an imagery that gets its fullest and most celebrated expression in Keats's 'To Autumn':

> Season of mists and mellow fruitfulness,
> Close bosom-friend of the maturing sun,
> Conspiring with him how to load and bless
> With fruit the vines that round the thatch-eves run;
> To bend with apples the mossed cottage-trees,
> And fill all fruit with ripeness to the core;
> To swell the gourd, and plump the hazel shells
> With a sweet kernel; to set budding more,
> And still more, later flowers for the bees,
> Until they think warm days will never cease,
> For Summer has o'er-brimmed their clammy cells.[48]

Such images of ripeness and fullness (for which words there are many synonyms in this stanza alone) are common in Keats's poetry. This excess may be interpreted as over-writing – Keats's poetry is too rich, too ripe, full, sticky ('clammy', reiterated in the last line of the second stanza: 'Thou watchest the last oozings hours by hours'), too dependent on lavish imagery, as in the apparently ridiculously metaphorical opening section of 'When I have fears'. But this poetic practice has clear links with Keats's aesthetic theories, his notion of the poem as an exercise in the creation of truth through beauty. If the poems strike readers as overly metaphorical, as full of image but lacking in sense, that, really, is the point: that is what they are 'about'. In a way, all of Keats's poetry is about beautiful poetry, about the creation of beautiful images – in other words, the poems are often about *themselves*. This is why Keats's poetry, unusually for Romanticism, so rarely refers to external events – it is entirely engaged in its own internal aesthetics. If his poems have 'subjects', these subjects are usually highly generalized abstractions or ideals – death, art, beauty, permanence, transience. The imagery of 'To Autumn' notwithstanding, Keats can hardly be called a 'nature poet' at all (certainly not when compared to a true Romantic nature poet like John Clare). 'To Autumn' uses nature as a vehicle for (an exercise in) the production of beautiful images; 'Ode to a Nightingale' isn't really about a nightingale at all, but uses the bird as a symbolic vehicle for a meditation upon abstractions (once again, death, transience, etc.). In other words, if Keats's poems are 'too metaphorical', this may be because, if they are about anything, they are *about* metaphors.

Endnotes

1 Victor Shklovsky, 'Art as Technique', in *Russian Formalist Criticism: Four Essays*, trans. Lee T. Lemon and Marion J. Reis (Lincoln, Nebr., and London,

1965), p. 5. Shklovsky's essay goes on to qualify this assertion, particularly with regard to 'the relative ease of the process'.

2 For the etymology of 'image' and its cognates, see *New Princeton Encyclopedia*, p. 559.

3 Paul Ricoeur, *The Rule of Metaphor: Multi-Disciplinary Studies in the Creation of Meaning*, trans. Robert Czerny (Toronto, 1977).

4 See Stephen Jay Gould, 'Four Metaphors in Three Generations', in *Dinosaur in a Haystack* (Harmondsworth, 1997), pp. 442–57, for this.

5 Steven Pinker, *The Language Instinct* (Harmondsworth, 1995), p. 230.

6 Ferdinand de Saussure, *Course in General Linguistics*, ed. Charles Bally, Albert Sechehaye and Albert Reidlinger, trans. Wade Baskin (New York, 1966), pp. 67–8.

7 Paul de Man, *Blindness and Insight: Essays in the Rhetoric of Contemporary Criticism* (Minneapolis, 1983), p. 11.

8 Ricoeur, *The Rule of Metaphor*, p. 110.

9 e. e. cummings, 'the Cambridge ladies who live in furnished souls', in *Norton Anthology of Poetry*, p. 1283.

10 T. S. Eliot, 'Preludes', in *Collected Poems, 1909–62* (London, 1963), p. 23.

11 For an analysis of this, see John Carey, *The Intellectuals and the Masses: Pride and Prejudice in the Literary Intelligentsia, 1880–1939* (London, 1992).

12 Bob Dylan, 'It's All Over Now Baby Blue', from *Bringing It All Back Home* (1964).

13 *The Bloomsbury Dictionary of Quotations* (London, 1991), p. 36.

14 *Norton Anthology of Poetry*, p. 139. Tichborne wrote the poem while imprisoned in the Tower of London accused of participating in a Catholic plot against Queen Elizabeth I; he was executed shortly after writing this poem.

15 Shklovsky, 'Art as Technique', p. 13. Italics in original.

16 *Norton Anthology of Poetry*, p. 1824.

17 Francis Thompson, *The Hound of Heaven*, in *The Norton Anthology of English Literature*, sixth edition, vol. 2, ed. M. H. Abrams *et al.* (New York and London, 1993), p. 1668.

18 Philip Larkin, *Collected Poems* (London, 1988), p. 89.

19 Larkin, *Collected Poems*, p. 148.

20 John Dryden, 'Discourse Concerning the Original and Progress of Satire', in *Dryden: A Selection*, ed. John Conaghan (London, 1978), pp. 575–606.

21 Samuel Johnson, 'Lives of the Poets' [Abraham Cowley], in *The Norton Anthology of English Literature*, fifth edition, vol. 1, ed. M. H. Abrams *et al.* (New York and London, 1986), p. 2419.

22 Donne, *Complete English Poems*, p. 72.

23 Geoffrey N. Leech, *A Linguistic Guide to English Poetry* (London, 1969), p. 156.

24 Big Joe Turner, 'Shake, Rattle and Roll', Atlantic 1026 (1954).

25 Madonna, 'Like a Virgin', Sire W 9210 (1984).

26 *Norton Anthology of Poetry*, p. 240.

27 *Norton Anthology of Poetry*, p. 767.

28 Milton, *Paradise Lost*, Book I, in *Complete Poems*, pp. 163–4.

29 Pound, *ABC of Reading*, p. 46.

30 See, for example, Paul Merchant, *The Epic* (London, 1971), p. vii and *passim*.

31 See Greil Marcus, *Dead Elvis: A Chronicle of a Cultural Obsession* (London, 1992), for Elvis symbolism.

32 See *New Princeton Encyclopedia*, pp. 1256–9, for the Symbolists.

33 Ben Jonson, 'To Penshurst', in *Norton Anthology of Poetry*, p. 297.

34 Blake, *Complete Poems*, pp. 216–17.

35 Eliot, *Selected Prose*, p. 95.

36 Eliot, *Collected Poems*, pp. 109–10.
37 W. B. Yeats, *Selected Poetry* (London, 1974), p. 95.
38 Quoted in Terence Brown, *The Life of W. B. Yeats: A Critical Biography* (London, forthcoming). We are grateful to the author for allowing us to consult the manuscript version of this book.
39 Yeats, *Selected Poetry*, p. 95.
40 Eliot, *Collected Poems*, p. 24.
41 The Rolling Stones, '(I Can't Get No) Satisfaction', London 9766 (1965).
42 Dylan Thomas, *Collected Poems*, p. 56.
43 John Keats, *The Complete Poems*, ed. John Barnard (Harmondsworth, 1977), p. 452.
44 *Selected Poems and Letters of Keats*, ed. Robert Gittings (London, 1966), p. 37.
45 *Selected Poems and Letters of Keats*, p. 41.
46 Keats, *Complete Poems*, p. 346. These lines are in inverted commas because they are 'spoken' by the urn in the poem.
47 Keats, *Complete Poems*, p. 221.
48 Keats, *Complete Poems*, p. 434.

|3|

Poem and tradition

I live, I let myself go on living, so that Borges may contrive his litera-
ture, and this literature justifies me. It is no effort for me to confess
that he has achieved some valid pages, but those pages cannot save
me, perhaps because what is good belongs to no one, not even to him,
but rather to the language and to tradition.

Jorge Luis Borges[1]

Several chapters in this book are concerned, to varying degrees, with the
legacy of Romanticism, with the ways in which it has profoundly altered
our practice as readers, the ways in which our expectations of what poetry
should be have been altered or even created by the Romantic aesthetics of
selfhood and self-expression, emotionalism and sincerity, encapsulated in
Wordsworth's famous dictum that 'Poetry is the spontaneous overflow of
powerful feelings: it takes its origin from emotion recollected in tranquil-
lity'.[2] Unscientific and anecdotal though this may be, straw polls taken in
tutorials on poetry over a number of years have revealed, quite consistently,
that while many students claim not to (claim not to be able to!) read poetry,
a fairly large number claim to have *written* poetry. Asked to describe this
poetry, three consistent factors are revealed: firstly, it is emphatically the
poetry of 'the spontaneous overflow of powerful feelings' (without neces-
sarily being 'recollected in tranquillity'); secondly, that it is written in *vers
libre*; thirdly, that it is an *entirely* private medium, not intended to be read
by anyone other than its author. Suggestions that this is a form of therapy
rather than poetry (that such writing belongs firmly in the genre known as
'angst' – or, better, 'wangst' – poetry) are often met with a disappointed
silence.

This is not necessarily, needlessly, to disparage such endeavours.
Certainly, Romantic poetics are as valid as any other, and have a rich cultural
heritage; but they are not the only poetics, nor, in spite of their dominance,
should they be considered normative, with all other poetics thought of as a
deviation from a Romantic mean (for one thing, this attitude bespeaks bad

historicism: Romanticism, not much more than 200 years old, is a relative poetic newcomer). Can one write poetry without really having read any? Not even the most extreme of the Romantics would say so (Wordsworth himself certainly would not have done).

In the abstract, the notion of 'tradition' can seem conservative and stultifying, far removed from the appealingly dynamic radicalism which we associate with Romantic poetics – such as Shelley's belief that 'Poets are the unacknowledged legislators of the world'[3] (making the highest claims for poetry), or Blake's assertion in *The Marriage of Heaven and Hell* that 'Milton . . . was a true poet, and of the Devil's party, without knowing it'[4] (for Blake, poetry was by definition a radical or even a revolutionary activity: Satan, the archetypal rebel or revolutionary, was also, therefore, the archetypal poet, a belief echoed and developed in Shelley's *Prometheus Unbound*). It is also true, we shall see, that many of the most influential appeals to the centrality of 'tradition' in poetics (such as T. S. Eliot's) have been predicated on a cultural conservatism. Nevertheless, a knowledge of tradition, of the place of a poem or genre within a tradition, of how partaking of or developing or deviating from a tradition can contribute to the force or the meaning of a poem, is an important element in the reading or studying of poetry. This chapter will begin with a critical account of some of the theories of 'tradition' put forward in poetics this century, and will end with an account of a specific poetic genre, the elegy, showing how the principles of 'tradition' and 'influence' have operated across the centuries.

The twentieth-century appeal to 'tradition' (or, more emphatically, 'Tradition') is closely associated with the cultural politics and aesthetics of Modernism. In a 1913 essay, 'The Tradition', Pound wrote:

> A return to origins invigorates because it is a return to nature and reason. The man who returns to origins does so because he wishes to behave in the eternally sensible manner. That is to say, naturally, reasonably, intuitively. . . . He wishes not pedagogy but harmony, the fitting thing.[5]

As previous chapters have argued, appeals to harmony, to a natural order of things, to organicism, are often predicated on a conservative or right-wing agenda (and so they are here: Pound, after all, was to become one of the most notorious anglophone fascists, incarcerated for treason as a consequence of his politics). Raymond Williams, in *The Country and the City*, an analysis of the history of 'golden age' organicism, writes:

> this kind of critique of capitalism enfolds social values which, if they do become active, at once spring to the defence of a certain kind of order, certain social hierarchies and moral stabilities, which have a feudal ring, but a more relevant and more dangerous contemporary application. Some of these 'rural' virtues, in twentieth-century intellectual movements, leave the land to become a charter of explicit

social reaction: in the defence of traditional property settlements, or in the offensive against democracy in the name of blood and soil.[6]

The title of Pound's 1934 volume of writings, *Make It New* (a slogan which has become inseparably associated with Modernist poetics) contains a profound paradox: reinventing poetic discourse for the twentieth century involved a return to the past, a 'return to origins'. This is why so much Modernist poetry can be said to contain its own traditions: think of the tapestry of allusion, quotation, translation, echo, and reference that comprises Eliot's *The Waste Land* or Pound's *Cantos*. As Stan Smith notes in his study *The Origins of Modernism*:

> By [their own] reckoning, none of the great Modernists could be called 'original', since a great part of their originality lies precisely in flaunting those traces and transformations, demonstrating self-consciously the operations they have performed on their sources. . . . Modernism's originality, that is, lies in making the transformative act of translation, adaptation, repetition its real content. . . . For what translation foregrounds is the fact of cultural relativity, at the very moment that it invents a 'timeless' tradition where all art co-exists.[7]

In part, this Modernist poetics is a response to, and a short-circuiting of, the Romantic poetics of revolution and self-fashioning, for what it does is attempt to dispense altogether with the notions of selfhood, individuality and personality. T. S. Eliot's essay 'Tradition and the Individual Talent' (1919) provides the most notable articulation of this kind of thinking, and may indeed be the most influential document of poetic theory of its century. As such, it's worth quoting at some length:

> Tradition . . . cannot be inherited, and if you want it you must obtain it by great labour. It involves, in the first place, the historical sense, which we may call nearly indispensable to anyone who would continue to be a poet beyond his twenty-fifth year; and the historical sense involves a perception, not only of the pastness of the past, but of its presence: the historical sense compels a man to write not merely with his own generation in his bones, but with a feeling that the whole of the literature of Europe from Homer and within it the whole of the literature of his own country has a simultaneous existence and composes a simultaneous order. This historical sense, which is a sense of the timeless as well as of the temporal and of the timeless and of the temporal together, is what makes a writer traditional. And it is at the same time what makes a writer most acutely conscious of his place in time, of his own contemporaneity.
>
> No poet, no artist of any art, has his complete meaning alone. His significance, his appreciation is the appreciation of his relation to the dead poets and artists. You cannot value him alone; you must set him, for contrast and comparison, among the dead.[8]

In part, this is a calculated affront to Romantic aesthetics: selfhood is subsumed into a mighty, atemporal tradition of literature, infinitely greater than any puny individual (we are a long way from Wordsworth's 'epic of the self' here), a tradition of which a poet (or any writer) can partake, a tradition to which he or she can add – but only *from within*. There can be no revolutionaries in the tradition.

Eliot also, of course, has a political as well as an aesthetic agenda here. Eliot's 'tradition' is a lofty, difficult affair: its burden, the burden of 'the whole of the literature of Europe from Homer' is, quite deliberately, one that most people (including, emphatically, the writers of this book) would find impossible to bear, even supposing that they wanted to. The tradition is the most exclusive of clubs. We might call this kind of thinking 'high cultural' – a kind of thinking which has its modern origins in the writings of Matthew Arnold, particularly *Culture and Anarchy* (1867–8). A characteristic of Modernism was that many of its practitioners (Eliot, Pound, Yeats, D. H. Lawrence, F. R. Leavis, and many others) were implacably opposed to *modernity*:[9] back in the 1860s, Arnold's volume – an attempt to define the parameters of 'high culture', parameters which, Arnoldian thinking believed, had not needed defining before but rather were accepted as a given, a shared cultural heritage on which all could agree – was a symptom of the insecurity of a cultural élite faced with the apparently unstoppable onslaught of modernity. In socio-political terms this meant industrialization, the demographic shifts brought about by the industrial revolution since the late eighteenth century, bringing large populations of working people together for the first time, in cities; in cultural terms, this had the effect of creating a visible, lively, influential 'mass culture', brought about both by a steady rise in literacy and by the availability of cheap and widely disseminable publishing, most notably in the form of newspapers. The newspaper, indeed, became a kind of a symbol of cultural degradation for Modernists, and the popular press was attacked by Eliot for 'affirm[ing] . . . a complacent, prejudiced and unthinking mass', and by Leavis for 'an overthrow of standards'.[10] Eliot clearly believed himself to be living through the development of an Arnoldian cultural crisis with its roots in the previous century: in 1921 he wrote, 'the twentieth century is still the nineteenth, although it may in time acquire its own character'.[11] By Eliot's time, in fact, this anti-modernity had become a stance of thoroughgoing reaction: as the famous line from *The Waste Land* has it, 'These fragments I have shored against my ruins'[12] – the 'fragments', that is, of the tradition, used to shore up the crumbling cathedral of high culture (though 'my ruins' here also suggests the possibility of another, more personal reading).

This accounts for the appeal of the Modernists to the past, to 'origins', to harmony, organicism, ruralism: it is an appeal to the pre-modern, a hearkening back to the pre-industrial. This appeal has understandably led to some powerful critiques, particularly from critics with left-wing sympathies such as Raymond Williams and, writing explicitly on Eliot, Terry Eagleton:

What Eliot was in fact assaulting was the whole ideology of middle-class liberalism, the official ruling ideology of industrial capitalist society. Liberalism, Romanticism, protestantism, economic individualism: all of these are the perverted dogmas of those expelled from the happy garden of the organic society, with nothing to fall back on but their paltry individual resources. Eliot's own solution is an extreme right-wing authoritarianism: men and women must sacrifice their petty 'personalities' and opinions to an impersonal order. In the sphere of literature, this impersonal order is the Tradition.[13]

Eliot suggested that readers of poetry should 'pass beyond the limitations of the nineteenth century into a new freedom'[14] – that is, they should imaginatively leapfrog the entire Romantic endeavour, for by that time the 'dissociation of sensibility' had set in. This is:

> something which had happened to the mind of England between the time of Donne or Lord Herbert of Cherbury and the time of Tennyson or Browning; it is the difference between the intellectual poet and the reflective poet. Tennyson and Browning are poets, and they think; but they do not feel their thought as immediately as the odour of a rose. A thought to Donne was an experience; it modified his sensibility.[15]

This is the condition of modern, industrial, post-Romantic humanity – alienated, dissociated even from their (our!) own sensibility, spiritually dead: 'A crowd flowed over London Bridge, so many, / I had not thought death had undone so many', Eliot wrote in *The Waste Land*.[16]

Eliot's anti-Romantic animus, and the limitations it imposed on his ideas of poetic tradition, can be clearly illustrated by his attitude to Blake:

> Blake was endowed with a capacity for considerable understanding of human nature, with a remarkable and original sense of language and the music of language, and a gift of hallucinated vision. Had these been controlled by a respect for impersonal reason, for common sense, for the objectivity of science, it would have been better for him. What his genius required, and what it sadly lacked, was a framework of accepted and traditional ideas which would have prevented him from indulging in a philosophy of his own, and concentrated his attention upon the problems of the poet. . . . The concentration resulting from a framework of mythology and theology and philosophy is one of the reasons why Dante is a classic, and Blake only a poet of genius. The fault is perhaps not with Blake himself, but with the environment which failed to provide what such a poet needed.[17]

This 'environment' was the background of eighteenth-century London working-class and artisan radical dissent which produced Blake. It was, as E. P. Thompson has shown, a background rich in intellectual debate, in the free exchange of just the kinds of theological and philosophical enquiry which Eliot suggests that Blake lacked.[18] It was also, however, by definition a background of religious and consequently intellectual nonconformity – setting itself quite deliberately, and on grounds of class, in opposition to mainstream culture and belief (working men, barred from study at the universities – that is, Oxford and Cambridge – were to set up their own, highly effective, 'Dissenting Academies', the symbolic ancestors of nineteenth-century industrial 'redbrick' universities). Although Blake's 'tradition' does contain some unproblematically canonical figures, notably Milton and Bunyan, as well as the various eighteenth-century hymn writers, ideologues, and eccentrics on whom he draws, this radical tradition, however complex, varied and intellectually engaged it was, was not one which Eliot's conservative aesthetics could accommodate. Thus, whilst grudgingly and patronizingly admitting Blake's 'genius' ('mere' though it may be), Eliot can clearly find no room for him in the tradition: Romanticism's achievements had to be acknowledged somehow, and here Eliot casts a major Romantic poet as ex-centric to the tradition, beyond the pale – an outsider, albeit an interesting one (which admittedly, though for very different ideological reasons – outsiderliness is a good thing, not a shortcoming – is how Blake would have viewed himself). Blake, effectively, is excluded from the tradition on class grounds.

The critic Harold Bloom recently wrote how, as a young academic, he found himself in reaction to Eliot's ideas (though it has to be admitted that, in the book from which the following quotation comes, *The Western Canon*, Bloom's position has come to resemble Eliot's):

> I began my teaching career nearly forty years ago in an academic context dominated by the ideas of T. S. Eliot; ideas that roused me to fury, and against which I fought as vigorously as I could.[19]

Bloom, a Romantic scholar who first came to prominence as the author of studies of Shelley and Blake, articulated his reaction to Eliot's 'tradition' most powerfully in his book *The Anxiety of Influence*.[20] Bloom's schema replaces an impersonal tradition with a highly personal, personalized model of 'influence': effectively, a kind of Freudian psychodrama of the Oedipal variety in which a poet wrestles creatively with a 'strong' precursor (a process Bloom has called the *agon*), writing out of the shadow of that precursor and shedding his influence through a process of misreading (a symbolically Oedipal 'killing of the father'). This is, of course, a thoroughly Romantic view of poetic creation, and it is a view which Bloom applies ingeniously to Romantic poetry. Wordsworth's 'strong' precursor, according to Bloom, is Milton; his sonnet to Milton enacts his struggle with his precursor, culminating in an act of 'misprision' in which Wordsworth deals with Milton's presence by symbolically making him a star, reducing him to a figure of speech (a simile) within the poem:

Milton! Thou shouldst be living at this hour:
England hath need of thee: she is a fen
Of stagnant waters: altar, sword and pen,
Fireside, the heroic wealth of hall and bower,
Have forfeited their ancient English dower
Of inward happiness. We are selfish men;
Oh! raise us up, return to us again;
And give us manners, virtue, freedom, power.
Thy soul was like a Star, and dwelt apart:
Thou hadst a voice whose sound was like the sea:
Pure as the naked heavens, majestic, free,
So didst thou travel on life's common way,
In cheerful godliness; and yet thy heart
The lowliest duties on herself did lay.[21]

It has to be said that most critics do not accept Bloom's ideas (though, melo-dramatic as they may be, they do offer a useful Romantic corrective to the dominant, impersonal, Modernist view of poetic tradition); certainly, many readers would not accept Bloom's reading of this poem. Nevertheless, a kind of Bloomian reading (though not one which Bloom himself offers) does make a certain sense here, in that the poem does seem to alternate between two conflicting registers of language. The first, hortatory and public (or even 'national'), we might call (in honour of Bloom) 'Miltonic'; the second, natural and private, we might call 'Wordsworthian'. The poem opens in Miltonic tones: 'Milton! Thou shouldst be living at this hour: / England hath need of thee'; shifting after the caesura in the second line to the Wordsworthian: 'she is a fen / Of stagnant waters'. The next lines are Miltonic: 'altar, sword and pen, / Fireside, the heroic wealth of hall and bower, / Have forfeited their ancient English dower'; however, all this is then renegotiated in Wordsworthian terms, figuring public experience in private language: '. . . their ancient English dower / Of *inward happiness*'. This 'inward' rhetoric is itself in turn interrogated ('We are selfish men'), the poem returning to the Miltonic: 'Oh! raise us up, return to us again; / And give us manners, virtue, freedom, power'. After this comes what is for Bloom the poem's crux – 'Thy soul was like a Star', following which the poem, its struggles over, concludes in Wordsworthian fashion, with a series of natural images. By the closing line, the grand public rhetoric of the poem's opening lines ('England hath need of thee') has been both feminized (a feminization anticipated by the 'bower' / 'dower' rhyme in an earlier Miltonic section) and consequently domesticized: 'The lowliest duties on herself did lay'. Saviour of the nation at the beginning of the poem, by its close Milton is figured as a housewife. Thus, there is indeed a sense in which the poem enacts a poetic conflict between Wordsworth and Milton.

One thing that Bloom and the Modernists share is an interest in the canon. The canon is effectively a list – a list of the great works which comprise Literature, and consequently contribute to Culture; a list upon whose contents, *in theory*, there should be broad agreement, an agreement based on shared evaluative criteria, or 'taste'. This, certainly, is how Arnold viewed the idea of Culture, at the same time as seeing it under threat from cultural 'Philistines' (the middle class, or anyway the petty-bourgeoisie) and 'Barbarians' (the working class); the role of the critic was to counter these tendencies through being a model of 'disinterestedness':

> And how is criticism to show disinterestedness? By keeping aloof from what is called 'the practical view of things'; by resolutely following the law of its own nature, which is to be a free play of the mind on all subjects which it touches. By steadily refusing to lend itself to any of those ulterior, political, practical considerations about ideas, which plenty of people will be sure to attach to them, which perhaps ought often to be attached to them, which in this country at any rate are certain to be attached to them quite sufficiently, but which criticism has really nothing to do with. Its business is, as I have said, simply to know the best that is known and thought in the world, and by in its turn making this known, to create a current of true and fresh ideas. Its business is to do this with inflexible honesty, with due ability; but its business is to do no more, and to leave alone all questions of practical consequences and applications, questions which will never fail to have due prominence given to them.[22]

By 'the practical view of things . . . those ulterior, political, practical considerations' Arnold means utilitarianism, the guiding ideology of nineteenth-century industrial capitalism, in which value was assigned an object or idea solely in terms of its material usefulness: thus Culture, an entity with no discernible material value (other than in crude terms, in the commercial value, say, of works of art), was highly problematic in utilitarian terms, and tended to be dismissed (John Locke, founding theorist of utilitarianism, testily asked, 'What is the *use* of poetry?').[23] As a reaction to this, Arnold's stance is understandable. It is also, however, either naive or disingenuous: in divorcing Culture from materialism, it also makes claims for his own class – the upper middle class, custodians of Culture – as beyond ideology, capable of transcending the material concerns of the rest of Victorian society in order to dwell in an unworldly Parnassus of Art. Culture was thus the province (in modern terms, perhaps, the *Provence*) of people very like Matthew Arnold, and nobody else.

The truth is that the canon has always been a profoundly ideological affair; far from the normative neutrality which Arnold envisaged (a still point upon which we can all agree), the canon and its constitution have explicitly become a site of ideological struggle. The two most influential figures in canon formation, T. S. Eliot and F. R. Leavis (in poetry and the novel respectively) were heavily motivated by ideology. Eliot, a great poet, was, it has to be admitted, an equally fine literary tactician. The poetic canon – the 'tradition' – which Eliot constructed in his critical essays at the same time as he was making a name for himself as a poet, is a canon in which Eliot himself appears as the major contemporary representative. As a consequence, those poets who do not influence or otherwise resemble Eliot himself (notably, we have seen, the Romantics) are strangely (or perhaps predictably) absent from the tradition, whereas those who do are in: Renaissance and Jacobean poets and tragedians; Metaphysical poets; and to a lesser extent figures such as Dryden and, with qualifications, Robert Browning. Indeed, a cynic could see the whole theory of the 'dissociation of sensibility' as a tactical manoeuvre – a soundbite which, at a stroke, succeeded in getting un-Eliotlike poetry out of the picture on theoretical grounds. Eliot was also, as it were, in on the ground floor of the professionalization of English Studies (the creation of an academic discipline, 'English', to be taught and studied at university): by influencing (and to no small extent, setting) the parameters for debate, the criteria for inclusion in a canon to be taught at universities, Eliot insured his own permanent inclusion in that canon – a successful gambit with immortality, perhaps, but certainly not an ideologically neutral, 'disinterested' endeavour.[24]

The problem with such *ex cathedra* judgements is that they can be *wrong* – or, rather, that subsequent history does not bear them out: even as great a critic as Leavis (and, with the knowledge that this parenthetical statement contradicts the force of its paragraph, he was one of the very greatest critics) got it wrong. Leavis's judgement (and his ability – or his belief in his ability – as a judge really is the cornerstone of his critical practice) could sometimes be suspect, as in this passage from *New Bearings in English Poetry* (1932), his groundbreaking, agenda-setting account of Modernist poetry:

> There is another young poet whose achieved work leaves no room for doubt about his future. Mr Ronald Bottrall's development has been remarkable rapid and sure – it is convincing – and his published volume, *The Loosening and Other Poems*, establishes him as a very considerable poet indeed.[25]

Mr Ronald Bottrall has, unfortunately, dropped out of literary history, except perhaps in the context of this quotation. (He may be back, though it is my suspicion that you cannot be a great writer if you are called Ronald.)

Writing in Istanbul between 1942 and 1945, having fled Nazi Germany, Erich Auerbach produced *Mimesis: The Representation of Reality in Western Literature*.[26] Written effectively from memory, Auerbach not having recourse to a research library, the book is a model of Arnoldian High Culturalism with an understandably apocalyptic subtext: Auerbach really is attempting to shore up all that he considered of value in western literature against the chaos raging through Europe, to commit to memory, and then hopefully to print, a record of a culture in the process of being systematically destroyed (its 'reality' implicitly opposed to the 'unreality' created by Nazism). It is difficult to conceive of such a project being undertaken now. In recent years the 'traditional' canon, and at times the whole *notion* of a canon, has come under strong criticism, particularly from parties who felt unrepresented or under-represented: from feminist critics over the relative paucity of women in the canon; from black critics over the total absence of black writers; from critics in Wales, Ireland and Scotland over the subsuming of writers from those nations into an 'English' canon. In extreme cases, the whole idea of a canon is said to bespeak élitism, sexism or colonialism. Thus a modern vindication of canonicity, Harold Bloom's *The Western Canon*, despite being almost absurdly inclusive and expansive (Bloom *cannot* have read all that! – or can he?), was almost by definition greeted in some quarters as an old-fashioned, even wistful project: an attempt to impose fixity where now there is only flux and difference.

For readers of poetry, ideas of a canon impinge most closely now on the contents of anthologies. Again, it is a mistake to think of anthologies as ideologically neutral: the criteria for inclusion often merit close scrutiny. Roger Lonsdale's remarkable *New Oxford Book of Eighteenth-Century Verse* (1987), by taking as its selection criterion any poem written between 1700 and 1800, succeeded in profoundly altering traditional conceptions about the poetry of that century: far from the old Augustan/Romantic binary traditionally thought of as characteristic of the eighteenth century (that is, a century characterized by discrete poetic *movements*), Lonsdale showed a wide and varied poetic culture, bringing into the century's canon women poets, hymn writers, industrial and peasant poets, creating a picture immeasurably more complex than the old model had allowed for.[27]

The 1928 anthology, *Great Poems of the English Language*, edited by Wallace Alvin Briggs, seems to be a vindication of Eliot's suspicion that, poetically, the climate of the nineteenth century lasted well into the twentieth: there is no real Modernist poetry in the volume.[28] In spite of the fact that, by 1928, Eliot had published *The Waste Land*, Pound his first volume of *Cantos*, and Wallace Stevens *Harmonium* (which admittedly sold only a handful of copies), there is no Eliot, Pound or Stevens in the anthology, though Yeats makes it in with 'The Lake Isle of Innisfree' and a couple of other early lyrics (certainly not 'Easter 1916'); nor is there any Hopkins (first published in 1918) or Wilfred Owen (though there are First World War poems by Ivor Gurney, Siegfried Sassoon and Alan Seeger, and Briggs does occasionally pleasantly surprise: the black 'Harlem Renaissance' poet of the 1920s, Countee Cullen, has a respectable five poems in the anthology). The nineteenth century is heavily represented: there are extensive selections from all the canonical Romantic poets, as well as Tennyson, both Brownings, both Rossettis, Swinburne and Arnold (though also Poe, Dickinson and Whitman). By 1936, when Michael Roberts edited *The*

Faber Book of Modern Verse, the twentieth century was well under way, at least according to Roberts (no doubt compiling the volume under the influence of Leavis's *New Bearings*): the volume opens with Hopkins, now recognized as a seminal proto-Modernist, and contains selections from Yeats, Eliot, Pound, Stevens, Conrad Aiken, H. D., William Carlos Williams, Dylan Thomas and many other great Modernists.[29]

Anthologies of this sort can also be used to support or confirm political or national agendas. When, in 1988, Kenneth Baker, then a Tory cabinet minister (Minister for Education, no less), edited *The Faber Book of English History in Verse*, many commentators noted that, as far as this volume was concerned, 'Englishness' was synonymous with 'Conservatism'; in 1993 Baker came clean and edited *The Faber Book of Conservatism*.[30] The twentieth-century (post-Yeats) section of Brendan Kennelly's *Penguin Book of Irish Verse* (1981) includes the work of seventy-three poets, an expansive agenda (Ireland is a nation of poets), whereas Paul Muldoon's *The Faber Book of Contemporary Irish Poetry* (1986), which also takes the year of Yeats's death (1939) as its starting-point, includes an austere ten poets (Muldoon is a hard aesthetic taskmaster; poetry is a difficult discipline, available only to the few); Patrick Crotty's *Modern Irish Poetry: An Anthology* (1995), the only one of these published in Ireland, attempts a medium, though still erring towards Kennelly-style, generosity of spirit.[31] Dannie Abse's anthology, *Twentieth Century Anglo-Welsh Poetry* (1997), was criticized for the over-expansiveness of its definitions of 'Welshness'.[32] Abse's criterion was to include 'the best poets of Welsh affiliation writing in English'; operating on what should be called the 'Jack Charlton principle' (in honour of the erstwhile Irish football manager who, by loosening the definitions of 'Irishness', created a successful national team), Abse brought in poets such as Wilfred Owen – born in Wales, of Welsh blood, but whose poetry betrays no real interest in 'the matter of Wales' (after all, he had more important things to write about): indeed, my own opinion is that Abse's selection was not expansive *enough* – the Jack Charlton principle would have allowed for the inclusion of such poets as Hopkins or Denise Levertov, neither of whom make it into Abse's anthology.

Is the whole complex of ideas surrounding tradition, influence and the canon, then, inherently bound up with ideology or with special interests? Not necessarily, but we have considered the politics of the canon at such length in order to convince readers that poetic or literary *value* is an astonishingly thorny subject – where many of the most influential critics of the first half of the century, such as Eliot and Leavis, were primarily *evaluative* (out to demonstrate, or anyway to assert, that X is better than Y), English Studies in recent years has become a far more 'decentred' discipline – a cause for lamentation to some – made up, as later chapters will show, of plural and often mutually incompatible methodologies. This is not necessarily to argue, though some do, for a complete relativism where anything carries the same value as anything else: most professional university teachers of English (and most of their students) still hold some notion, however sceptically articulated, of literary value and the place of the canon (few, for example, would dissent from the desirability of studying Shakespeare; the authors of this book have spent a good deal of their professional lives teaching and writing about Jane Austen and Herman Melville, two solidly canonical writers). 'English' exists – thrives, in fact – as an academic discipline, and it therefore follows that there should be a subject which that discipline studies: literature. In spite of the critiques which this chapter has offered, both Eliot and Leavis were wholly successful in establishing *some of* the parameters of the canon – many university teachers of English owe their jobs (and many of their students their vocations) to this success. It also has to be admitted that, in questions of canonicity and value, most of us are still to some degree Arnoldian, holding some belief, however loose, in a system of shared values (for example, the belief that the study of literature is itself of value). It is not difficult to live, and certainly not to work, with such contradictions. We live with contradictions all the time: few socialists would want entirely to do without consumer capitalism (this one would not); physicists know that, since relativity makes travel into the future theoretically possible, then the future must in some meaningful, provable way be already 'out there', co-existent with the present, but this does not necessarily make them all into powerlessly extreme fatalists. It is not difficult to live with such contradictions, *provided that we are aware of them*: this is why many critics today are less comfortable with the idea of their discipline as primarily an evaluative one, but tend rather to be more 'self-reflexive', consistently questioning the parameters and ontology of this discipline – a set of practices called critical theory.

This chapter will end with an exercise in reading which is also an exercise in literary history, focusing on one genre: the elegy. Looking at a few notable examples of the genre, we will examine the ways in which the ideas of tradition and influence have operated. Do genres themselves form a 'tradition'? Do we need to know the genre of a poem, or the history of that genre, in order to understand it?

The elegy was originally a ceremonial form used for commemoration – typically, to commemorate a life on the occasion of a death, using death as a means of remembering (or re-membering, putting back together) the meaning or achievements of a life. Thus, though elegies are generally associated with death, not all poetry about death is elegiac. For example, there is a medieval and Renaissance genre of 'timor mortis' (fear of death) poems which usually comment on the transience of mortality, sometimes, as in poems by John Audley and by William Dunbar, ending their stanzas with the refrain 'Timor mortis conturbat me' ('fear of death confounds me'). As an example of this kind of poetry, this is the opening stanza of Thomas Nashe's 'Adieu, farewell, earth's bliss' (sometimes called 'A Litany in Time of Plague'):

> Adieu, farewell, earth's bliss;
> This world uncertain is;
> Fond are life's lustful joys;
> Death proves them all but toys;
> None from his darts can fly;
> I am sick, I must die.
> Lord, have mercy on us![33]

This is not an elegy but a 'memento mori' poem, a poem whose trope is a meditation on the transience of life and the certainty of death (here, during a plague, more certain than ever). Other poems of this kind would include Shakespeare's sonnet 'No longer mourn for me when I am dead', Keats's 'When I have fears that I may cease to be', or Christina Rossetti's 'Remember'.

The elegy, then, was originally a poem of commemoration, usually though not always the commemoration of a death (Donne wrote elegies on love). Coleridge suggested that the elegy was a form 'natural to the reflective mind'[34] – thus the elegy became a genre for the writing of serious meditation, though most often upon the death of an individual: Tennyson's *In Memoriam*, Whitman's 'When lilacs last in the dooryard bloom'd', Dylan Thomas's 'A Refusal to Mourn the Death, by Fire, of a Child in London', Allen Tate's 'Ode to the Confederate Dead', and Robert Lowell's 'For the Union Dead' are all examples of elegies.

When the poem figures this individual in exemplary terms, it is known as a pastoral elegy. Milton's *Lycidas* is amongst the most famous examples, written on the occasion of the death of his college acquaintance Edward King, drowned in the Irish Sea in 1637:

> Yet once more, O ye Laurels, and once more
> Ye Myrtles brown, with Ivy never sere,
> I come to pluck your Berries harsh and crude,
> And with forced fingers rude
> Shatter your leaves before the mellowing year.
> Bitter constraint and sad occasion dear,
> Compels me to disturb your season due:
> For *Lycidas* is dead, dead ere his prime,
> Young *Lycidas*, and hath not left his peer:
> Who would not sing for *Lycidas*? he knew
> Himself to sing, and built the lofty rhyme.
> He must not float upon his watery bier
> Unwept, and welter to the parching wind,
> Without the meed of some melodious tear.[35]

As we noted in the previous chapter, contemporary readers of this poem often ask why it is so impersonal. Why poetically transmute Edward King, a known, named individual, into Lycidas, an archetypal pastoral shepherd?

And why, too, would Shelley do the same to Keats, transforming him elegiac-
ally into Adonais upon his death? After all, has Yeats not impressed upon
us modern readers in 'Easter 1916' the significance of naming for commem-
oration, for re-membering?:

> I write it out in a verse –
> MacDonagh and MacBride
> And Connolly and Pearse
> Now and in time to be,
> Wherever green is worn,
> Are changed, changed utterly:
> A terrible beauty is born.[36]

This is a problem which, from a modern perspective, seems to have haunted
poetry up until Romanticism – how to represent private grief in an essen-
tially public medium, poetry. What the pastoral elegy did was to give form
to grief. However, its impersonality can genuinely be problematic, as it is in
this section of perhaps the best-known of all English pastoral elegies,
Thomas Gray's 'Elegy Written in a Country Churchyard':

> Let not Ambition mock their useful toil,
> Their homely joys, and destiny obscure;
> Nor Grandeur hear with a disdainful smile
> The short and simple annals of the poor. . . .
>
> Perhaps in this neglected spot is laid
> Some heart once pregnant with celestial fire;
> Hands that the rod of empire might have swayed,
> Or waked to ecstasy the living lyre.
>
> But Knowledge to their eyes her ample page
> Rich with the spoils of time did ne'er unroll;
> Chill Penury repressed their noble rage,
> And froze the genial current of the soul.
>
> Full many a gem of purest ray serene,
> The dark unfathomed caves of ocean bear:
> Full many a flower is born to blush unseen,
> And waste its sweetness on the desert air.
>
> Some village Hampden, that with dauntless breast
> The little tyrant of his fields withstood;
> Some mute inglorious Milton here may rest,
> Some Cromwell guiltless of his country's blood. . . .
>
> Far from the madding crowd's ignoble strife,
> Their sober wishes never learned to stray;
> Along the cool sequestered vale of life
> They kept the noiseless tenor of their way.

Yet even these bones from insult to protect
Some frail memorial still erected nigh,
With uncouth rhymes and shapeless sculpture decked,
Implores the passing tribute of a sigh.

Their name, their years, spelt by the unlettered Muse,
The place of fame and elegy supply;
And many a holy text around she strews,
That teach the rustic moralist to die.[37]

The poem cannot represent the figures it describes, figures about whom Gray knows and wants to know nothing, other than pastorally, as figures in a landscape – honest rustic folk, poetic types – or else in terms of what they are *not*, by comparison with the named individuals who *are* fit poetic subjects (Hampden, Milton, Cromwell – all figures connected with the English Civil War). This, then, is not an elegy for individuals, but an exercise in the formal production of elegiac poetry. Gray's 'Elegy' is, in fact, a sustained exercise in the creation of a mood: melancholy ('Implores the passing tribute of a sigh'). The poem's elegiac figures are primarily cyphers used to facilitate this mood.

The industrial revolution made the writing of pastoral (originally a genre pertaining to the activities of shepherds, later taken to signify any idealized representation of rural life) a difficult, if not impossible, act to perform in good faith. The poetry of John Clare enacts this difficulty. With the landscape being enclosed to make way for new forms of agriculture (an early form of what we would now call agribusiness), with urbanization rampant, and with the small farmer or shepherd increasingly under strain, it was no longer as easy to represent these rustic types ideally. Clare's poem 'To a Fallen Elm' is a good illustration of the historical changes to country life which he saw happening around him in the early nineteenth century:

It grows the cant terms of enslaving tools
To wrong another in the name of right
It grows a licence with oer bearing fools
To cheat plain honesty by force of might
Thus came enclosure – ruin was her guide
But freedom's clapping hands enjoyed the sight
Tho comfort's cottage soon was thrust aside
And workhouse prisons raised upon the site
Een natures dwelling far away from men
The common heath became the spoilers prey
The rabbit had not where to make his den
And labour's only cow was drove away
No matter – wrong was right and right was wrong
And freedom's brawl was sanction to the song[38]

Here, common land (land which was available to all in order to graze their livestock) has been enclosed – fenced up – by private concerns, and is metaphorically transformed into a 'workhouse prison' – this rhetoric of the workhouse takes us back to Blake and forward to Dickens, both notably urban (metropolitan) writers – but here, the workhouse is built in the country. Symbolically, this signifies the invasion of the urban into the rural, the subordination of rural economies to strict capitalism which meant impoverishment for labourers, figured here as enslavement or imprisonment.

The problems of naming and representation, and of traditional poetic forms being at variance with harsh modern realities, are all given expression in Tony Harrison's 1980s elegy, *v.* The poem is set, like Gray's 'Elegy', in a graveyard, though no longer an idyllically 'English' country one but a nineteenth-century industrial-municipal necropolis going to seed in Leeds during the miners' strike of 1984. The poet visits his parents' grave, to find that it has been desecrated by graffiti (a spraypainted 'V'). This was a period of massive unemployment and one which, it now transpires, marked the end of working-class identity in Britain as it had been constructed since the industrial revolution: the poem is consequently an elegy for the British working class. *v.* is quite deliberately written in the same metre as Gray's 'Elegy' (a metre called the elegiac quatrain), and begins with a passage of naming, identity and employment of the kind which Gray refused:

> Next millennium you'll have to search quite hard
> to find my slab behind the family dead,
> butcher, publican, and baker, now me, bard
> adding poetry to their beef, beer and bread.
>
> With Byron three graves on I'll not go short
> of company, and Wordsworth's opposite.
> That's two peers already, of a sort . . .
>
> Wordsworth built church organs, Byron tanned
> luggage cowhide in the age of steam . . .[39]

Gray recognized, melancholically, that 'Full many a flower is born to blush unseen, / And waste its sweetness on the desert air', but that 'Chill Penury repressed their noble rage, / And froze the genial current of the soul'; Harrison insists on giving a voice to the twentieth-century equivalent of Gray's (or, better, Clare's) dispossessed peasants, an unemployed skinhead who has desecrated his parents' grave, and who functions as Harrison's poetic alter ego. The skinhead's 'rage' has not been 'repressed' by 'Chill Penury', nor is it 'noble', but rather made up of 'uncouth rhymes'; their dialogue (with the skinhead's voice in italics) is one which questions the nature of poetic representation:

> *Ah'll tell yer then what really riles a bloke.*
> *It's reading on their graves the jobs they did –*
> *butcher, publican and baker. Me, I'll croak*
>
> *doing t'same nowt ah do now as a kid. . . .*
> *This lot worked at one job all life through.*

> Byron, 'Tanner', 'Lieth 'ere interred'.
> They'll chisel fucking poet when they do you
> and that, yer cunt, 's a crude four-letter word.
>
> 'Listen, cunt!' I said, 'before you start your jeering
> the reason why I want this in a book
> 's to give ungrateful cunts like you a hearing!'
> A book, yer stupid cunt, 's not worth a fuck![40]

This poem takes us beyond questions of poetic form, genre or language, to ask whether it is appropriate or even possible to write an elegy for a society post-industrial and unemployed. Do 'traditional' poetic forms have *anything* to say about the condition Harrison describes? Is poetry really intrinsically bound up with class and ideology after all? Indeed, the poem questions the validity of poetry itself: as John Locke, in another context, said, 'What is the *use* of poetry?':

> Don't talk to me of fucking representing
> the class yer were born into any more.
> Yer going to get 'urt and start resenting
> it's not poetry we need in this class war.
>
> Yer've given yerself toffee, cunt. Who needs
> yer fucking poufy words. Ah write mi own.[41]

Endnotes

1 Jorge Luis Borges, 'Borges and I', trans. James E. Irby, in *Labyrinths: Selected Stories and Other Writings* (Harmondsworth: 1970), p. 282.
2 Wordsworth, 'Preface' to *Lyrical Ballads*, p. 266.
3 Shelley, 'A Defence of Poetry', in *Romanticism: An Anthology*, p. 969.
4 Blake, *Complete Poems*, p. 107.
5 Quoted in Stan Smith, *The Origins of Modernism: Eliot, Pound, Yeats and the Rhetorics of Renewal* (New York and London, 1994), p. 5.
6 Raymond Williams, *The Country and the City* (London, 1973), p. 36.
7 Smith, *The Origins of Modernism*, p. 6.
8 Eliot, *Selected Essays* (London, 1961), pp. 14–15.
9 For a penetrating analysis of this, see David Harvey, 'Modernity and Modernism', in *The Condition of Postmodernity: An Enquiry into the Origins of Cultural Change* (Oxford, 1989), pp. 10–38.
10 See Carey, *The Intellectuals and the Masses*, pp. 6–10 and *passim* for this. This attitude is still with us: in Martin Amis's millennial 'Condition of England' novel, *London Fields*, the working-class thug, Keith Talent, a tabloid newspaper perpetually rolled under his arm, talks in a 'misery of stringer's clichés' because this is *'what he actually sees'*. Martin Amis, *London Fields* (London, 1989), p. 98.
11 Eliot, 'John Dryden', in *Selected Essays*, p. 305.
12 Eliot, *Collected Poems*, p. 79.
13 Eagleton, *Literary Theory*, p. 39.

14 Eliot, 'John Dryden', in *Selected Essays*, p. 306.
15 Eliot, 'The Metaphysical Poets', in *Selected Essays*, p. 287.
16 Eliot, *Collected Poems*, p. 65.
17 Eliot, 'William Blake', in *Selected Essays*, p. 322.
18 See E. P. Thompson, *Witness Against the Beast: William Blake and the Moral Law* (Cambridge, 1993).
19 Harold Bloom, *The Western Canon: The Books and School of the Ages* (London, 1995), p. 517.
20 Bloom, *The Anxiety of Influence: A Theory of Poetry* (Oxford, 1973). See p. 126 for his reading of Wordsworth's sonnet to Milton.
21 William Wordsworth, *The Poems*, ed. John O. Hayden, vol. 1 (Harmondsworth, 1977), pp. 579–80.
22 Matthew Arnold, 'The Function of Criticism at the Present Time', in *Selected Criticism of Matthew Arnold*, ed. Christopher Ricks (New York, 1972), pp. 102–3.
23 John Locke, *Essay Concerning Human Understanding*, ed. Maurice Cranston (New York and London, 1965), p. 9.
24 For an analysis of Eliot's profound and long-lasting influence on canon-formation, see the chapter 'Ideology and Canonical Form: The New Critical Canon', in John Guillory, *Cultural Capital: The Problem of Literary Canon Formation* (London and Chicago, 1993), pp. 134–75.
25 Leavis, *New Bearings in English Poetry* (Harmondsworth, 1963), p. 148.
26 Erich Auerbach, *Mimesis: The Representation of Reality in Western Literature*, trans. Willard R. Trask (Princeton, 1953).
27 *The New Oxford Book of Eighteenth-Century Verse*, ed. Roger Lonsdale (Oxford, 1987).
28 *Great Poems of the English Language*, ed. Wallace Alvin Briggs (London, 1928).
29 *The Faber Book of Modern Verse*, ed. Michael Roberts (London, 1936).
30 *The Faber Book of English History in Verse*, ed. Kenneth Baker (London, 1988); *The Faber Book of Conservatism*, ed. Kenneth Baker (London, 1993).
31 *The Penguin Book of Irish Verse*, ed. Brendan Kennelly (Harmondsworth, 1981); *The Faber Book of Contemporary Irish Poetry*, ed. Paul Muldoon (London, 1986); *Modern Irish Poetry: An Anthology*, ed. Patrick Crotty (Belfast, 1995).
32 *Twentieth Century Anglo-Welsh Poetry*, ed. Dannie Abse (Bridgend, 1997).
33 *Norton Anthology of Poetry*, p. 254.
34 Quoted in Cuddon, *A Dictionary of Literary Terms* (Harmondsworth, 1982, 1986, p. 214.
35 Milton, *Complete Poems*, p. 42. We have modernized the spelling here.
36 Yeats, *Selected Poetry*, p. 95.
37 *Norton Anthology of Poetry*, pp. 610–11.
38 John Clare, *John Clare*, ed. Eric Robinson and David Powell (Oxford, 1984), p. 98.
39 Tony Harrison, *v.* (Newcastle, 1985), p. 7.
40 Harrison, *v.*, pp.18–19.
41 Harrison, *v.*, p. 22.

P A R T
II

CRITICAL APPROACHES

|4|

Poem as object

The stanza is neither true nor false; it is an object that exists.

Allen Tate[1]

If we are to lay hold of the poetic act to comprehend and evaluate it, and if it is to pass current as a critical object, it must be hypostatised.

W. K. Wimsatt[2]

The concept of the poem as an autonomous object, liberated from its author and from the circumstances of its origin, is a recent one. Viewing the poem as an object may not at first seem the most compelling way of looking at it. But the thinking underlying this approach has been very influential in the reading and analysis of poetry, to the extent that many of our critical and readerly assumptions about poetry have been based on it. The idea occasionally surfaces explicitly in statements about poetry: for example, in 1995 Carol Rumens defended selections for an anthology by stating that she chose poems which seemed to her to be 'strongly made, free standing verbal objects'.[3]

This phrasing and the sentiment behind it derive directly from New Critical theory, perhaps the major critical movement of the twentieth century with regard to the reading of poetry. Not, it needs to be said, that New Criticism was a movement in terms of its being a group with shared, stated aims; when John Crowe Ransom used the term New Criticism in his book of that title in 1941, some of the writers whom he called New Critics explicitly dissociated themselves from the label. It was more of a loose confederation of individual critics and teachers in the United States and Britain who participated in the professionalization of literary studies from the 1920s onwards, and included I. A. Richards, John Crowe Ransom, Allen Tate, William Empson, Yvor Winters, R. P. Blackmur, Cleanth Brooks, Robert Penn Warren, W. K. Wimsatt and Monroe C. Beardsley. Some of the critical judgements of T. S. Eliot and Ezra Pound have also been loosely termed New Critical. In terms of critical practice, these writers often differed considerably. But they were to some extent united in the value that they placed on the text before the reader, and in their insistence that critical judgement needed to pay close attention to the text. The most influential 'New Critical' book in this respect was I. A. Richards' *Practical Criticism* (1929), in which Richards used the responses of Cambridge undergraduates to demonstrate that in spite of their expensive education they had not developed the skills appropriate to the reading of poetry; they needed what Richards called 'useful training'.[4]

The fact that *Practical Criticism* originated from classroom experience and was intended to highlight the deficiencies of classroom practice indicates a significant feature of New Criticism. That is, it was primarily concerned with the teaching of poetry and with the poem as something experienced in the classroom. At a period of expansion in higher education and of the growth of departments of English, the point that poetry needs to be read differently from other language was a crucial one for the New Critic. One of the major New Critical texts, *Understanding Poetry* by Cleanth Brooks and Robert Penn Warren (first published in 1938 but revised and expanded thereafter) was basically a book for classroom use. Brooks and Warren wrote chapters on aspects of poetry and also printed selections of poems with questions designed to sharpen the reader's attention to the words on the page. Certainly, behind New Criticism there are sometimes implicit beliefs regarding the autonomy of art and the supposedly non-political nature of the aesthetic. It is these assumptions which have stimulated hostile accounts such as those of Terry Eagleton.[5] But in practice, the New Critical focus on the text had a fairly modest aim: that of making the reader pay attention to the words the poet had used, the ways in which they had been used, and the formal elements of the poem. At times this enforced attention might seem restrictive, or to be positivistically demanding evidence for any statement about the poem, but it is because of this pragmatic aspect that New Criticism survived for a long time as a classroom technique. Furthermore, it survives as a way of reading poetry in particular. Although New Criticism was ostensibly an approach to all literary genres, poetry was in fact central to it. This was because poetry represented the most concentrated use of language, and was also where the formal difference between uses of language could most readily be seen. The New Critics tended to privilege formal poetry over free verse, and the short lyric over other, longer forms.

In some respects, the New Critics' emphasis on the poem as an object was a reaction against a debasement of the Romantic belief in the poem as an expression of the author's feeling. They saw that this approach to the poem potentially limited the ways in which the poem might exist as objective knowledge. Although New Criticism was indebted to much Romantic theorizing about poetry, particularly that of Coleridge, it mistrusted the ways in which an emphasis on feeling could be incorporated into the actual study of poetry, and was uncertain of how critical judgement could be exercised in its assessment.[6] An emphasis on feeling seemed to invite reading itself to become subjective, whereas the New Critical endeavour was about objective assessment: thus William Hazlitt's influential statement about poetry and feeling was anathema to the New Critic. Hazlitt wrote that poetry was 'the language of the imagination and the passions . . . the universal language which the heart holds with nature and itself'.[7] The dangers in this were of reducing the role of criticism to that of providing an emotional response to the poem, and of reducing poetry itself to being only about the author's feelings when writing the poem. Hazlitt's formulation could exist in the classroom only as an emotional appeal, an invitation to each reader to privilege an individual and subjective response to the poem, or an exercise in reconstituting the mind (or heart) of the poet. Both were seen by the New Critics as improper approaches to poetry. We value a poem as a structure of words, as a particular use of language; it is a mistake, they asserted, to think of those words as transparent, as providing a clear window into the poet's life or feeling. Allen Tate, for example, complained that:

> The poem as a formal object to be looked at, to be studied, to be construed . . . dissolved into biography and history, so that . . . the poetry was only a misunderstood pretext for the 'study' of the sexual life of the poet, of the history of his age, of anything else that the scholar wished to 'study'; and he usually wished to study anything but poetry.[8]

Nor is it proper criticism to respond emotionally to the poem or, at least, only to respond emotionally to it, since that privileges the emotive rather than the cognitive power of language and erodes any basis for a serious and shared discussion of poetry.

The New Critical distrust of emotion in poetry may be seen to emerge partly from its perceived function as a teaching method and partly from its emphasis on the objective nature of the poem. A poem is a linguistic object, a machine rather than a window through which to view the author; it is an objectification of the poet's feelings, not the feelings themselves. T. S. Eliot's phrase about the need for an 'objective correlative' in art had a special resonance for the New Critics. In his 'Essay on *Hamlet*' (1919) Eliot claimed that Shakespeare's play was problematic because of its failure to create adequate common ground between character and audience. The emotions involved in the play remained too personal to Hamlet. Working from this observation, Eliot went on to propound a much-quoted hypothesis:

> The only way of expressing emotion in the form of art is by finding an 'objective correlative'; in other words, a set of objects, a situation, a chain of events which shall be the formula of that *particular* emotion; such that when the external facts, which must terminate in sensory experience, are given, the emotion is immediately evoked.[9]

The objective correlative – a symbol, for instance – objectifies the emotion of the author (and hence, to use another Eliotean idea, liberates the author from it) and permits the reader to evaluate the emotion in a detached way.[10]

Today Eliot's essay might seem tenuous and almost casually provocative, not least because of its assumption of the failure of *Hamlet*. But Ransom and Tate in particular developed the idea of the objective correlative more fully as part of their abhorrence of the direct statement of feeling in poetry. In this respect, particular censure was reserved for Shelley in 'Ode to the West Wind': 'I fall upon the thorns of life! I bleed!' The New Critics were not *opposed* to the expression of feeling in poetry. Indeed, both Ransom and Tate repeatedly stressed that poetry was valuable precisely because it combined intellect and emotion, but these have to be in balance. Poetry can restore the union between mind and feeling: a union which, many Modernists felt, had become lost in the emergence of modernity. The New Critics highlighted the importance of mind over feeling, cognition rather than emotion, because they feared that one of the results of the debasement of Romanticism was an emphasis on the emotive element in poetry. Thus one aspect of seeing the poem as an object is to lay stress on it as cognitive. As a young man learning the craft of poetry in the late 1930s, Robert Lowell chose Allen Tate as a mentor. Later he remembered Tate saying that a good poem had 'nothing to do with exalted feelings or being moved by the spirit'. Rather, a poem was 'simply a piece of craftsmanship, an intelligible or *cognitive* object'.[11] Tate himself insisted that literature was 'the complete knowledge of man's experience'.[12]

A poem, then, is a structure of words, a linguistic object, a 'verbal icon', and must be judged as such. It must function successfully in an autonomous way. It must exist as knowledge, and is a unique way of knowing the world. Assessing a poem means paying close attention to the words on the page; it exists there freed from the intentions of the poet and distinct from whatever feelings it might arouse in us. While we might recognize that a poem moves us, this is only one of the ways in which it is important to us. Such statements about poetry are closely bound up with seeing the poem as an object, and this view has been of great significance in the professionalization of literary criticism in the twentieth century. With its assistance, the New Critics thought, criticism could become established as a distinct and properly intellectual discipline.

We have probably inherited in a fairly unconscious way the concept of the poem as an object, and this is partly due to the success of New Criticism in so deeply establishing a classroom methodology for the understanding of poetry that it now appears normative. Often the essays on poetry by Ransom or Tate refer explicitly to the practice of teaching poetry, which they considered at a crisis point because of what Tate termed 'the decline of the art of reading'.[13] In one essay Tate cites a manual's advice that:

Comprehending a poem need not involve any intellectual or formal concern with its technique, prose content, type, moral, diction, analysis, social implications, etc. Comprehending a poem is essentially an organic experience, essentially a response to the poetic stimulus of the author.[14]

Outraged, Tate commented that when you respond 'you are not doing more than a chimpanzee or a Yahoo would be doing'.[15]

At the other end of the scale, as it were, lay those who taught poetry mainly as an instrument for teaching something else. The New Critical tendency to dehistoricize the poem, and to 'de-author' it, was closely bound up with the recognition of it as an autonomous entity. It also developed from a belief that one of the ways that poetry, indeed literature, had often been taught in universities was as a form of historical enquiry. Criticism, the New Critic argued, has to do more, must take account of the poem as utilizing language in a special way. Seeing the poem as an object lays emphasis on the durability, the lasting value of the poem; the poem survives the historical context in which it was created and speaks to us not of things locked in the past but of our present, our permanent, necessary truths. Someone who would read Keats's 'Ode on a Grecian Urn' as if it could tell us something about life in Georgian England is as deluded as Tate's 'Yahoo' in responding only emotionally to the poem. Both have ignored the poem as an object in its own right, a unique form of knowledge, a unique structure of words. Poetry is a distinct genre with its own generated rules and conventions; it is not a historical narrative, or a historical document, and should not be utilized in a way that would reduce it to the status of one.

Similarly, a poem cannot provide us with unproblematic access to the life of the poet, and an approach which treats the poem as if it could is biography, not literary criticism. In both the historical and biographical approaches there is a failure to see the poem as a poem, to acknowledge the formal elements that mark poetry as an exceptional use of language. Also, once a poem is published, it exists quite apart from the life of its author, who consequently has no control over the interpretations that it generates. In Eliot's terms, the poem ideally exists as an objective correlative and not as a private effusion of the author to which the reader is granted special access. Certainly there are many examples of readers and critics using poems as if they provided straightforward access into the lives of the poets, and there are poets whose poetry seems explicitly to invite such an approach. For the New Critic such readers and poets are mistaken in overlooking the formal distinguishing characteristics of the poem, which make it an 'object' rather than a 'window'.

The relation between the poem and the author will specifically be considered in the next chapter. Here, it is important to emphasize that seeing the poem as an autonomous object is a way of liberating the reader from the control of the poet. Whatever the poet *intended* to write is irrelevant because what finally matters to us as readers are the words on the page. This attack on intentionality as a factor in interpretation occurs most famously in an essay by W. K. Wimsatt and Monroe C. Beardsley called 'The Intentional Fallacy' (1946). They argued that 'the design or intention of the author is neither available nor desirable as a standard for judging the success of a work of literary art'.[16] It is fallacious to believe that by somehow being familiar with the intention of the poet, the poem can be explained. Like the concept of sincerity, intentionality can exist only by relativizing the poem, that is, by providing a point of comparison to something outside it. Sincerity and intentionality have no role to play in the understanding or criticism of poetry, because they depend on the invocation of considerations quite disconnected from the poem itself. How might we judge from the words on the page whether the poet was sincere? How can we know by those words what the poet intended? After all, we can only assume that the poet intended to write the words on the page in the order and form in which they appear before us.[17] If the poem is a machine, then it does not matter who made it as long as we perceive that it functions in the way that it should.

The New Critical ideas on sincerity and intentionality are of course intimately bound up with belief in the autonomy of the object. But as readers and critics of poetry we rarely encounter a poem only as words on the page; there are usually factors and contexts outside of the poem which help determine and guide the act of interpretation. In practice, most New Critics were unsympathetic to extreme formalistic readings of the individual poem, even though their theoretical orientation emphasized poetry's formal properties. Furthermore, we often read the poem *for* something; and that may well be to find out about the life of its author. One problem with seeing the poem as an object is that we rarely see it as an object detached from a context. There is also a way in which intentionality is significant, indeed essential, in our understanding of poetry. That is, as we saw in Chapter 3, it is often important to know about the exact poetic genre in which the poet is working. To put this another way, genre itself crucially reveals intention. A good example of this is Milton's *Paradise Lost*. C. S. Lewis began his book on the poem with the uncompromising assertion that:

> The first qualification for judging any piece of workmanship from a corkscrew to a cathedral is to know *what* it is – what it was intended to do and how it is meant to be used. . . . The first thing the reader needs to know about *Paradise Lost* is what Milton meant it to be.[18]

We need to know that Milton planned the poem as an epic because then we have the grounds for assessing it. Lewis explicitly states that recognition of intentionality is essential to understanding poetry, precisely because our judgement must take account of genre. It would be absurd to conclude that *Paradise Lost* is a failure because it does not rhyme, or because it is too long or because there is no humour in it.

Cogent as Lewis's point is, it should be remembered that such intentionality is present *in* the poem as well as extra-textually. We must assume that what we have in front of us is what the author intended, otherwise the poem would not have been published and made available to us. There are notable exceptions to this inscription of intentionality. Emily Dickinson's poetry is one of those exceptions. Since her work was effectively unpublished in her lifetime we cannot assume that the version of the poems that we have reflects her intention. Milton's epic intentions are made very clear in the opening lines of the first book of *Paradise Lost*, so we do not in this instance need anything from outside of the poem to provide a point of comparison between intention and performance; Milton effectively tells us what kind of poem we are to read.

Seeing the poem as an object, then, involves paying attention to the special use of language in the poem before us rather than invoking the author's life or something beyond the poem. As noted earlier, I. A. Richards's *Practical Criticism* was an important starting-point for this approach due to Richards's demonstration of how his students seemed to lack the skills in reading poetry as a distinctive kind of language. Certainly *Practical Criticism* and the approach to the text which it encouraged have been criticized for being a particular form of British empiricism (if it is not in the text then it does not exist). But it might be pointed out that reading poetry is largely an empirical act, and that the poet has given us only the words on the page to contain and transmit meaning. Again, underlying Richards' approach is the wish to see the poem rather than the poet or the poem's historical basis, and to consider poetic language as distinct from the language of prose. Logically, this led to what Cleanth Brooks called the 'Heresy of Paraphrase'. He argued that since a poem existed only in the language that the poet had created for it, it was heretical to reduce the poem to a prose statement or paraphrase. Not only would the special use of language be lost, but the entire complex experience of reading the poem would be simplified or abstracted.[19]

When the concept of the poem as object is invoked, it is noticeable that the imagery used is often that of the container. For the New Critics the poem existed spatially. It set up a boundary, it enclosed a set of ideas. As we shall see, this concept is challenged by reader-response critics, who emphasize that the reader's experience of the poem is temporal rather than spatial, and by 'open field' critics who resist the assumption that the poem is defined by boundaries. Cleanth Brooks's image of the poem as a 'well wrought urn' (the phrase is from John Donne's poem 'The Canonization') is a significant one in this respect. The poem is a well-crafted object which encloses, seals off, holds.

Seeing the poem as an object had a particular influence on poetry from the 1930s to the 1950s. This is apparent in several ways. It is there in the renewed interest from the 1930s in the poem's formal elements, as a 'piece of craftsmanship' to use Tate's term. It is there in the preference for the lyric and the short poem and, in a related way, to the idea of the poem as a self-contained unit. With regard to this last topic, it is often interesting to look at how a poem concludes, as a way of seeing how the poem is made concrete or substantial, how it is hypostatized. Poetic closure, how poems end, is an oddly neglected topic, although it is the subject of a valuable study by Barbara Herrnstein Smith.[20] The neglect is odd because the ending of the poem can tell us a great deal about what the poet understands poetry to be and about what the poem accomplishes. When reading a poem it is worth paying attention to how it concludes. Does it end inconclusively, opening up the theme or themes without resolving them? The poems of Emily Dickinson tend to do this, even turning the poem over to the reader as if it were something the reader had to complete. This is entirely appropriate for a poet who insisted in her poem 501 that 'This World is not Conclusion'. By contrast the sonnets of Shakespeare often close firmly, suggesting the completion of a thought explored in the poem; critics have often complained that the concluding couplets weaken the sonnets (Robert Lowell once wondered whether Shakespeare wrote them all in one afternoon).[21]

Some poems (those of William Carlos Williams are often striking in this respect) end with an ellipsis or without punctuation, implying a refusal or failure to close or resolve, and implying also that the poem is less a logical pattern and more like something shaped to reflect experience. Some poems by Walt Whitman end by invoking 'you', thereby creating a point of contact between the poem's persona and the implied reader. This is notably true of his masterpiece 'Song of Myself'. The poem begins with the word 'I' and ends with the line 'I stop somewhere waiting for you'. This suggests a transfer of the mystical experience recounted in the poem from writer to reader; suggesting also that the poem is not a spatially perceived object handed over from poet to reader but part of a process which must engage both. In such cases closure seems not exactly to perform the job of closing the poem in the sense of establishing a boundary between the poem and the outside world, but seems instead something provisional, uncertain, as if the poet draws attention to the epistemologically incomplete status of the poem, that there can be no ready resolution to the themes and that the reader must be involved in the poem.

In particular, the ending of a poem can indicate whether the poet thinks of the poem as an object or thinks of it as more like a process. Poems such as those by John Ashbery, James Tate or Jorie Graham, for example, typically follow patterns of thought and may reach no conclusion at all, existing as dynamic processes rather than as static, completed objects. For example, Ashbery's poem 'This Configuration' begins:

> This movie deals with the epidemic of the way we live now.
> What an inane cardplayer. And the age may support it.
> Each time the rumble of the age
> Is an anthill in the distance.[22]

The words are dynamic, lacking a stabilizing, accommodating register that would fix meaning for the reader and, characteristic of Ashbery's poems, the poem in its entirety does not provide such a register at its conclusion. In an interview Ashbery agreed with the suggestion that his poetry 'consists mainly in the fluidity of thought rather than the objects of thought'.[23]

By contrast, some poems have an exceptionally strong sense of an ending. The critic David Bromwich has suggested that lyric poetry in particular 'delights in gestures of completion'.[24] If the poem can be seen as a container then strong closure is the lid on the box. It declares the independent, self-enclosed nature of the poem, perhaps seeking to resolve the issues raised and contain them in some way. Again it is thus often illuminating to consider what the poem's ending tells us about the poet's concept of poetry that drives the poem. A poem by John Ashbery will have a different kind of ending from one by Robert Frost or Seamus Heaney, for instance. Heaney's early poem 'Mid-term Break' is a good example of a self-contained lyric which, like a good prose paragraph, clearly delineates its boundaries and explores one topic within them. The narrator tells of the death of his infant brother killed in a motor car accident. It is an almost perfect example of a New Critical poem, with its techniques of punning, suggestions of irony and ambiguity, in its clear exposition of a single theme, in its deft use of iambic pentameter and in its skilful creation of common ground between poet and reader. The poem's closure is resoundingly strong, its final couplet being: 'No gaudy scars, the bumper knocked him clear. / A four-foot box, a foot for every year'. William Carlos Williams once characterized some poems as ending with a 'click'.[25] 'Mid-term Break' ends more resoundingly than with a little click. Another good example of a poem with strong closure is the one quoted in Chapter 7, Jon Dressel's 'Let's Hear It For Goliath', which does actually end with the word 'thud'.

As well as noting how poems end, it is useful to consider how the titles of poems can indicate whether the poet sees the poem as an object or a process. Some poems have titles that give the reader some necessary information: one example is the poem we discussed earlier, John Donne's 'A Nocturnal upon S. Lucy's Day', another is Yeats's 'Easter 1916'. Such titles tell us something we need in order to understand the poem, and therefore they help to ensure the poem's autonomy or its objective status. Titles may well be supplied by editors, or they can serve to create a distance between the poet and the persona of the poem: Yeats does this in his earlier work, where he often uses an archaic form of titling. This is especially evident in his 1899 collection *The Wind Among the Reeds*, which includes titles such as 'The Lover tells of the Rose in his Heart' and 'The Lover asks Forgiveness because of his Many Moods'. Titles used by Modernist and Post-modern writers tend to be more oblique or playful, indicating that the process of imaginatively reading the poem must begin with considering how its title is related to it. Both Wallace Stevens and John Ashbery are renowned for oblique or playful titles. Stevens wrote poems entitled 'The Revolutionists Stop for Orangeade', 'Saint John and the Back-ache' and 'The Woman Who Blamed Life on a Spaniard'. (It has been suggested that Stevens thought of his titles long before he wrote the poems that went with them.) Ashbery often seems to parody the very convention of titles. He uses titles that seem borrowed from other genres such as painting (the marvellous comic sestina 'Farm Implements and Rutabagas in a Landscape'), from film and cartoons ('Forties Flick', 'Daffy Duck in Hollywood'), that refer back to poetic traditions ('The Picture of Little J. A. in a Prospect of Flowers') or which are scraps of inert prose ('The Instruction Manual', 'The Wrong Kind of Insurance', 'And I'd Love You to Be in It'). He has one delicious poem called 'Untilted' which unravels the paradox involved in the convention of calling a poem 'Untitled'. Again, it is worth asking what a title is telling us about the poet's theory of poetry.[26]

One criticism of treating the poem as an object involves the assumption made about how knowledge exists. The idea that the poem may contain knowledge, hold truth, has been challenged by those who emphasize that knowledge is a process rather than a thing. This is an old distinction, and it is familiar partly through Joseph Conrad's narrator in the novel *Heart of Darkness*, who distinguishes between the yarns of seamen which contain truth 'within the shell of a cracked nut' and the tales of Marlow, to whom 'the meaning of an episode was not inside like a kernel but outside, enveloping the tale which brought it out only as a glow brings out a haze'.[27] Seeing the poem as a container indicates that it holds truth as the shell holds the nut. This containing aspect is often indicated by the kind of closure that the poem enacts.

One of the legacies of seeing the poem as an enclosed artefact has been a preference in the twentieth century for lyric poetry and for short poems. There are of course a variety of reasons behind this preference. But one of them which is intimately related to New Critical practice is the liking for poems that 'work' in the classroom. One of the effects of the way that poetry came to be taught, particularly after *Practical Criticism*, has been that poetry is generally studied by concentration on individual short poems. This is evident in several ways. Anthologies are very specifically designed for the teaching of the poems in courses. For instance, in successive editions of *Understanding Poetry* the section of 'poems for study' has considerably expanded, becoming by the fourth edition (1976) a fairly considerable anthology of poems for classroom study. The understandable tendency in *Understanding Poetry* and in classroom-bound anthologies is to concentrate on shorter poems or on supposedly autonomous extracts from longer poems. This combination of classroom and anthology practice has given the short lyric a powerful ascendancy. Similarly, when individual named poets are selected for syllabi, the syllabus will usually specify a list of the poet's individual poems for study. Anyone involved in the teaching of poetry, as a student, pupil, teacher or lecturer, will be conscious of how a canon of short poems has been recurrently, if perhaps unconsciously, endorsed through both the ideals and practicalities of teaching. We know which poems 'go' in class and which do not; the likelihood is that the most attention is given to short poems.

In a related way, the New Critical emphasis on features such as symbol, pun, irony, paradox and ambiguity was certainly given an impressive justification, as was the elimination of the author as a factor in judging the poem. But the powerful influence of New Critical thought may have had less to do with the persuasiveness of the theoretical foundation underlying these features than with the fact that they are valuable for classroom discussion of individual poems. Poets who exploit ambiguity or whose poems are centred in symbols are more 'teachable' than poets of direct statement or decentred imagery.

The twentieth-century preference for the lyric and the shorter poem is, however, far from entirely based on one form of pedagogy. The sustained force evident in great lyric poetry also indicates something of the vital difference between poetry and prose: the concentration of language, the excess of meanings generated by poetry. Many long poems have been described as 'too prosy'. That is, they show a failure to sustain the concentrated effect, or they rely upon a narrative in which the potential richness of poetic language is moderated in order to generate a denotative meaning. Certainly, some of the great long poems in the English tradition, those by George Crabbe or William Morris or George Meredith, for instance, are stories in verse, and in order to be stories there is necessarily a curbing of the ambiguities and suggestive possibilities of language. It is the non-narrative lyric which shows language at its most intense. If we compare, for example, the opening lines of Morris's poem 'The Haystack in the Floods' with the opening line of Yeats's lyric 'The Sorrow of Love', we can see the differences in the kind of language. Morris writes: 'Had she come all the way for this, / To part at last without a kiss?' Yeats's line reads 'The brawling of a sparrow in the eaves.' Morris's opening is a narrative gesture in which the suggestive force of language is appropriately muted. The scene is set and the reader is made curious about the story that is to follow. Yeats sets up an image filled with suggestive possibilities. It is not that one opening is better than the other, since both are serving different purposes – remember that intentionality can be inscribed in the poem. Yet we are tempted to say that Yeats's line is more 'poetic' because by that term we tend to mean the suggestibility and concentration of image and language; in being so tempted, we have internalized New Critical beliefs.

This distinction between forms of poetic language will be considered in the next chapter in terms of the reader's constructive attention to the poem. That is, these differences may exist because the reader gives richness to them where this is considered appropriate rather than because there is any inherent difference in the properties of the language. Here, though, it is important to see that the preference for the lyric has developed to such an extent that the lyric might be said to represent 'real' poetry in a way that other forms – dramatic, narrative – no longer do.

One useful starting-point for this operating distinction is Edgar Allan Poe's 1846 essay 'The Philosophy of Composition'. Poe's distinction between poetry and verse rests precisely on this matter of concentrated effect. He writes that a poem is defined as a poem 'inasmuch as it intensely excites, by elevating, the soul; and all intense excitements are, through a psychal [*sic*] necessity, brief'. Thus, 'what we term long poem is, in fact, merely a succession of brief poetical effects' and 'at least one half of the "Paradise Lost" is essentially prose'.[28] Poe declares that the maximum length for a poem is about 100 lines.

While much of Poe's essay is contentious, his view that concentrated moments form the essence of poetry was profoundly influential in the subsequent elevation of the lyric and in the aspiration to 'poésie pure' that we saw in Chapter 1. Even though Poe's poetry has frequently been derided, it does have the excess of meaning and register that has come to be considered essential to lyric poetry. It was because of this that C. S. Lewis complained of the reader approaching *Paradise Lost* as if it were a lyric, searching the poem for 'little ebullient patches of delight'.[29] This excess, or extravagance, is exactly what Poe's French admirers, among them Mallarmé and Baudelaire, valued in his poetry. Also, the emphasis on poetry as heightened, concentrated language has frequently surfaced in other writing about poetry. In the twentieth century it was made familiar by Ezra Pound and his elaboration of the theory behind Imagism. Pound wrote a stimulating account of how he composed his two-line poem 'In a Station of the Metro'. In it he distinguishes between 'bad writing' in which the image is used as an ornament, and Imagism, in which the image is central, 'the word beyond formulated language'. He goes on to explain how having had the experience which formed the basis of 'In a Station of the Metro' he wrote a poem of 30 lines. He destroyed this as it was 'of second intensity'. He then wrote another of 'half that length' and then, eighteen months after the first attempt, he wrote the two-line poem.[30]

For Pound the Imagist the process of composing was one of gradual distillation of thought into image; narrative had to be transformed into intense moment. Poetic quality, Pound argues, is to do with the intensity of the communicating image rather than with a narrative of 'secondary intensity'. It is this way of seeing the poem, as well as his recognition of its breadth of cultural and historical reference, that leads to Pound's description of *The Waste Land* as 'the longest poem in the English langwidge'.[31] Placed alongside *The Fairie Queen*, Michael Drayton's *Poly-Olbion*, *Paradise Lost*, Wordsworth's *The Prelude*, Herman Melville's *Clarel* and Browning's *The Ring and the Book*, this claim for the 433 lines of Eliot's poem is patently absurd. But it is true given the terms Pound uses for the definition of poetry: thanks largely to Pound's own editorial interventions, *The Waste Land* is a work of 'first intensity' where the ideas that could have animated a much longer poem have been distilled into a series of images.

The emphasis on image and lyric is strongly related to seeing the poem as an object, because it is in the lyric that language is most obviously different from non-poetic usage. In our time this has gradually led to a repudiation of longer poems. Of course, narrative and dramatic poems are still written and published, such as Vikram Seth's *The Golden Gate* (1986) and James Merrill's *The Changing Light at Sandover* (1982). In the last 25 years there have also been many sonnet sequences and, interestingly, collections of short poems which handle a single event or provide a kind of narrative. John Berryman's *The Dream Songs* (1964–68), Douglas Dunn's *Elegies* (1985) and Tony Harrison's *The School of Eloquence* (1978) are important in this respect, utilizing a mode of writing reminiscent of Tennyson's *In Memoriam*, where short lyrics achieve a degree of autonomy but take their fullest meaning from the larger context. This practice of the short poem in the context of other short poems is interesting because it represents a combination of the apparently individual lyric and a variation of the long poem. Thus Berryman, Dunn and Harrison satisfied the preference for the short lyric while achieving some of the overall effects associated with the long poem.

Another and related result of the preference for the lyric has been the presentation of extracts from long poems as if they were autonomous lyrics. Many anthologies of poetry have taken parts of longer texts from, say, Shakespeare, Milton or Wordsworth and published these without reference to their context as part of a longer narrative. Some anthologists even provide a title for the extract, thereby heightening the illusion that it is a self-contained poem, and occluding its actual status as an extract. Thus, many readers of poetry are familiar with what is apparently a poem by Tennyson called 'Tears, Idle Tears' but which is in fact an untitled song from the narrative *The Princess*. We are accustomed to reading a poem by Blake called 'Jerusalem' which is in fact taken from a poem called *Milton*. Similarly, readers of anthologies often encounter apparently autonomous poems by Wordsworth which are actually extracts from *The Prelude*.

There are many examples of anthologies decontextualizing some lines and thereby transforming them into an apparently self-contained poem with a title. In fact, some poets have themselves made extracts from longer works and published these separately; others, though, have refused permission for extracts to be made from long poems. Clearly, for the anthologist there may be practical considerations involved which make it better to include excerpts from a longer poem, which might for reasons of space be impossible to publish in its entirety, than altogether ignore its existence. Given this choice, it seems better to have part of *The Prelude* rather than none at all. Nevertheless, this practice does once again testify to the desire for seeing the poem as an object, as a short, autonomous unit, even where this means that the editor must supply the elements which indicate that autonomy. Also, the practice helps to maintain and further a limited sense of how poetry may be defined.

The belief in the poem's autonomy arose at a very particular time in the history of poetry. For all of the many recurring movements to popularize poetry, the reading and the assessment of poetry has become more and more a specialized activity, taking place mainly in the classroom, the library and the study. One of the recognitions fundamental to New Critical theory was the shift of poetry from being a natural activity open to all to being something difficult, demanding specialized and informed attention. Certainly, the supposed obscurity of much Modernist poetry helped to develop this attitude; a poem as allusive and apparently inaccessible as *The Waste Land* appeared to demand explicators mediating between poem and reader. When they perform a mediating function, critics need to see the poem as autonomous because it is only through this assumption that common ground could exist between poem, mediator and reader. When a critic provides notes for a poem, explaining, for instance, the story of Tiresias, the effect is to widen the common ground between reader and poem. Actually this explanation preserves, shores up, the autonomy of the text because without the annotation and the information provided, the poem would be seen as incomplete in the sense of the words on the page carrying their meaning whole. Like titles, footnotes can supply something whose absence would challenge the self-contained nature of the poem. Instead of widening the poem's terms of reference outwards, they help to preserve the text in an urn-like enclosed space.[32] It is in this regard that Tate wrote that, for the New Critic, history no longer 'devours' the text but it 'survives as contributory knowledge'.[33] The poem's independence is thereby guaranteed where it had been threatened; if the reader knew nothing about Tiresias the gap creates a rupture in the supposed autonomy of the text.

It is also true that, for the New Critics, poetry existed almost exclusively in the print medium. This underscored the belief in the poem as an integral unit, because the words existed demonstrably and empirically *there*, on the page, not in the ear or in the memory of the audience as oral poetry had. The poem exists as a printed artefact.

What are the advantages of approaching the poem as if it were a self-contained unit? What are the disadvantages? Here is W. H. Auden's poem 'If I Could Tell You':

> Time will say nothing but I told you so,
> Time only knows the price we have to pay;
> If I could tell you I would let you know.
>
> If we should weep when clowns put on their show,
> If we should stumble when musicians play,
> Time will say nothing but I told you so.

There are no fortunes to be told, although,
Because I love you more than I can say,
If I could tell you I would let you know.

The winds must come from somewhere when they blow,
There must be reasons why the leaves decay;
Time will say nothing but I told you so.

Perhaps the roses really want to grow,
The vision seriously intends to stay;
If I could tell you I would let you know.

Suppose the lions all get up and go,
And all the brooks and soldiers run away;
Will Time say nothing but I told you so?
If I could tell you I would let you know.[34]

Although there is an expression of feeling in this poem, it is apparent that Auden has depersonalized the emotion (who is 'you'?), has restrained it, and has decontextualized it from the specifics of time and place. The traditional form of the villanelle, described in Chapter 1, is here slightly modified and the entire poem has a formal, slightly detached tone to it. While appropriate to many subjects, the villanelle has often been used to express a sense of the inevitable – of, for instance, mortality and the passing of time. Good examples include Tennyson's 'Tithonus' (echoed in William Empson's 'Missing Dates'), Dylan Thomas's 'Do not go gentle into that good night' and Elizabeth Bishop's 'One Art'. In Auden's poem the iambic pentameter is fairly regular, though there is perhaps a modification in line 14, 'The vision seriously intends to stay'.[35]

The poem is concerned with our inability to see the future, but also with the knowledge that after a certain period of time everything will come to have seemed inevitable. Even if the totally unexpected occurs, over time this will seem to have been anticipated, even expected. In some ways the strength of the poem lies in the considerable force of its language and its memorability, combined with the excision of the self. It tells no story nor does it rely on individual memorable images. It works by generalizing an attitude and then presenting specific examples or illustrations of that attitude. The poem is also strikingly self-contained, each image and example is clear, and the repetitions characteristic of the villanelle here indicate a closed form, a thought completed as well as complete in itself.

Can we be persuaded that the poem is successful because Auden has depersonalized it, objectifying emotion and experience? Its lack of specificity regarding time or individual identity can be seen as a strength. Like a proverb it has an applicability to a variety of circumstances rather than being specific only to one person or one event or one moment in time. Hence we could say that the poem's success derives partly from the very excision of whatever personal circumstances led to it. Had he included them, the poem's general applicability would have been seriously reduced. Auden has hypostatized his subject, giving it independence from the circumstances of its creation. While there is an 'I' in the poem, it is depersonalized and distant.

Although Auden's excisions of historical context and personal circumstances are crucial to the poem, we could ask how differently we might read the poem if it could be seen to invoke public and private history. Auden, or an editor, could add something to the poem which would direct interpretation in a particular way. For instance, when this poem appeared in Auden's posthumous *Collected Poems*, the editor, Edward Mendelson, attached a date to the end, 'October 1940'. This supplementary date disturbs the notion of the poem as self-contained, as detached from public events as Auden had made it seem. The date precipitates a shift in our perception of the poem, making it seem more directly to be about the Second World War and a confrontation of the anxieties and uncertainties that thinking about the war generates. The poem's sense of an uncertain future, of patterns going wrong, we could say, makes it both of its time and about its time. Adding 'October 1940' seems to make much more topical, less generic, the reference to 'soldiers' in line 17, and the references to decay and death become more concrete. With 'October 1940' even the innocent-sounding 'lions' of line 16 seem to have a resonance, suggesting the lions that represent England (as they do in Ted Hughes' 'The Dream of the Lion', discussed in Chapter 8). Perhaps that line really is saying 'Supposing England fell?' as seemed likely in October 1940. Is there also a direct reference to the war in line 4? The word 'show' had been a slang word for battle since the First World War, and if '1940' is invoked, it seems to refer more directly to the kinds of 'show' these militaristic 'clowns' are going to mount this time. Given that, then it is likely we will 'weep' at this 'show'.

Certainly, adding the date of composition as Mendelson did changes how we read the poem. The same is true, incidentally, of Edward Thomas's short poem 'In Memoriam':

> The flowers left thick at nightfall in the wood
> This Eastertide call into mind the men,
> Now far from home, who, with their sweethearts, should
> Have gathered them and will do never again.

What seems a generic lament for the absent men, reminiscent of a poet like A. E. Housman, is transformed into a very specific lament for the dead of the First World War when an editor adds the date 'Easter 1915' to the poem.[36] The point is that Thomas and Auden deliberately kept their poems undated, and this gave them a more objective, generic significance and that this is transformed when an editor supplements the poem. The poem loses something of its perceived autonomy.

Alternatively, or additionally, a biographer could discover and draw our attention to the fact that October 1940 might have been a time of personal crisis in Auden's life. He might have been distressed over his lover and their future together. In fact, biographies of Auden indicate that this was a period during which he began to return to the Christian faith of his childhood and this may have precipitated a crisis in his relationship with his lover, the Jewish Chester Kallman. A biographer might try to demonstrate that the poem is rooted in deeply personal circumstances. Certainly, we would read 'If I Could Tell You' differently in the light of such knowledge, and one recent authority has stated, as if it were unproblematically the case, that the poem is 'another encouragement to Kallman'.[37] The supposedly generic 'we' of the poem would thus seem to be more specifically individuated as Auden and Kallman; the 'I' Auden, the 'you' Kallman. The possible modification of iambic pentameter in line 14 is explicable if a personal context is invoked, because 'the vision' who might or might not stay could be Kallman, and this may actually be the emotional centre of the poem. The poem's evident reticence could be explained by Auden's reluctance to write openly at this time about his homosexuality; in other poems, such as 'Lullaby' he carefully used language in which gender was unspecified. It is also possible that an editor persuaded by the weight of evidence for a personal interpretation of the poem could give it a different title. How differently would we respond to this poem if it were called something like 'To Chester Kallman' or, to use a title comparable to Yeats's early poetry, 'The Lover Addresses his Love and Wonders at Their Future Together'? The change of title is not entirely far-fetched; the titles of many Auden poems have been altered or titles added to previously untitled poems, and at different times this particular poem has had three different titles.[38] Furthermore there are some outstanding examples of editorial additions of titles which then come to direct subsequent readings in ways that point to the personal life of the poet. One example is that of Milton's Sonnet xix, which begins 'When I consider how my light is spent'. This came to be titled 'On His Blindness' and the title guided readers in a particular direction. Another famous example is that of Keats's poem which begins 'This living hand, now warm and capable'. Although an untitled fragment, editors have often called the poem 'To Fanny Brawne' as if it were addressed to Keats's beloved. This turns the 'you' of the poem into Fanny and transforms the sense of what the poem is expressing.

It could be said that the supplementary information given by a changed title or by the addition of a date of composition enriches our appreciation of a poem by filling some lacuna. But it may also limit or even impoverish our appreciation of the poem through restricting its generation of multiple possible interpretations. That is, by seeming to give us something by which to understand the poem, the information actually acts as a limiting device to our free interpretation of it. I might propose that Auden's poem is primarily concerned with his doubts over being a poet and concerns a crisis over whether he will write again. I have no biographical evidence for this, and might not be interested in looking for any, but I do have the words on the page. For example: feeling helpless about loss of inspiration (a 'vision'), the poet tries to write in a highly traditional form (at one time the poem was titled 'Villanelle') through which he hopes to make contact with the great stream, 'the brook' of poetic thought. The association of the villanelle with pastoral accounts for much of the imagery as the poet tries to find inspiration in thinking on traditional subjects for poetry: clowns, soldiers, musicians. Nevertheless the poet feels a failure and tries to will a poem into being through craft in an act which he hopes will connect him to a restorative poetic tradition.

Seeing the poem as an object involves a certain sleight of hand. The poet may fashion a cognitive object freed (or so the poet thinks) from the self, and if poems are to mean anything more or different from biography, then we must accept this fiction. But the paradox is that for the poem to mean anything to us, we must locate it in a context. To do so involves the breaking down of that very boundary between poem and world, since contextualizing necessarily involves the disruption of the poem's supposed integrity. The act of interpretation involves reducing the remoteness of the poem by invoking comparisons associations and contexts; if it did not, then poetry might mean very little to us, because its capacity to enter our lives would be lost. The ideal of free-standing autonomy for the poem is an important ideal. But the act of interpretive reading necessarily and, rightly, disrupts any sense of the poem as an object.

Endnotes

1 'Three Types of Poetry' (1934), in Allen Tate, *Essays of Four Decades* (London, 1970), p. 194.
2 W. K. Wimsatt, *The Verbal Icon: Studies in the Meaning of Poetry* (Lexington, 1954, 1982), p. xvii.
3 Carol Rumens, letter to *The Times Literary Supplement*, 28 July 1995, p. 17.
4 I. A. Richards, *Practical Criticism*, 1929 (London, 1978), p. 309. It was Richards who stated that his students were 'products of the most expensive kind of education', p. 310.
5 Eagleton's account in his *Literary Theory: An Introduction* (Oxford, 1983, 1989) analyses the covert political ideology in the New Criticism, arguing that it was 'a recipe for political inertia, and thus for submission to the status quo' (p. 50).
6 The New Critical indebtedness to Romanticism and to Coleridge in particular is especially important, and in his Preface to *Essays of Four Decades*, Tate acknowledged this debt.
7 William Hazlitt, *Lectures on the English Poets* (1818), 'Lecture 1: On Poetry in General', in *The Selected Writings of William Hazlitt* ed. Duncan Wu, 9 vols (London, 1998), vol. 2, p. 165.
8 'Understanding Modern Poetry' (1940), in Tate, *Essays*, p. 161.
9 T. S. Eliot, *Selected Essays*, p. 145.
10 In 'Tradition and the Individual Talent' (1917) Eliot wrote that poetry was 'an escape from emotion' and an 'escape from personality'. *Selected Essays*, p. 21.

11 'Visiting the Tates' in Robert Lowell, *Collected Prose*, ed. Robert Giroux (London, 1987), p. 59.

12 'The Present Function of Criticism' (1940), in Tate, *Essays*, p. 210.

13 'Understanding Modern Poetry' (1940), in Tate, *Essays*, p. 159.

14 Quoted in Tate, *Essays*, p. 159.

15 Tate, *Essays*, p. 164. Although human, the 'Yahoos' represent degraded irrational bestiality in Swift's *Gulliver's Travels* (1762).

16 Wimsatt, *The Verbal Icon*, p. 3.

17 With regard to this point, it is worth noting Gareth Reeves' poem recording the reaction of his father, the poet James Reeves, to the inclusion of a poem of his on an examination paper:

> *Write down in your own words what the poet means by* . . . 'Means, my foot. It means what I bloody well wrote,' barked Father when they set him for O Level prac. crit.

Although obviously restricting the imaginative free play of signifiers, the point should not be overlooked; intention is inscribed in the poem. Gareth Reeves, *Listening In* (Manchester, 1993), p. 8. We are grateful to Amanda Piesse for bringing this poem to our attention.

18 C. S. Lewis, *A Preface to Paradise Lost* (Oxford, 1942, 1979), p. 1.

19 See Brooks, *The Well Wrought Urn*, pp. 176–96.

20 Barbara Herrnstein Smith, *Poetic Closure: A Study of How Poems End* (London, 1968). Murray Krieger also wrote on the topic in *A Reopening of Closure* (New York, 1989).

21 See Smith, *Poetic Closure*, p. 214.

22 John Ashbery, *Selected Poems* (London, 1987), p. 279.

23 Quoted in Peter Baker, *Modern Poetic Practice* (New York, 1986), p. 152.

24 David Bromwich, 'Parody, Pastiche and Allusion', in Chariva Hosek and Patricia Parker, eds, *Lyric Poetry: Beyond New Criticism* (New York, 1985), p. 329.

25 Quoted in Smith, *Poetic Closure*, p. 237.

26 Anne Ferry's book *The Title to the Poem* (Stanford, 1996) is a stimulating account of a topic which, like closure, is oddly neglected.

27 Joseph Conrad, *Heart of Darkness* (1902, Harmondsworth, 1981), p. 8.

28 Poe, *Essays and Reviews* (New York, 1984), p. 15.

29 Lewis, *Paradise Lost*, p. 1.

30 Pound, *Gaudier-Brzeska: A Memoir*, quoted in Cleanth Brooks and Robert Penn Warren, *Understanding Poetry*, fourth edition (New York, 1976), p. 72.

31 Pound, *The Selected Letters of Ezra Pound 1907–1941*, ed. D. D. Paige (London, 1982) p. 169.

32 With regard to the explanatory notes that *The Cantos* have generated, Lawrence S. Rainey has written 'The annotation was intended not to provide "facts," but to defuse their troublesome presence by containing them in an illusory immutability. Only so could the poem "demonstrate its own purposes," assume its true status as "an object of art." ' Rainey, *Ezra Pound and the Monument of Culture* (Chicago, 1991), p. 137.

33 Tate, 'A Note on Critical "Autotelism" ' (1949), in *Essays*, p. 169.

34 W. H. Auden, *Collected Poems*, ed. Edward Mendelson (London, 1976), pp. 244–5.

35 The possible modification occurs because of the question of how many syllables there are in the word 'seriously'. If the word is pronounced with three syllables then it can be scanned as regularly iambic. If pronounced with four, then it is a modified iambic. The *Oxford English Dictionary* indicates that 'serious' is to be

pronounced with two syllables, whereas the *Merriam-Webster Dictionary* indicates three syllables (if you ever experienced the American tennis player John McEnroe shouting his famous line 'You cannot be *serious*' then you'd have heard the three distinct syllables). The distinction between American and standard English usage is important, then, though unresolved in this case because the question of whether Auden is an English or an American poet is also a vexed one.

The disagreement between the two authors of this study on the scanning of 'seriously' bears out exactly what Philip Hobsbaum expresses with admirable succinctness: 'There will always be a certain amount of choice in rhythmic scansion, since rhythm is a matter of hearing the verse rather than counting the syllables, and no two people are going to hear the verse in exactly the same way' (*Metre, Rhythm and Verse Form* (London, 1996), p. 13).

36 Edward Thomas, *Collected Poems*, ed. R. George Thomas (Oxford, 1981), p. 58.
37 John Fuller, *W. H. Auden: A Commentary* (London, 1998), p. 400.
38 See Fuller, *W. H. Auden*, p. 400. The poem has been called 'Villanelle', 'But I Can't' and 'If I Could Tell You'.

|5|

Poem and author

He is this afternoon writing a poem with great spirit: always a sign of well being with him. Needless to say, it is an intensely dismal poem.
Florence Hardy[1]

In the preceding chapter we examined the idea of the poem as a free-standing autonomous entity. As we saw, this ideal involved the concept of the poem as an object available to public interpretation, regardless of whatever intentions the poet may have had for it. This chapter explores this concept further, by focusing more on the author. How does our knowledge (if any) of the poet direct our interpretation of the poem? If we read a poem and have no knowledge of the author (and remember that some poems have no author) then how do we see an author constructed, or implied, in the poem itself? How does the concept of sincerity function in the understanding and interpretation of poetry?

Perhaps the first point that needs to be made is that the concept of the author is a relatively recent one in the history of literature, and that the assumption of a literary work growing out of the life of the writer is even more recent. In western Europe the author, as the owner of a work, developed as print developed from the fifteenth century onwards (even though in Britain there was no copyright act until 1709, and that was not enforced until later in the century). For us today the idea of the author is inevitably involved with the published writing of the author, but this was by no means always the case. In oral cultures the 'author' of a poem or story may not have been that work's 'author' at all, in our sense of the term, but may have been rather an elaborator of existing poems or songs or stories as performances. Further, because it would have been a performance, the story or poem could not be fixed (like an object) but depended on collaboration, audience involvement and recognition. In an oral culture the performance functioned as a statement *of* community more than a statement *to* the community, because the performance itself formed part of the communal recognition of its own group members. The sense of community arising from performance is quite transformed by print culture. There, the 'performance' is fixed in print and is consumed (usually) privately by the individual in a solitary act of reading, rather than communally through listening and seeing.

Oral traditions do survive, however much they may be modified. The printing of an anonymous ballad such as 'Sir Patrick Spens' or 'Lord Randal' preserves the idea that the ballad is a product of, and an expression of, a community or a culture rather than of an individual. Contemporary writers of ballads (whether the ballads are sung or not) often use the form as a way of suggesting that their concerns are communal and public rather than private. One of the best examples of a sung ballad in this tradition is Bob Dylan's 'A Hard Rain's A-Gonna Fall' (1963), echoing 'Lord Randal' and existing as an expression of communal horror at the likelihood of nuclear devastation. In Britain the work of poets such as Linton Kwesi Johnson also demonstrates the current vitality of an oral tradition. While his poems are printed, Johnson's dub poetry exists primarily as performance. Some contemporary American Indian writers such as Leslie Marmon Silko, Louise Erdrich, Joy Harjo, Simon Ortiz and N. Scott Momaday have been very much concerned with how elements of an oral tradition with which they align themselves might be adapted in order to become a means of expression in a predominantly print culture.

The adaptation and survival of orality into the world of print is itself a rich and significant theme. But print culture has come to be dominant, and remains powerful in spite of repeated predictions of its demise. With it has developed the idea of the author as legal owner of the words on the page. This is bound up with many other developments. In particular, a series of copyright acts in the eighteenth and nineteenth centuries assisted in the professionalization of authorship by guaranteeing that payment would be given (or, at least, would be expected) for what was published (and sold). This inevitably changed the sense of what an author was, to the extent that in an interesting complaint made in a letter in 1818 Byron complained of Wordsworth's being described as 'at the head of his profession'. Byron scathingly commented 'I thought that Poetry was an *art*, or an *attribute*, and not a *profession*.'[2] Byron is of course disputing whether Wordsworth is at the head of this 'profession' at all, but his comment is revealing in its perception of how the sense of the author is changing.

However, we are more concerned here with the effects that various factors have had on our view of the poet and the poem. Because of a complex web of issues, some having to do with print, law and money, we now tend to think of the author as an important presence in the poem. Also, one of the effects of the shift from an oral to a print medium has been that the poem itself has become more individualized. This act of individuation exists on several levels. The poem is no longer the property of all, or part of a collaborative, communal expression, but is considered the personal expression of the individual. Also we are inclined to privilege the poem, rather than prose, as if it provided direct access to the mind and the feelings of the poet.

Thomas Hardy is a remarkable example of a poet whose work incorporates both an oral, public basis and also has the status of a written, private expression. Hardy was born in 1840 and many of his poems (and, indeed, numerous episodes in his novels) make reference back to a pre-industrial, pre-urbanized England in which communal identity is affirmed through story-telling and through performance.[3] His sense of poetry is of a public, performative act in which a theme is reiterated or a story told, perhaps in ballad form. Hence, poems such as 'The Bridge of Lodi', 'A Trampwoman's Tragedy' and 'The Revisitation' are narratives embodying themes also present in traditional ballads, and sets of Hardy's poems are explicitly called 'songs' as in the section of poems entitled 'A Set of Country Songs'. In 1922 – the year in which Modernism came to its fullest bloom with the publication of *The Waste Land* and *Ulysses* – Hardy published his preface to *Late Lyrics and Earlier*. There he characterized himself as 'a man of letters concerned to keep poetry alive'.[4] For Hardy, keeping poetry alive meant keeping it in touch with what he considered its vital origins in orality, where the author is an indiscernible presence. At the same time, though, Hardy's work also demonstrates exactly the shift to personalized poetry in which the individual feelings and expression of the poet are predominant. This aspect of his work is seen most strikingly in the poems he wrote after the death of his first wife, Emma, and included in his 'Poems of 1912–13' in *Satires of Circumstance* (1914). There Hardy renegotiates the view of the poem as unauthored record of the communal and transforms it into the expression of deeply felt individual experience and pain. Poems such as 'The Going', 'The Voice' and 'Where the Picnic Was' are today likely to seem more considerable poems than others of Hardy, because our sense of poetry as a record of deeply felt experience is very strong, and likely to be much stronger than our sense that the author is an uninvolved storyteller. The poems written after Emma's death seem to give us entry to 'the real Thomas Hardy', entry that is blocked in, say, 'The Rash Bride' or 'A Trampwoman's Tragedy', and we are in an age which places high value on such authenticity and on sincerity.

While it is frequently invoked in judgements of poetry and of poets, sincerity is not really a helpful concept in critically evaluating poetry. Certainly, we might value sincerity in a person as a moral attribute, but it becomes a difficult matter in judging poetry; as one critic has written, sincerity is 'a moral and not an aesthetic virtue'.[5] This is partly because to judge sincerity involves invoking something from outside of the text, and partly because the invocation of sincerity as if it were a critical concept makes reading poetry into something almost circular, as if a poem were to be judged only by whether it is a valid expression of the mind of the poet. That is, sincerity is only about the author and the author's relation to the work, rather than being an enlargement of the terms of the poem.

Nevertheless, sincerity is highly valued, particularly in appreciation of lyric poetry, and often becomes a form of validation for the lyric, or in any poem in which we feel that the poet is writing directly and personally, rather than through a persona.

The first problem we encounter in trying to invoke sincerity in reading poetry is that we cannot look at the words on the page and decide from them alone whether or not they were meant sincerely. For instance, Weldon Kees has a poem titled 'For My Daughter' in which he writes movingly of his daughter, in a way reminiscent of Yeats's 'A Prayer for My Daughter':

> Looking into my daughter's eyes I read
> Beneath the innocence of morning flesh
> Concealed, hintings of death she does not heed.[6]

The poem concludes, though, with the line:

> I have no daughter. I desire none.

We cannot decide from the poem alone whether Kees has a daughter or not and therefore the issue of sincerity is invalidated. We might make a useful distinction here between dramatic poetry and lyric poetry, but this distinction is less useful than it might be supposed when we are discussing sincerity. For instance, here is a speech from Shakespeare's *Cymbeline* in which a character called Posthumus, believing that his wife, Imogen, has been unfaithful, inveighs against women:

> Could I find out
> The woman's part in me – for there's no motion
> That tends to vice in man but I affirm
> It is the woman's part; be it lying, note it,
> The woman's; flattering, hers; deceiving, hers;
> Lust and rank thoughts, hers hers; revenges, hers;
> Ambitions, covetings, change of prides, disdain,
> Nice longing, slanders, mutability,
> All faults that man can name, nay, that hell knows,
> Why, hers in part or all, but rather all . . .
>
> (Act 2, scene 5, 19–28)

It would be naive or even foolish to read these lines and then ask whether or not Shakespeare was sincere and, therefore, whether he must have hated women. We know the question is naive because these are lines given to a character in a drama, and for the purpose of the drama the audience must be convinced that the speaker really feels a hatred of women, and is utterly sincere in this belief (even though he is mistaken regarding Imogen). Thus we might note the violent intensity of the language, the syntax which seems so cluttered because of the relative absence of verbs, and how this produces an effect of overwhelming rage and hatred bordering on the inarticulate. The speech is carefully managed by Shakespeare to give the impression of

unshakeable and violent hatred. But we cannot say that this intensity testi-
fies to Shakespeare's own depth of feeling, and is therefore evidence of his
own sincerity.

The example from *Cymbeline* is a useful one because we may think it
bizarre that the author's sincerity could be invoked with regard to a char-
acter in a drama (though there are those who believe that here and there in
his plays Shakespeare included a speech about what he 'really felt' about a
subject). The point is not that sincerity has no place in considering dramatic
poetry, but that in any poetry the intensity and quality of the language alone
is no guide to sincerity. Indeed, Oscar Wilde went so far as to say that 'all
bad poetry springs from genuine feeling'.[7] Poetry is language shaped,
ordered, intellectually controlled.

We might regard Shakespeare's sincerity as irrelevant to our understand-
ing of Posthumus's speech, because the presence of the dramatic persona
blocks any direct route from the author to us. But the principle that the
language before us is no guide to sincerity is equally true of lyric poetry as
of dramatic. For example, we might think that Shakespeare's sonnets give
us more direct access to what he was really thinking or feeling, because they
are unmediated, apparently, by dramatic personae. So when Shakespeare
begins Sonnet 144 with the lines: 'Two loves I have, of comfort and despair,
/ Which like two spirits do suggest me still' we are tempted to think that the
sonnet is more sincere than Posthumus's speech. But, just as in the speech,
we have no way of ascertaining sincerity unless something from outside of
the text is utilized. The words alone are no guide; after all, these lines from
the sonnet are as crafted as the words Shakespeare wrote for Posthumus. In
fact, poets themselves are (a little inconveniently, perhaps) apt to remind us
that poetry is artifice, that as Touchstone puts it in *As You Like It,* 'the
truest poetry is the most feigning', even as we might wish it were truth (Act
2, scene 3, 19–20). Poets are masters of language, and it is naive for us to
be persuaded of the truth or sincerity of a feeling because the expression of
it is so powerful. As David Hume wrote in 1739: 'Poets . . . tho' liars by
profession, always endeavour to give an air of truth to their fictions.'[8]

This, again, is one of the problems with sincerity when reading poetry: it
presupposes a straightforward, unproblematic relation between author and
text. It also, as one of the theoretical preconditions for judging sincerity,
presupposes that the poem is a narrative of a prior event. Those who invoke
sincerity as an important concept assume that the poet offers a narrative
version of things from her or his own life. Hence the poem is a form of
journal, a kind of diary entry, and its truth (and, consequently, its value) can
be apprehended by comparing what the poem says with what actually
happened. It is important to remember that poems, like novels or other
narratives, create their own version of reality which is independent of any
prior event or series of events. Even when poems and novels have a factual
basis ('based on a true story') we should not forget that they are narratives
that are carefully shaped and selected, to the extent that they necessarily

distort the very shape of events. We might like to ask 'what really happened?' but we must remember that this question presupposes a straightforward relation between art-work and reality, a relation which is often quite absent from the poem or novel. It is this independence from reality that is overlooked when something extraneous like sincerity is used in critical judgement.

Ideally, the sincerity of the poet should be irrelevant to our critical evaluation of the poem, especially if we see, in New Critical terms, the poem as an object. After all, we do not need to know whether a builder is 'sincere'; we just want to be sure that the roof over our heads is securely attached to the house. Nevertheless, it is generally true that sincerity probably does affect our appreciation and judgement of some poems. If we admire a love poem and then discover (again, recalling that sincerity is always invoked extra-textually, that it cannot exist in the text itself) that the poet actually hated the subject of the poem, we would tend to feel that the poem was weakened by being insincere. We would also, perhaps, feel that the poem was more an exercise in language than an expression of something deeply felt, and consequently it might mean less to us. Some critics and readers have been uncomfortable with Milton's *Lycidas* because of the fact that the poem seems 'insincere'. Milton was far less friendly with the drowned Edward King than the poem suggests and it is unlikely that the death caused as much weeping on Milton's part as is implied in the poem. Writing on *Lycidas*, Northrop Frye stated sternly: 'Personal sincerity has no place in literature, because personal sincerity as such is inarticulate.'[9] Judgements regarding sincerity might become inevitable as we know more about a poet's life, but when we make such a judgement we should also be conscious that it depends on contextualizing the poem in the author's life; we are no longer only reading the poem but are undertaking a comparison between the poem and the life of the writer. This awareness should make us pause and ask whether we are reading the poem as if it were autobiography.

While we should be wary of invoking sincerity in textual judgement, doing so can indicate how much we value poetry as expression. We want it to be sincere and we might well be suspicious of insincerity because it seems to make poetry into a mere exercise in language. This is certainly a modern ideal; it has been argued that sincerity was an irrelevant concept before the rise of Romanticism, and that the skill and ingenuity of the poet were valued much more highly than emotional sincerity. In fact, there have been different periods in history when poetry has been valued particularly as expression, and thus a high estimation is placed on sincerity. Towards the end of the 1950s in the United States, there was a reaction against what many poets and readers thought of as the overly impersonal, academic poetry encouraged by the dominance of New Criticism. In the 1950s and 1960s many poets tried to make their poems as authentic as possible to their experience. Some, like Allen Ginsberg, consciously attempted to refashion a poetic tradition stemming from the Romantics, cherishing poetry which emphasized the value of subjective self-expression, and had sincerity at its basis. Further, audiences for poetry valued its immediacy, relevance and the authenticity of performance. Sincerity came to be valued very highly and Lionel Trilling tried in his influential 1974 book *Sincerity and Authenticity* to restore sincerity to critical vocabulary as a moral authority.

Such uses of the self have important implications for reading poetry, implications beyond the question of sincerity. As readers of poetry we are being asked about why we value poetry. Is it because it is an expression of personal feeling with which we can identify, or because the poem creates something memorable, opening up for us a different way of seeing the world? These are of course by no means exclusive; again, we need to be self-conscious about how we are reading poetry and what we might unconsciously be asking of it. Our judgements of poems might well rely upon criteria which we have not fully established consciously for ourselves.

When we consider questions of sincerity and of intentionality, the very role and even existence of the author is called into question. Of course, these questions, of intentionality and of sincerity, are not unique to poetry: they are valid also for any literary study. They do, though, have a special resonance for poetry because poetry, especially lyric poetry, has so often been considered the most suitable medium for self-expression. With their emphasis on the 'words on the page' the New Critics attempted to exclude the author from consideration of the poem; otherwise the necessary attention to the poem's special language would be in danger of being lost. For them, removing the author from the text was a strategy to enable reading. For structuralist and post-structuralist thinkers, however, the absence of the author has been an essential premise for quite different textual manoeuvres. When Roland Barthes famously announced 'The Death of the Author' in 1968 he was attempting to move criticism away from the privileging of the author by emphasizing the autonomy of the text beyond individual agency. Such a move was essential for establishing structuralist readings, since structuralism emphasizes that language is a socially determined structure in an arbitrary relation to 'real life'. The idea of the individual author in control of language is a nostalgic fiction; the author is not independent of discourses but is situated by and in them. The text must be seen, writes Barthes, not as 'a line of words' delivered by the 'Author-God' but as 'a multi-dimensional space in which a variety of writings, none of them original, blend and clash'.[10] Michel Foucault's equally famous essay 'What is an Author?' (1969) both built upon Barthes's essay and redirected it towards emphasizing the way that an authorial figure exists in the text. Foucault insists that the author is repeatedly invoked as a means of limiting interpretation and discussion of the work; the author is 'a certain functional principle by which, in our culture, one limits, excludes, and chooses; in short, by which one impedes the free circulation, the free manipulation, the free composition, decomposition, and recomposition of fiction'.[11]

When we include the author in our interpretations of poetry, we should consider whether the author is being used mainly as a way of limiting interpretations, and whether we are implicitly considering the author as a figure fully in control of the poem. Using the author can be a means of restricting interpretation and denying the fuller possibilities of the poem; the idea for instance, that a poem might mean different things to different people at different times would be denied if everything were referred back to the author and the experiences of the author. Taken to its extreme, this restriction of interpretation would result in our interpretations of Shakespeare being restricted to everything that Shakespeare could have known or thought; that is, interpretation could not refer to anything that had happened after his death in 1616. Rather than being creative or imaginative in responding to the poetry, interpretation would be a form of historical reconstruction of the author's life.

Perhaps because they recognized this interpretative restrictiveness, many poets have been keen to dissolve any perceived bond between the poem and their own lives. Poets have repeatedly emphasized the free play of self that the poem allows, thereby deflecting interpretation away from their personal circumstances. Keats wrote that the poet was the 'most unpoetical thing in existence', without identity and always imaginatively investing an identity in others. He also wrote that 'A Man's life of any worth is a continual allegory. . . . Lord Byron cuts a figure but he is not figurative – Shakespeare led a life of Allegory; his works are the comments on it.'[12] Emily Dickinson seemed wryly to anticipate kinds of inquiry into her own life when she began her Poem 288 with the line: 'I'm Nobody! Who are you?' It is as if we go to her poems expecting that they will reveal to us the 'real' Emily Dickinson but what they actually demonstrate is the self-reflexive nature of interpretation. We should end up asking questions about ourselves and our motives and identities, not expecting that the poems are windows on Dickinson's life. Indeed, Joyce Carol Oates has memorably expressed how far the experience of reading Dickinson's poetry dissolves any sense of a coherent individual self behind the poems. Oates writes that despite the 'voluminous biographical material' and the 'extraordinary intimacy' of Dickinson's poetry, the 'common experience of reading her work' is that 'we come away seeming to know nothing'.[13] Indeed, Dickinson seems to have revelled in the possibilities of flexible and multiple identities that poetry provided and to have feared the imposition of a limited, single identity. Poetry may be an escape from the self and a realization of alternatives; it was in this sense that T. S. Eliot wrote of the progress of an artist being a continual extinction of personality.[14]

The force of such statements is to depersonalize the poem, and, as it were, release it from the restrictions that reference to an author might place upon it. It could also be pointed out that such statements serve to broaden out the poem; that the poet is attempting to give the poem a very broad frame of reference by refusing the potential reduction of it to personal terms. When Ezra Pound was editing with Eliot the poem that became *The Waste Land*, Pound dissuaded Eliot from using lines which he felt would lead to a dismissal of the poem as personal. In particular, a section planned for the poem was excised by Pound and published separately as the poem 'Gerontion'. This poem ends with the line 'Thoughts of a dry brain in a dry season' and it is obvious that if the line were included in *The Waste Land* it would be seen as an invitation to see the poem as an expression of private despair. Pound wanted the poem to be read as expressive of a generation, not as something personal to one individual.

It might also be pointed out that a poet may claim that the poem is not based on personal experience in order to deflect inquiry into her or his life. To take the case of Eliot and *The Waste Land*, for instance, we know much more about Eliot than the first readers of the poem did, and because of what we know we are likely to understand the poem in a different way from those first readers. Certain lines of the poem which once seemed puzzling are now explicable by reference to Eliot's life. Thus, we know that the lines

> On Margate Sands.
> I can connect
> Nothing with nothing

refer to a particular period in Eliot's life when he was afflicted by extreme anxiety over the mental state of his wife. They were both recuperating at the coastal resort of Margate. Knowing this, we might be much more inclined than the poem's first readers were (or could have been) to personalize the poem and read it as a personal lament. In fact, our knowledge of Eliot and his private life might be an obstruction to seeing the poem in the public terms that Eliot and Pound had proposed for it. For many critics the kind of personal inquiries that have been made into the private life of Eliot have been distasteful and unjustified by any illumination of the poetry. It is perhaps on these grounds, and not only on the grounds that biographical knowledge limits the interpretation and, ultimately, the significance of poetry, that some poets have taken steps to ensure that biographical information will be kept secret or hidden. Some poets have requested that no biographies be written of them. In recent times, Eliot, Auden and Philip Larkin each made such a request. Eliot left instructions intending to restrict access to his unpublished papers. Larkin went so far as to request that his papers and unpublished manuscripts be destroyed. Those executors, Anthony Thwaite and Andrew Motion, not only did not do so, but Thwaite published much previously unpublished poetry in the *Collected Poems* of Larkin and published letters in *The Selected Letters of Philip Larkin*, and Motion published a controversial biography of Larkin knowing that his friend expressly did not want one. These actions certainly have ethical and legal ramifications, and many people considered them grossly unethical. Unsurprisingly, we also have several biographies of Eliot and Auden, in spite of their clear wishes. Even though there are ethical and legal issues involved here, it is important to remember that there is a fundamental critical issue at stake; that is, the biographies are considered important because it is assumed that knowing the facts of the author's life will illuminate the poetry in some way.

Of course, that last statement may be an exaggeration. We live in an era when biographies command large readerships, and top biographers are accordingly well rewarded. But the strong evident interest in biography should make us all the more wary about how we actually use biographical knowledge in reading poetry, particularly when poets may have explicitly wished to keep certain details of their private lives away from public scrutiny. It is as if publishing a poem, however much the poet has tried to depersonalize it, means giving permission for intimate inquiry into one's personal life, and some critics have certainly expressed their view that this process has gone too far. But at the same time, some kinds of poetry do seem actually to invite, or even demand, a knowledge of the author's life which is not mentioned explicitly in the poem itself. That is, interpretation requires some supplementary, extra-textual knowledge. When we read one of the many biographies of Sylvia Plath we may feel that the poetry is gradually disappearing and is being replaced by gossip and speculation about whatever remains of a private life. But we should also recall that some of the poems in *Ariel* were highly personal, in which Plath used details of her private life with only the thinnest of disguises. These poems provoked probing into Plath's life (seemingly made more justifiable because of her suicide), because they seemed to require that the reader possess particular information in order to understand them. We will deal more with this question and how it affects interpretation at the end of this chapter.

One way out of the problem of reductive biographical interpretations is to maintain a strict demarcation between the actual author of the poem and what has been called the 'implied author'. The implied author is a useful concept in that it recognizes an authorial presence in the poem while at the same time noting a distinction between that presence and the actual poet. Although the term 'implied author' is most readily used with regard to prose, all poems have some kind of implied author, or even narrator, even where we may know little or nothing about the actual author. (Poems have an implied reader too, of which more in the next chapter.) We can also talk about the speaker of the poem, or the persona of the poem, again in an attempt to mark a sometimes crucial distinction between the poet and the authorial presence in the work. Thus, Robert Frost's celebrated poem 'Stopping by Woods on a Snowy Evening' has a narrative presence which may be distinguished from the actual author. Indeed, this is an interesting example in that readers of this poem sometimes fail to notice that the speaker is not gendered at all. Frost is often very specific about whether his speakers are male or female, but in this case the gender is left open. While the signifiers associated with the speaker, such as work, duty, desire for independence, can be associated with masculinity, it is probable that most readers who imagine a male protagonist are assuming an unproblematic link between the actual author and the implied narrator of the experience recorded in the poem. This assumption necessarily limits interpretation of the poem, either by insisting that the experience be grounded in Frost's own life (in which case the question of 'Whose woods these are' may be literally answerable) or by maintaining that the poem is fundamentally concerned with masculinity. Using the convention of the implied author, or persona, though, permits us to engage with alternative readings of the poem. For example, we may note that the non-gender of the speaker means that the poem has been dissociated from Frost's own life, and biographical details are accordingly irrelevant. We then read the poem as being concerned with a struggle between duty and pleasure, relevant to both men and women.

In spite of the existence of the implied author convention, it is often difficult to maintain this convention, especially where understanding the poem seems to require some knowledge of the author's life. We noted above that this was the case with parts of Plath's *Ariel*. Although it is worth noting that the version of *Ariel* which Plath planned was never published, some of the poems which Plath had always planned on including have such a powerful personal element that reading them seems almost like reading Plath's diary.[15] Indeed, the later publication of Plath's *Journals* and of her letters to her mother provided an often necessary supplement to the poems. The problem here is that while we might wish to preserve a conventional New Critical distinction between author and persona in reading the poems, the poems themselves appear to have invalidated that distinction. There is also a further issue, though. Some readers of *Ariel* have felt that Plath's use of highly personal details in her work involved other people so that, without their permission, they have had their private lives held up to public scrutiny. In one way this involves a broader question which, again, might have legal implications. That is, does the poet have a right to put anything into a poem? What if the poet uses details which bring a kind of unwelcome attention to individuals, especially given that such individuals may have no voice within the poem itself? Are there some subjects which should not be appropriated for poetic ends? Is Plath's use of Holocaust imagery and Jewish history to depict personal anguish, notably in the *Ariel* poems 'Daddy' and 'Lady Lazarus', a sickeningly inappropriate use of public atrocity?

One might distinguish here between a legal and an ethical issue. Poetry is, after all, subject to the laws of libel pertaining to any publication. Given this, some poets have been careful to disguise, however lightly, the identity of an individual who is the subject of their poem. We might regret this to some extent. Moral outrage drives Shelley's poems on Castlereagh ('I met Murder on the way / He had a mask like Castlereagh') and George III ('An old, mad, blind, despised, and dying king') and is best expressed without devious disguising of the subject.[16] The ethical question is different, though. While a poet may not be prosecuted in the courts if there is no actual defamation of individuals, is there a moral element, an ethical limit to what the poet might write? Also, how as readers do we respond critically to references to living people in the poem?

These questions arise very clearly in the following poem, 'Records' by Robert Lowell.

> '. . . I was playing records on Sunday,
> arranging all my records, and I came
> on some of your voice, and started to suggest
> that Harriet listen: then immediately
> we both shook our heads. It was like hearing
> the voice of the beloved who had died.
> All this is a new feeling . . . I got the letter
> this morning, the letter you wrote me Saturday.
> I thought my heart would break a thousand times,
> but I would rather have read it a thousand times
> than the detached unreal ones you wrote before –
> you doomed to know what I have known with you,
> lying with someone fighting unreality –
> love vanquished by his mysterious carelessness.'[17]

The poem was published in 1973 as part of a sequence entitled *The Dolphin*. Like Lowell's immediately preceding books, which were also sequences, it is concerned with the break-up of his marriage and his leaving America to live and work in England. 'Records' has a special place in the book, as it is about the effect of Lowell's news of his affair on his wife and on his daughter. The poem is narrated by the wife (we know her as Elizabeth from other poems) and Harriet is the daughter who is named in the poem.

The Dolphin is loosely based on the sonnet form, and Lowell employs a metre based on the iambic pentameter. Here, lines 2, 4, 6, 9 and 12 are regularly iambic, and the ghost of the iamb hovers over all of the lines. Rhyming is erratic, giving the poem an air of conversational informality, even if what is spoken moves towards the climactic rhetoric of the final lines. Although, then, the poem is only loosely a sonnet, it does have some of the characteristics associated with the sonnet: the iambic base, the strong caesuras of some of the lines (5 and 7), and a climactic two-line conclusion. As in traditional sonnet sequences, the theme is love and the revelation of the individual's affections.

Thematically, the poem is very much concerned with what its title suggests, 'records'. It is about the forms which records take, about how things are recorded and about the responsibility, however difficult, of recording accurately. The speaker and Harriet cannot listen to the voice in the recording because it is too accurate, too close to recalling the living figure who has abandoned them. At the same time, though, the speaker expresses a preference for the letter which was received, the accurate letter, over the previous 'detached unreal' ones previously received. There is a notable conflict in the poem between the 'real' and the 'unreal'. While the speaker expresses a preference for the real, it is with the realization that reality is painful and damaging.

In a way the poem is about its own status, its own 'reality'. In a later poem, called 'Epilogue' Lowell expressed his preference for exactness in poetry as a form of truth, asking 'Why not say what happened?' and praying for 'the grace of accuracy' to be the true basis for poetry.[18] The quotation marks around this poem invite the reader to read it as an accurately transcribed statement made by the figure who, we know from the other poems in the sequence, is Elizabeth, the deserted wife. So, in this way, the poem seems to provide a valid sense of its own authenticity at the same time as thematically it is a justification of authenticity, of the need for accurate 'records'.

Although we could discuss the theme of 'Records' as though that exists apart from the real life of Robert Lowell, the poem does raise a significant ethical question. For several of the poems in the sequence Lowell had apparently transcribed letters and telephone calls made by his wife, Elizabeth Hardwick. The words of 'Records' are, actually as well as apparently, those of Hardwick, sent in a letter. Lowell may be the author of the poem in that he has arranged the words into a recognized formal structure and has invited us to read them as a poem rather than as prose, but the actual words were apparently written by Hardwick. Was Lowell wrong, somehow unethical, in doing this? That is, Hardwick did not intend her letter to be published and enter the public domain – and, along with it, the details of her marriage. Furthermore, we as readers cannot know how far Lowell has altered the letters in order to make them conform to the demands of the poem. In fact, this is in itself a significant ethical consideration, and one which greatly upset Lowell's friend Elizabeth Bishop when she commented on *The Dolphin*. In a letter to Lowell, quoting Hardy, Bishop wrote that the 'infinite mischief' of using the letters lay in the 'mixture of fact & fiction' that they represented.[19]

While Bishop identifies a significant issue, especially for a poem about 'records', the other issue had to do with whether Lowell had any right to appropriate Elizabeth's words. In a review of *The Dolphin* Adrienne Rich wrote that 'the inclusion of the letter poems stands as one of the most vindictive and mean-spirited acts in the history of poetry, one for which I can think of no precedent'.[20] The alternative view is that authors have a right to use whatever material comes their way, and this right is withdrawn only at great cost to art. As Alan Brownjohn said, 'There is a kind of entitlement of poets to transmute, to use any kind of material that life, personal and public, offers them.'[21] In a perspective made possible by the passing of time, Brownjohn is probably right. It might also be pointed out that 'Records' is anyway a highly unusual poem, because what it urges is also being enacted in it: the need for accurate 'records' however painful;

and what might be more accurate than the very words of the person involved?

There are no easy answers to the many critical questions posed in this chapter. It is tempting to conclude that different kinds of poem demand different reading strategies and make the author present (or invisible) in various ways. That is, we might read a poem by Lowell in a different way from a poem by someone who is much more reticent about the use of the self and of personal experience. It would certainly be possible to read *Paradise Lost* and look for clues as to the state of Milton's marriage, but were we to do so we should also be aware that we are sacrificing a thematic richness in order to privilege one element. Poets use the self and their own experiences in different ways, and many poets do not want to write of themselves at all. Currently, the author may be a very strong presence in the reading of poetry, but this is certainly not true for all poets.

Endnotes

1 Florence Hardy, letter to Sidney Cockerell, quoted in Henri Peyre, *Literature and Sincerity* (London, 1963), p. 308.
2 Byron, letter to Thomas Moore, 1 June 1818, *Byron's Letters and Journals*, ed. Leslie A. Marchand, 12 vols (London, 1976), vol. 6, p. 47.
3 In 'The Storyteller' Walter Benjamin refers to the ways in which listening to a told story was a means of reinforcing a communal identity. See Walter Benjamin, *Illuminations*, trans. Harry Zohn (New York, 1969).
4 Thomas Hardy, 'Apology' to *Late Lyrics and Earlier*, in *The Works of Thomas Hardy* (Ware, 1994), p. 529.
5 Herbert Read, *The Cult of Sincerity* (London, 1968), p. 18.
6 Weldon Kees, *Collected Poems* (London, 1975), p. 14.
7 Quoted in Lionel Trilling, *Sincerity and Authenticity* (London, 1974), p. 119.
8 David Hume, *A Treatise of Human Nature* (1739), ed. L. A. Selby-Bigge and P. H. Nidditch (Oxford, 1978), p. 121.
9 Northrop Frye, 'Literature as Content: Milton's *Lycidas*', quoted in Peyre, *Literature and Sincerity*, p. 329.
10 Roland Barthes, 'The Death of the Author', in David Lodge, ed., *Modern Criticism and Theory: A Reader* (London, 1988), p. 170.
11 Michel Foucault, 'What is an Author?', in Lodge, *Modern Criticism and Theory*, p. 209.
12 John Keats, *The Letters of John Keats*, ed. Robert Gittings (Oxford, 1977), pp. 157, 218.
13 Joyce Carol Oates, 'Soul at the White Heat: The Romance of Emily Dickinson's Poetry', *Critical Inquiry* 13 (1987), p. 806.
14 T. S. Eliot, 'Tradition and the Individual Talent', in *Selected Essays*, p. 17.
15 Plath had planned a version of *Ariel* which made apparent how far the book was planned as a thematic sequence. The posthumously published *Ariel* did not preserve this sequence. See Sylvia Plath, *Collected Poems*, ed. Ted Hughes (London, 1988), p. 295.
16 Shelley, 'The Mask of Anarchy', 'England in 1819', in *Romanticism: An Anthology*.
17 Robert Lowell, *The Dolphin* (London, 1973), p. 31.

18 Robert Lowell, 'Epilogue', in *Day by Day* (London, 1977), p. 127.
19 Elizabeth Bishop, *One Art: The Selected Letters* ed. Robert Giroux (London, 1994), pp. 561–3.
20 Adrienne Rich, quoted in Ian Hamilton, *Robert Lowell: A Biography* (New York, 1982), p. 433.
21 Hamilton, *Robert Lowell*, p. 424.

6

Poem and reader

In attempting to make explicit what one does when reading or interpreting a poem one gains considerably in self-awareness and awareness of the nature of literature as an institution. As long as one assumes that what one does is natural it is difficult to gain any understanding of it. . . . Reading is not an innocent activity. It is charged with artifice.

Jonathan Culler[1]

So far we have seen how the New Criticism presented a certain view of poetry and of the poem. The poem was seen as if it were an object, removed from the control and intention of the author. The poem was seen as a form of knowledge, and it was thought improper to invoke one's subjective impression of reading the poem as if that were criticism. It was the words on the page which mattered, and all critical interpretation of the poem had to be based on empirical reference to the text, and not to something outside of it. Seeing the poem as an object had particular implications for the role of the reader. In New Critical approaches to the poem, the reader came to be seen as the passive receiver of the meaning contained in the poem, and not as an active participant in the construction of the poem and of its meaning. One of the most important essays on the reader in New Criticism is by W. K. Wimsatt and Monroe Beardsley, called 'The Affective Fallacy' (1949). Wimsatt and Beardsley tried to remove the responses of the reader from critical evaluation because they feared subjectivity: 'the objective critic' could not take the 'purely affective' reports of readers into account.[2] They exhorted the maintenance of a clear distinction between the poem and its 'results':

> The Affective Fallacy is a confusion between the poem and its *results*
> . . . the outcome of either fallacy, the Intentional or the Affective, is
> that the poem itself as an object of specifically critical judgement,
> tends to disappear.[3]

As already suggested in Chapter 4, the New Critics tended to see the poem in spatial terms, a formal arrangement of words on the page. This view of the poem has been challenged by critics who involve the reader as a crucial factor in the making of the poem. Such critics are sometimes loosely termed 'reader-response' critics and they recognize how the reader experiences the poem sequentially, that is, temporally rather than spatially. The New Critics saw meaning contained in the text, the words on the page. Reader-response critics see meaning resulting from a process of interaction between poem and reader. Where the New Critics saw the poem as if it were a room or an urn or a house or a closed box, reader-response critics see it more as a process. In some way the poet has actually recognized the necessity of the reader and encoded this recognition into the poem, organizing it as a temporal, shifting experience rather than a fixed object.[4]

Even a moment's reflection leads to the conclusion that it would be ridiculous to think of poetry existing without the reader. Reading is an activity, we do it; it is not passive, done to us. Words lie there inertly on the page before us and we have to become active in order to make them mean anything. As Sartre famously wrote, 'the literary object is a peculiar top which exists only in movement'.[5] Also, as W. H. Auden has reminded us, 'That is one of the wonderful things about the written word: it cannot speak until it is spoken to.'[6] There is no such thing as passive reading. Certainly there may be inattentive reading, and certainly different kinds of book or poem demand different levels of attention or concentration, but all reading is active.

It is also important to recognize how far poets can exploit the reader's sequential apprehension of the poem. Understanding a poem obviously must begin with reading it, but the first reading of a poem is usually very different from subsequent readings. In the first reading a variety of potential meanings engage us, usually much more so than in later readings, when the field of possibilities has tended to narrow. Certainly, poets can and often do exploit the very way in which the reader makes sense of the poem sequentially. Sometimes there may even be a kind of teasing of the reader, a teasing that relies on how the reader builds up expectations. A good example of this comes in William Carlos Williams's lines:

> I saw a girl with one leg
> over the rail of a balcony[7]

The enjambment is arranged so that for a moment it seems as if we are seeing a one-legged girl, but this impression is corrected when the fuller sense of the phrase is revealed over time. But we might also claim that the line is mimetic, in that if we really saw a girl with one leg over a balcony we might at first think she was one-legged. Although there is a playful element to this example, Williams is also making a serious point about impressions, about how we both perceive and construct meaning. The line's potential meanings are not contained in them but arise through activity.

Another very common conventional poetic technique is that of the poet setting up a regularity in the poem which is then slightly varied. The reader apprehends the pattern which is established, and is then surprised by the shift which takes place. Much humorous verse relies on this technique – it can be used to make puns or to give a bathetically comic ending to a line – but so too does much serious poetry. For instance, a poet may start a poem using full rhymes but then shift to half-rhyme, thereby disturbing the reader's sense of order and arrangement. These shifts in pattern may not seem remarkable, in that they are so basic to what many poets do, but it is worth remembering that the effectiveness of this strategy depends on the way that the reader reads the poem in time, and is unable to apprehend it all at once.

While this variation of an initial regular pattern is a typical element of poetic practice, there are also poets who have emphasised that they see the poem itself as a process in which the reader plays a significant part. We noted in Chapter 4 how John Ashbery commended one description of his poems as consisting 'of the fluidity of thought rather than the objects of thought'[8] and it is such fluidity in particular which requires special attention from the reader, who follows and indeed participates in, the very fluidity of the thought. The poem is, to use the title of William Carlos Williams's influential essay, 'a field of action'; a process, not something handed over to the reader for consumption.[9] While Ashbery is outstanding in his development of a poem which is fluid, escaping boundaries, the technique is by no means new, and by no means necessarily related, as it sometimes is by critics, to a specifically post-modernist aesthetic. Some of the reader's intense engagement with Keats's 'Ode to a Nightingale' for instance comes from the poem's apparently almost improvisational quality. Keats gives the impression of following a thought through the poem, and this can be seen in the stanza division. Here is the end of stanza 2 and the opening of stanza 3:

> That I might drink, and leave the world unseen,
> And with thee fade away into the forest dim –
>
> Fade far away, dissolve and quite forget

The effect is more than that created by the stanzaic enjambment or alliteration; the repetition of 'fade' creates a powerful sense of process. Keats uses the same technique between stanzas 7 and 8:

> Charmed magic casements, opening on the foam
> Of perilous seas, in faery lands forlorn.
>
> Forlorn! the very word is like a bell
> To toll me back from thee to my sole self!

It is as if we are engaged with the very thought process of the speaker, and through this involvement the poem becomes one of dynamic exploration of thought rather than the fixed presentation of an idea. Keats involves the reader in the poem, directing imagination and thought: the poem needs the reader and acknowledges the reader's presence.

Poems differ considerably in the creative demands that they make on the reader; a fact which Roland Barthes recognized in using the terms *lisible* and *scriptible* to distinguish between sorts of literary text. The *lisible*, 'readable', text allows us mainly to read it without demanding that we read creatively, whereas the *scriptible*, 'writerly' text demands that we become like a writer in the creative construction of meaning. According to Barthes, the writerly text is more valuable than the readerly text because it is 'a galaxy of signifiers, not a structure of signifieds': and 'the goal of literary work . . . is to make the reader no longer a consumer, but a producer of the text'.[10]

One familiar example of a 'writerly' text is T. S. Eliot's 'The Love Song of J. Alfred Prufrock'. The reader of this poem participates in the gradual unfolding of a consciousness whose perception of reality is shifting and developing during the dramatic monologue. There are gaps and absences, unstated things, for which the reader must supply meaning, reference and, ultimately, language. Eliot's poem could certainly be transformed into a stable narrative, a readerly text, but to do this would be to eradicate the kind of imaginative demand which it makes on the reader.

Again, even this sort of demand on the reader is very familiar in poetry (as indeed it is in prose). In Robert Browning's 'My Last Duchess' the reader must supply meaning to the dramatic monologue by filling in what the Duke does not say. If we were to read the poem without supplying such a meaning, then the poem itself might seem rather pointless to us. It is only when we fill the gaps in the Duke's self-serving narrative, and supply a language to fill his linguistic absences, that the poem's implicit and unstated tragedy is available to us. In studying poetry it is crucial to realize that we are never just consumers of the poem's stable meaning; we are required to respond to suggestion and possibility, to be creatively engaged with the text.

There are other ways in which poets have acknowledged the existence of (and the necessity for) the reader. Robert Frost once said that every poem should have a 'door' in it. Although his remark is consistent with seeing the poem as a room or a space, it is striking that Frost emphasizes how the reader must have some point of entry into the poem. Frost's 'Stopping by Woods on a Snowy Evening', cited in the previous chapter, provides an interesting example of such a 'door'. In the line 'The woods are lovely, dark and deep' the word 'lovely' is arrestingly vague. Actually, editors today would probably reject a poem that included the word 'lovely'; it suggests that the poet is too lazy (or has too limited a vocabulary) to think of a more specific adjective. However, 'lovely' is a key word *because* it is vague: it is the door by which the reader can participate in the poem. It invites a subjective response, invites us into the poem. Since we all have different ideas about what is 'lovely' and what may tempt us from the world of work and duty, then the poem can become imaginatively ours.

So one way of including the reader in the poem is by generalizing rather than particularizing an experience, making the reader as it were fill a gap in the poem. Another way is simply by choosing to write, as did William Carlos Williams, about the ordinary, everyday world that he shared with the people around him. This was part of Williams's belief in the need to make poetry available to all, an attack on everything that he felt T. S. Eliot's poetry represented. Instead of the remote Tiresias (inaccessible except through the classroom), Williams would write of everyday shared reality: of a widow in springtime, of a poor woman eating plums on the street, of the road to the hospital.

In some poems there is a direct address to the reader, as an essential part of the poem. This technique is especially true of poems which are allied with an oral or even an oratorical tradition, where the poet is like someone making a speech to an audience. The forms and the effects of such direct address to the reader vary considerably. Sometimes the poem places the reader in the passive position of mere listener. In his Prefaces to his master-piece *Leaves of Grass* Walt Whitman continually emphasized the necessary presence of the reader as someone who completed, made possible the poems, and many of Whitman's poems involve the presence of a 'you', the reader. For Whitman such recognition was a vital component of his sense of a democratic aesthetic; the reader was to be seen as an equal and even as the co-creator of the poems. However, the poetic technique of addressing the reader is often a means by which the poet acknowledges the reader and the need for the reader as a vital part of the poetic process – someone who makes the poet's work live in the present. When 'you' is used in the poem we might consider whether that 'you' is the implied reader. For example, 'The Love Song of J. Alfred Prufrock' begins with the line 'Let us go then, you and I', possibly indicating the need for a creative imaginative reader in the poem's journey. Keats also uses 'you' in the poetic fragment usually known as 'This Living Hand':

> This living hand, now warm and capable
> Of earnest grasping, would, if it were cold
> And in the icy silence of the tomb,
> So haunt thy days and chill thy dreaming nights
> That thou wouldst wish thine own heart dry of blood
> So in my veins red life might stream again,
> And thou be conscience-calm'd – see here it is –
> I hold it towards you.

The status of this poem is uncertain as it was found among Keats's papers only as a fragment. It is a Gothic poem, vampiric and chilling not only because of the central image of the speaker's outstretched hand, but also because of the technique of implicating the reader in the act of making the speaker live. There is a request for a sort of literary blood transfusion by which we make the speaker live once more through the act of reading the poem; through reading we touch and give blood back. Notably, the first seven lines of the poem are in regular iambic pentameters, but the last line is less perfectly iambic and consists of only three feet rather than five. The poem seems incomplete, as if lacking some response from the reader to make it whole. The sense of the poem is a request for blood, for life, while the form requires two more iambic feet. The poem's unforgettable power is in its formal embodiment of the idea that a poem is a living hand between reader and writer, forming a bond between them, a bond which the reader must acknowledge.

Remembering that the status of this poem was uncertain, it is entirely possible that the poem is a kind of puzzle, and that there is a missing name of four syllables which, if added to the poem, would fit the metre and complete the poem. This is not meant as a fatuous proposal, in that many poets, especially in love poems, have used acrostics and other forms of word-play to communicate a secret longing. In some works the name of a lover is cleverly concealed, ready to be discovered by the alert reader. In his sequence of sonnets written in 1947 John Berryman wittily uses devices and techniques from Renaissance sequences, and in one sonnet the first letters of each line reveal the real names of the two lovers. This is a straightfor-wardly traditional technique from a poet who was also a significant Renaissance scholar.[11] While such poems usually testify primarily to the skill and the wit of the writer, they do represent an interesting technique of including the reader in the poem, and there have been so-called 'puzzle poems' which challenge the reader to a kind of creative involvement in the work. Again the reader's status is not only of understanding the poem but of actively constructing and contributing to it.

In his book *The Implied Reader* Wolfgang Iser, a prominent reader-response theorist, wrote:

> The phenomenological theory of art lays full stress on the idea that, in considering a literary work, one must take into account not only the actual text but also, and in equal measure, the actions involved in responding to that text.[12]

Among important issues that Iser dealt with was the concept of the 'implied reader', that is, each piece of literature creates or includes a reader. A poem or a novel implies a reader by a series of assumptions built into the text about how the reader might respond. Although the book from which the above quotation comes, *The Implied Reader*, is mainly about prose, Iser's points are relevant also for poetry. We have seen above how poets assume the presence of the reader, or even have the reader participate in the making of the poem. But can we go further and suggest that in all cases the reader is the maker of meaning; that Roland Barthes's distinction of *lisible* versus *scriptible* text breaks down because even in the *lisible* text the reader is the active maker?

In some basic sense, of course, the reader participates in a poem simply by reading it and updating it from whenever it was written, making it part of the present reality. Readers can invest something of themselves in poems, especially those which have a powerful emotional referent at their centre. This is a significant form of interaction with the text, a way of 'making it ours'. We do not then just 'respond' to a text but we add to it something of ourselves and our own experiences.

Asserting that literature is 'in the reader' is one way of challenging the idea of the poem as a self-enclosed, autonomous unit. Another is to shift the locus of critical inquiry altogether, away from the words on the page towards the way that the reader constructs meaning for and from them. This approach is associated with the critic Stanley Fish. In his influential essay 'Literature in the Reader: Affective Stylistics' (1970) Fish proposed exactly this relocation. As he later commented on the essay:

> I was encouraged . . . to advance the general claim that all poems . . . were, in some sense, about their readers, and that therefore the experience of the reader, rather than the 'text itself' was the proper object of analysis.[13]

Of course this statement directly contradicts the New Critical concept of the importance of only the 'text itself'. Fish is challenging this by developing the fact that words cannot exist in themselves, that a poem might have life only when a reader, to use Sartre's image, sets it in motion. In his work on Milton's poetry, Fish was struck by the apparent gap between explications of the poetry and the actual experience of reading the poems. This gap existed because critical explication represented the poem spatially, whereas the reader experiences the poem temporally. For instance, in the line from *Paradise Lost*:

Nor did they not perceive the evil plight

the reader's apprehension of the line's meaning is deferred by the second negative.[14] Milton, Fish argued, often made use of the fact that reading poetry is a dynamic, temporal process, and that one of the effects of reading Milton was to be placed in a position of uncertainty. Milton repeatedly deferred meaning, disallowing the reader the certainty that might come only when all of the poem has been read and, in effect, when the poem has been translated from the temporal (as it exists in the act of reading) to the spatial (where it exists, for example, as recapitulation). Thus Milton performed a kind of serious toying with the reader. Critical accounts of Milton's poetry, however, relied on a spatial explication of the poems rather than on taking into account this demanding experience of reading them. Fish's emphasis on the presence of the reader and the constant fluctuation of potential meanings were especially relevant for Milton. Fish argued that there was a theological dimension to this uncertainty, crucial to *Paradise Lost*, in that the uncertainties of the reader embodied one of the truths of the poem, that the reader, like Adam and Eve, was fallen into time, into uncertainty, imperfect.

Fish followed this line of thought, away from Milton in particular, towards a more general proposal that in effect the reader makes the poem. Poetry is not characterized by formal features but is produced by the activity of the reader. That is, poems are not poems because the poet has shaped words into a formal arrangement, but because the reader has taken that arrangement as a cue to give a special kind of attention to the words. It is this attention, the way that we read poetry differently from how we read prose, that creates the poem. 'It is my thesis,' writes Fish, 'that the reader is always making sense', adding that he intends the word 'making' 'to have its literal force'.[15]

There are several assumptions, and many implications, involved here. Perhaps the most obvious and, for our purposes here, the most striking is that for Fish poetry is not characterized by formal arrangement whereby it exists differently from prose. It is the activity of the reader which enforces a distinction between poetry and prose, if indeed such a distinction is at all significant. Definitions of poetry usually involve a contrast with prose. But if we invoke, as Fish does, the experience of the reader as the maker of the poem, then the formal properties of the words on the page matter much less, and cannot be said to form any distinguishing or defining principle. That is, poetry is generically characterized not by any formal quality distinguishing it from prose, but by the activity of the reader, who gives one kind of attention to prose and another kind to poetry. Nor does the supposed rich excess of meaning provide a useful means of defining poetic language, since the reader can readily supply that excess in the act of reading.

So, can it be determined, without regard to the author's intention, that any words comprise a poem? The answer is certainly yes, if we consider the case of 'found' poems, where words not intended to comprise a poem are presented as if they did. However, it might be objected that found poems are a special case. After all, someone presents the poem to us, often having arranged the words in a certain way (almost always having arranged them so that they look more like poetry than prose) and, perhaps most crucially, having called them a poem.

This calling of the found poem a 'poem' is crucial because we could say that the reader responds to the word 'poem' and brings into play all of the resources and activities involved in making sense of a poem. When we read a poem we tend to think of the language as loaded with an excess of possible meanings, carefully chosen. Perhaps the paying of a particular kind of attention actually results in the making of a poem; hence Fish's proposal that the reader literally *makes* sense of a poem. Moreover, it is important to point out that as readers we rarely come across poems innocently, or unexpectedly. Poems are flagged in ways that are sometimes obvious but are sometimes subtle, and perhaps as readers we set into motion the activities involved in making sense of a poem, because we are responding to a cue received consciously or unconsciously. We almost always know when we are reading poetry, or are expecting to read poetry; we have opened an

anthology of poetry, we are in a classroom, or we know that the author is
a poet, or, quite simply, the poem is clearly signalled as a poem. Even when
we encounter poems in public places, on posters or being displayed on
public transport, it is interesting that the poem is always named as a poem,
held apart from the other forms of language and image that might surround
it. Thus we are primed to initiate the kind of activity that results in a poem
whenever we respond to the cues given to us.

Given the potential erasure of the distinction between poetry and prose
in terms of the formal arrangement of the words on the page it is important
to emphasize that when poets include prose extracts in their poems they
often demarcate these as poetry, by, for instance, breaking up the prose into
shorter lines. Thus in a way the formal difference between poetry and prose
is actually maintained, as the prose extract is arranged so that it looks like
a poem, the most obvious difference being that prose runs continually to the
end of the page whereas poetry conventionally does not.

We saw in the Introduction how W. B. Yeats 'created' a poem from
Walter Pater's prose through certain acts of reorganization. In a more
general sense, we could ask how far readers are actually 'makers' of poems.
Stanley Fish once told a class of his students that the words on the black-
board comprised a poem, and asked them to 'make sense' of it. The class
duly came up with possible meanings and an interpretation. Writing on
their constructive activity Fish related how the 'poem' was in fact a list of
names left on the blackboard from a previous class.[16] In analysing the way
that the students had made the poem, Fish concluded:

> we do *not* have free-standing readers in a relationship of perpetual
> adequacy or inadequacy to an equally free-standing text. Rather, we
> have readers whose consciousnesses are constituted by a set of
> conventional notions which when put into operation constitute in
> turn a conventional, and conventionally seen, object. My students
> could do what they did, and do it in unison, because as members of a
> literary community they knew what a poem was . . . and that knowl-
> edge led them to look in such a way as to populate the landscape with
> what they knew to be poems.[17]

(It is interesting, incidentally, to note Fish's distinction between the active
process of reading and the conventional way of seeing the poem as an
object.) Similarly, Jonathan Culler argued that one could take a 'piece of
banal journalistic prose', write it 'as if it were a lyric poem' then 'the words
remain the same but their effects for readers are substantially altered'.[18]
Looking at Fish's experiment, though, it is worth pointing out that the
students came to the situation by no means innocently. There is a significant
institutional force behind the experiment, deriving not only from Fish's
authority in the classroom but also from the student's expectation that they
were 'doing poetry' that day.[19] Again, although the final effect of Fish's
experiment is the same as Yeats's 'poeticization' of Pater – that is, a poem

has been made by the creation of and the reader's acceptance of certain cues – it is important to remember that these cues might exist elsewhere than the 'words on the page' and extend to the very material situation in which those words are mediated: in a classroom or in a book of poems.[20]

We are trained to look for things in poetry, to read with attention and not to read just for information, as if a poem were a newspaper or a computer manual. When we read poetry we usually expect to find ambiguity, irony, language richer than in its normal usage. We might think of poetry as the most compelling, forceful use of language, but we must also consider whether that is because *we* give that force and that richness to the language. That is, poetry may be demanding to read because we think of a poem as a powerful, concentrated use of all of the resources of language. That is why, properly to read poetry, we must read with alertness and with a sensitivity to connotation that we normally withhold from non-poetic language, in which the news or the idea conveyed may be more important than the suggestibility of the language through which it is mediated. But could we in effect make any piece of prose into poetry by giving the words the same sort of attention that poetry requires?

The answer seems to be yes, although the reasons why this is so are often diffuse and difficult to prove. Indeed, the answer might be 'yes' simply because there is no definition of poetry which holds true for all poems and on which everyone agrees. As we have seen, the most obvious distinction, that between poetry and prose, frequently breaks down. It breaks down through poetic practice, which has resulted in something which ought not to exist, but which does, called the 'prose poem', and it has resulted in poets transforming prose to poetry merely by the lightest of editorial touches, by which the prose appearance is transformed into what looks on the page like a conventional poem. In one anthology of poetry the editors included sections of prose works by James Joyce and Djuna Barnes, without editing them to 'look like poems'. They defended this practice on the grounds that there was really no difference between poetry and 'imaginative prose of the highest order'.[21] Though this is certainly arguable, they themselves had erased the difference by simply requiring that the reader approach extracts from *Finnegans Wake* and *Nightwood* as if they were self-contained poems.

If the reader really does make the poem, as it has been claimed, then another danger, surely, is of the development of highly individual 'responses' to the poem. That is, we might all be making different, and highly individual readings. This danger of subjective response has been tackled in different ways. For the New Critics it could be countered by the demand that every statement about the poem be empirically grounded in the poem itself, the words on the page. For Stanley Fish, though, there could be no such empiricist appeal, because, as he claimed, he was more concerned with the 'experience of the reader' than with the 'text itself'. What if those experiences are so disparate that there is no point of contact between individual readings?

Fish himself has answered this question by insisting that the interpretive activity is not performed in isolation. It takes place as an interaction with others, whether those others are previous readers of the poem who have published their ideas about it, or are other people in a classroom. Hence, Fish has emphasized the importance of the 'interpretive community' by which judgements and experiences are shared and tested by others.[22]

A concomitant question, often posed, is simply 'Can you read too much into a poem?' The phrase itself, and it commonly appears in this form, is interesting, because it contains the acknowledgement that we must read *something* into the poem, the question being then, when have we read too much? One answer to the question might simply be that it depends what you are reading the poem *for*. If you read poetry primarily for pleasure, as a solitary activity, then you can be perfectly happy with whatever readings of a poem satisfy you. As part of an academic exercise your readings should be backed up by some sort of evidence, rather than relying simply on your individual response to the words before you. Certainly, you would be reading too much if you did not read the poem at all – that is, did not pay attention to the specific use of language or to the kind of vocabulary. But in many ways 'reading too much into' a poem is less of a danger than of reading too little into it. There are certainly readings of poems that we might consider eccentric and say that too much has been 'read into' them, but there are also readings which impoverish the richness of poems by making them seem one-dimensional, existing only in one context. We read too narrowly if we say that a poem has only one meaning, or that it is about only one thing, or is only about the life of the author or the time in which it was written, or if we disallow the suggestive possibilities of alternative meanings. Certainly one recurring argument for the quality of poetry has been that great poetry supports multiple readings and re-interpretations, whereas lesser poetry offers only a limited opportunity for re-reading; that great poetry is always about the present in some way, available to us, whereas lesser poetry or verse is stuck in the time in which it was written; this is the force of Ezra Pound's statement that literature is 'news that STAYS news'.[23] In this regard it is important to respond to the possible multiple levels of meaning, even if you are afraid that you are 'reading too much into' a poem, rather than think there is only one meaning and consequently read too little.

In the quotation at the top of this chapter, Jonathan Culler emphasized how far reading is governed by institutional practices and norms. As we have seen, there are a variety of institutional and normative cues, not all of them overt, which suggest how we should read the text in front of us and what kind of attention we ought to pay it. This basic point might be developed in several ways. We could insist that, in spite of appearances to the contrary, reading is a social activity as well as a personal one, in that we read according to certain traditions and standards of which we may not be consciously aware. As Culler wrote, reading is not an innocent, natural, activity. It might also be pointed out that learning to read poetry, learning to pay very close attention to language and to the use (or misuse) of words itself has a social dimension, because we are surrounded by language, and are to a large degree governed by it as to how we see the world. Hence a sensitivity, an alertness, to language may help us to develop our consciousness of power.

We noted above some of the different ways in which poets might acknowledge and include the reader in the poem, and might exploit the very activities involved in reading. Adrienne Rich's poem, 'The Burning of Paper Instead of Children' is a particularly good example of a poem which explores the possibilities (and anxieties) of reading while demanding that the reader experience those same possibilities and insecurities.[24] Published in 1968, the poem is in five sections in which lyric poetry is mingled with prose to give a collage effect. Sharply different styles of writing are included. The poem begins with a paragraph of descriptive prose concerning the punishment given to two boys by a neighbour for burning a mathematics text book. The neighbour sees the burning as a terrible act, that 'arouses terrible sensations in me, memories of Hitler'. The incident is a starting-point for a complex and at times disordered series of reflections on the poet's own privileged, bookish childhood, on anger, on burning, inequality, the Vietnam War, the propriety of speech, the burning of draft cards, of silencing and censorship. Other voices enter the poem, including this one in section 3 which, a note tells us, is written by one of Rich's students:

> People suffer highly in poverty and it takes dignity and intelligence to overcome this suffering. Some of the suffering are: a child steal because he did not have money to buy it: to hear a mother say she do not have money to buy food for her children and to see a child without cloth it will make tears in your eyes.

The poet cannot easily assimilate her anger and self-contradiction into a coherent, ordered poem and so we are left with a collage of different styles of writing. We are presented with a fractured surface; this is definitely not a poem being given to us as if it were an object. The ideas that the poem explores are ideas in progress; this is not a finished poem giving the impression that the poet has thought out the issues carefully and has reached a conclusion. Here the poet is dynamically exploring the possibilities of thought, possibilities which must be confronted but which cannot be brought to a satisfactory conclusion. The ideas are being worked through in the process of the poem. While it begins with a form of prose narrative, relating the incident that comprises the starting-point for the thought processes, it does not reach a conclusion. Nor does the poem seem highly patterned. Rather than providing us with a set pattern, a poem of clarity and organization, the poet gives a sense of including the reader in the poem, an effect created partly through the use of the present tense. The poem seems to come closer and closer to the immediate present, culminating in section 5 where it appears that these words are being mediated to us in the very moment that they appear 'hot' on the poet's typewriter:

> Some of the suffering are: it is hard to tell the truth; this is America; I cannot touch you now. In America we have only the present tense. I am in danger. You are in danger. The burning of a book arouses no sensation in me. I know it hurts to burn. The typewriter is overheated, my mouth is burning, I cannot touch you and this is the oppressor's language.

On the one hand the poet laments her failure to control language, to make it into something clear; this is the terrible impotence and despair that is expressed. But on the other hand, the poem's great power comes through the forceful expression of this powerlessness, where form brilliantly expresses content by the very inability to find finished form. It is a poem of rage and of impotence, in which the very dilemma from which that rage springs cannot be expressed in a way that is not contradictory. Language is a state in which we exist, through which we are controlled, from which we can find no escape and in which we might happily or unconsciously imprison ourselves; the encyclopedias of the bookish childhood can form a protective wall against the world rather than a window on it. Yet while we can see ourselves imprisoned in language, we have no means of communicating our imprisonment except through language.

Rather than work that contradiction up into an organized form, a completed thought where it might be expressed as irony or paradox, Rich brings us closer to the very making of the poem, insisting, as it were, that the readers share in the effort of managing its recalcitrant raw materials. Thus the reader experiences this shifting dilemma also, and experiences it shifting through time, rather than being allowed to reflect coolly on it once it has been shaped into some other form of discourse. Hence the poem also leads to no conclusion but seems to continue after the ending, passing on the dilemma and the rage to the reader; it is a poem that asks what we are doing as we read. The crisis tormenting the poem involves the relation between language, knowledge, reading and power. Rich engages strongly with the contemporary political situation, as the Vietnam War expands the dilemma of language towards the problem of how power is maintained and controlled.

The poem is an open text, displaying a kind of democracy of form. The student's fractured prose invites us to realign our assumed preference for the well written, the well made, in that these broken words testify so movingly to powerlessness and vulnerability. The poem insists on the necessity of creative reading, of finding truth behind language, beyond language, of finding value in fractured language as well as in 'pure' English. We may also need to undo language, to become selfconscious about the fact that reading is not an innocent activity. The open text invites us to enter it, rather than somehow setting up a wall, another barrier, between reader and writer.

Similarly, the poem never acquires any kind of centre, or any sort of unifying symbol. It is important that we experience the poem temporally, seeing how Rich echoes possibilities and potential motifs without ever privileging one of these to be the centre of the poem. For example, the image of burning keeps surfacing as we read; it is there implicitly from Fr Berrigan's statement that serves as epigraph to the poem: 'I was in danger of verbalizing my moral impulses out of existence' (Fr Berrigan was imprisoned for burning draft cards in protest at the Vietnam War). Images of burning recur: the burning of the book, of Joan of Arc, the flames of napalm. Burning is not a fixed, static image, but one that keeps altering and shifting and accumulating fresh possible meanings. The final images of burning ('The typewriter is overheated, my mouth is burning') do not conclude the poem by bringing it to a satisfactory ending, but continue to enrich the possibilities of the tormenting imagery. The image is continually in flux, as the writer's (and consequently the reader's) thoughts shift and change, unable to reach sure language or conclusion. There is no centre to the poem, no image, or even any sure moral centre; these are all unavailable to the poet in a time of crisis, anger, uncertainty and indignation. The poem can really thus exist only in the form which Rich has made for it; it properly exists only sequentially, by making the reader experience the dilemma, and not by making it readily available for easy resolution and consequent readerly consumption. We too must become uncertain about our ideas, unfixed: in short, must experience the poem and learn to reflect on our activity of reading. Nor can we readily translate this experience into a straightforward summary of the poem, because to do so is to falsify what is important about it – that the poem exists only as our experience of it: it is about reading.

Endnotes

1 Jonathan Culler, *Structuralist Poetics* (New York, 1975), p. 129.
2 W. K. Wimsatt, *The Verbal Icon: Studies in the Meaning of Poetry* (Lexington, 1954, 1982), p. 32.
3 Wimsatt, *Verbal Icon*, p. 21.
4 Ian Maclean provides a good overview of reader-response criticism in Ann Jefferson and David Robey, eds, *Modern Literary Theory: A Comparative Introduction*, second edition (London, 1992), pp. 122–44. See also the introduction to Jane Tompkins, ed., *Reader-Response Criticism* (Baltimore, 1980).
5 Jean-Paul Sartre, *What is Literature?* trans. Bernard Frechtman, 1948 (London, 1978), p. 28.
6 Quoted in Charles Osborne, *W. H. Auden: The Life of a Poet* (London, 1979), p. 330.
7 The lines are from Section XI of *Spring and All*, in Williams, *Collected Poems*, 2 vols (London, 1991), vol. 1, p. 206.

8 Quoted in Charles Altieri, *Act and Quality* (Brighton, 1981), p. 126.

9 Williams, 'The Poem as a Field of Action' (1948), in *Selected Essays of William Carlos Williams* (New York, 1969), pp. 280–91.

10 Roland Barthes, *S/Z*, trans. Richard Miller (London, 1975), pp. 5, 4.

11 John Berryman, Sonnet 87, in *Collected Poems 1937–1971* (London, 1990), p. 114.

12 Wolfgang Iser, *The Implied Reader* (Baltimore, 1974), p. 274.

13 Stanley Fish, *Is There a Text in this Class?* (London, 1980), p. 21.

14 Fish, *Is There a Text?*, p. 25. The line is from *Paradise Lost*, I, l. 335.

15 Fish, *Is There a Text?*, p. 162.

16 The list read:

> Jacobs-Rosenbaum
>> Levin
>> Thorne
>> Hayes
>> Ohman (?)

and comprised a list of names for a bibliography. ('Ohman' is followed by a question mark because Fish was unsure of the spelling.) Fish, *Is There a Text?*, pp. 322–7, at 323.

17 Fish, *Is There a Text?*, p. 332.

18 Culler, *Structuralist Poetics*, p. 161.

19 Fish's writing about poetry is similar to much New Critical writing in being strongly based on classroom experience; much of the appeal of Fish's lucid and attractive work is related to this communal, classroom engagement. For Fish we 'make sense' of poetry in the study or in the classroom as part of an engagement with other readers.

20 With regard to Fish's experience, it is interesting that he relied upon names to cue poetic significance. Names or proper nouns themselves, we might say, are often symbolic, carrying connotations of place, occupation, history and social position.

21   Passages from this work [*Nightwood* by Djuna Barnes] need only be spaced as free verse in order for the concentrated use of the rhythms, allusions and tropes of modern poetry to become apparent . . . we are content to make slow beginnings of what we hope will be a widening recognition of the breakdown between poetry and prose in modern times, and of the similarity between poetry and imaginative prose of the highest order (Kimon Friar and John Malcolm Brinnin, eds, *Modern Poetry, American and British* (New York, 1951), p. x).

22 Fish, *Is There a Text?*, pp. 338–55. His emphasis on the 'interpretive community' is another demonstration of how far Fish sees reading poetry as an activity that takes place in the university rather than anywhere else.

23 Pound, *ABC of Reading*, p. 29.

24 Adrienne Rich, *Collected Early Poems 1950–1970* (London, 1993), pp. 363–6. We intended to quote the poem in its entirety here but the interpretive conditions imposed by Adrienne Rich for the granting of permission were unacceptable to us. Given both the subject of the poem and of this chapter, we find this rather ironic.

P A R T

III

INTERPRETING POETRY

|7|

The poem in history

We have to refuse the short cut so often proposed, by which the 'truly creative' is distinguished from other kinds and examples of practice by a (traditional) appeal to its 'timeless permanence'.

Raymond Williams[1]

Poems – all poems – are historical artefacts. They are all produced at specific historical moments, and their meanings are in many ways produced *by* these moments. This chapter will look at the relationship between poetry and history, and at the importance of context for the study of poetry. We will also examine the often complex theoretical accounts of the relationship between poetry and history – although for most of the twentieth century poetic theory tended to downplay or even ignore this relationship. We will begin this chapter by asking why this might be so.

In our analysis of the considerable successes of New Criticism as a method of analysing poetry, we have also been concerned with its weaknesses. In its relentless focusing on 'the words on the page', its treatment of the poem as a self-contained, free-standing 'verbal icon', New Critical analysis rejected (and presented powerful theoretical arguments for rejecting) the idea of bringing to the poem any extrinsic knowledge. Simply put, in its rigorous concentration on the *text* of a poem, it tended to neglect its *context*.

This was an understandable tactic, for two reasons. Firstly, it was a reaction against nineteenth-century 'logical positivist' theories, which argued that only material fact was relevant to the study of literature – thus poetry was understood in effect as autobiography, telling the reader things about the poet's life and thoughts (a thoroughly Romantic view of the function of poetry). A more 'historical' poem – by Milton, for example, or Dryden – existed as a straightforward account of a historical event, and was to be understood simply by reference to its historical background. This straightforward relationship between poetry and people or events was obviously simplistic, an inadequate response to the complexities of many poems.

Secondly, one must understand New Criticism in its own historical context. Its rise coincided with the rise of English Studies as an academic discipline: New Criticism, then, must be understood in its *institutional* context, as a pedagogical tool. As Stanley Cavell writes:

> It seems reasonable to suppose that the success of the New Criticism in the academic study of literature is a function of the way it is *teachable*: you can train someone to read complex poems with sufficient complexity, there is always something to say about them.[2]

Again, it is this teachability which accounts for the dominance of New Critical models for the teaching of poetry in schools, even today – as an approach it is very portable, doing away with the need for well-stocked research libraries (one might say that New Critical models substituted *depth* of reading for the traditional *breadth*, or substituted 'reading' for 'culture').

The previous chapter offered an outline of some of the theories of Stanley Fish on the role of the reader in the creation of the poem, most notably as they appear in his book *Is There a Text in this Class?* (Again, we suggested that Fish's theories derive from the institutional teaching of literature: the book contains many useful strategies for the effective teaching of poetry in the classroom.) Discussing his reader-centred theories, Fish writes:

> In its operation my method will obviously be radically historical. The critic has the responsibility of becoming not one but a number of informed readers, each of whom will be identified by a matrix of political, cultural and literary determinants. The informed reader of Milton will not be an informed reader of Whitman, although the latter will necessarily comprehend the former. . . . This raises the problem of the consideration of local beliefs as a possible basis of response. If a reader does not share the central concerns of a work, will he be capable of fully responding to it? Wayne Booth has asked the question: 'But is it really true that the serious Catholic or atheist, however sensitive, tolerant, diligent, and well-informed about Milton's beliefs he may be, enjoys *Paradise Lost* to the degree possible to one of Milton's contemporaries and co-believers, of equal intelligence and sensitivity?' The answer, it seems to me, is no.[3]

These are important questions, and they are questions which *Is There a Text in this Class?* does not really address. While Fish does shift the focus on the poem's status from that of spatial object ('the words on the page') to temporal process (the act of reading), which might suggest a gesturing towards history, his technique is nevertheless fundamentally an adaptation of New Critical close reading models, and thus does not allow for (or seem interested in) the kinds of historicism suggested by the quotation above.

Many critics *have*, however, addressed themselves to the relations between poetry and history. John Barrell's book *Poetry, Language and*

Politics begins by suggesting a few of the questions which we should ask if we are to begin to view a poem as a historical artefact: 'when it was written, . . . whom it addressed, . . . what was the function of any particular literary activity – writing epic poems, reading novels – at any particular period for any particular kind of reader'.[4] These are the kinds of question this chapter will be addressing.

In his book *Historicism*, Paul Hamilton writes:

> We can call the first focus of historicism hermeneutical. The past is to be understood on the model of interpreting a text; and texts, literary or otherwise, only have meaning within an economy of other texts, which both limits their possibilities and facilitates the distinctiveness of their utterance. A poetic statement, for example, amounts to one thing in Plato's philosophy, but it might possess an altogether different status in Renaissance, Enlightenment, Romantic or postmodern treatises. In each case, its value is relative to that accorded to adjacent discourses of science, politics, history and so on.[5]

Part of Hamilton's argument here is readily understandable on a semantic level – words acquire new meanings with the passing of time. Thus if we were to analyse Andrew Marvell's poem 'The Nymph Complaining for the Death of her Faun' with the assumption that 'complaining' here carries its modern meaning of moaning or grumbling about, rather than its seventeenth-century meaning of 'lamenting', we would run the risk of misinterpreting not only the title but potentially the whole poem. On a more complex level, the work done by Raymond Williams (an important figure in historicist literary theory) in *Keywords* on the semantic shifts, and their ideological significance, of certain significant terms would also be an example of this idea. For instance, Williams notes, the meaning of the word 'culture' has undergone an important semantic shift from its original meaning as 'a noun of process: the tending of something, basically crops and animals', to its contemporary usage as 'the independent and abstract noun which describes the works and practices of intellectual and especially artistic activity'.[6]

But what of texts 'only hav[ing] meaning within an economy [that is, organization] of other texts'? This is certainly an emphatic denial of the autonomy of the poem as offered by New Criticism. Historicist theories of poetry insist on the necessity for understanding poems not in isolation but in the context of other contemporary textual artefacts, that is *in their historical context*. However, as the phrase 'an economy of other *texts*' suggests, such theories do not accept the notion of a single, simple historical 'truth' to which poems refer. Rather, modern historicism insists that our knowledge of the past is always mediated through texts (it *textualizes* the past): as Barrell notes, 'all we can hope to recover of the past is other representations of it'.[7] This statement amounts to a central article of faith for the most influential strains of modern historicist thinking, American 'New

Historicism' and its British cousin, 'Cultural Materialism', both of which derive much of their impetus from Marxist theory (for obvious reasons – traditional Marxist thinking is deeply concerned with the dialectics of historical process). 'New Historicism' (a term coined by the critic Stephen Greenblatt) is especially difficult to define – 'a phrase without an adequate referent', according to H. Aram Veeser, who nevertheless offers five 'key assumptions' common to its practitioners:

1. that every expressive act is embedded in a network of material practices;
2. that every act of unmasking, critique and opposition uses the tools it condemns and risks falling prey to the practices it exposes;
3. that literary and non-literary 'texts' circulate inseparably;
4. that no discourse, imaginative or archival, gives access to unchanging truths nor expresses unalterable human nature;
5. ... that a critical method and a language adequate to describe culture under capitalism participate in the economy they describe.[8]

At its most extreme, in insisting on the impossibility of stable, objective history, New Historicism would deny the existence of (deny the very possibility for the existence of) historical 'facts' at all; rather history is a 'discourse' (a critical term denoting the language with which a subject is discussed or represented) or more properly a complex web of often conflicting discourses; that is to say, mediated through a collection of texts all of which are by definition partial and subjective, and none of which should therefore be privileged above the others as 'authoritative' or 'true'. While the premises of this argument seem reasonable, its conclusion (the non-existence of historical fact) has been attacked as untenable or even absurd. In a volume dedicated to New Historicist theory, Elizabeth Fox-Genovese writes:

> Contemporary critics tend to insist disproportionately on history as the ways in which authors have written about the past at the expense of what might actually have happened, insist that history consists primarily of a body of texts and a strategy of reading or interpreting them. Yet history also consists, in a very old-fashioned sense, in a body of knowledge – in the sum of reliable information about the past that historians have discovered and assembled. And beyond that knowledge, history must also be recognized as what did happen in the past – of the social relations and, yes, 'events', of which our records offer only imperfect clues.[9]

Clearly, there are such things as historical fact – the French Revolution took place in 1789, Elvis Presley died in 1977 – but what is up for debate here is the significance accorded these facts. A political conservative, for example, might consider the French Revolution an infamous episode in European history; for him or her this historical fact would be mediated through Edmund Burke's *Reflections on the Revolution in France*, a violently anti-Revolution tract which lays many of the foundations for modern conservative thinking. A socialist, however, might consider the French Revolution as the golden dawn of a new, enlightened political order; for him or her, this historical fact would be mediated through Thomas Paine's *The Rights of Man*, a violently pro-Revolution tract which lays many of the foundations for modern socialist thinking.

What has all this to do with poetry? This is a poem by Jon Dressel:

LET'S HEAR IT FOR GOLIATH

who never asked
to be born
either, let alone
grow nine feet

tall and wind
up a metaphor;
fat chance he
had of avoid-

ing the shove
from behind;
his old man
no doubt gave

him a sword
to teethe on,
and a scout
for the Philistine

host probably
had him under
contract by
the end of

junior high;
it was a fix;
and who wouldn't
have cursed

at the sight
of that arr-
ogant runt with
the sling, who,

for all his
psalms, would later
buy one wife
with a hundred

bloody pecker-
skins, and another
with a King's X
on Uriah; bah,

let's hear it
for Goliath, a big
boy who got
bad press but

who did his job,
absorbed a flukey
shot, and died
with a thud.[10]

How do we read this poem? We could attend to its overriding metaphor, whose vehicle is sport and whose tenor warfare, and, marking its appropriation of the language of sport in a description of warfare, conclude that the poem has ironic points to make on the nature of sport as aggressive competition, and by extension on the nature of masculinity. We could attend to the – again ironic – disparity between the poem's language and that which it signifies, its use of contemporary American vernacular to represent biblical antiquity, and conclude that this is a poem concerned with *anachronism* – a humorous poem whose humour lies precisely in this anachronistic, inappropriate use of language. This might in turn take us back to the previous point about warfare and sport, and to the conclusion that the poem is a deflationary exercise in exposing the mock-heroic rhetoric associated with sports commentary.

We might want to read this poem in a specifically cultural light. Dressel is an American poet writing from Wales: the poem, in fact, appears in a volume entitled *Out of Wales* (1984), which should itself be a cue to the reader. The named figure missing from this poem, of course, its unnamed Other, is David, which is also the name of the patron saint of Wales. Might Goliath, then, be America, and the poem a (sympathetic) metaphorical account, for Welsh readers, of the American military psyche, published around the same time as the American invasion of Grenada?

More widely read readers might want to draw connections with Joseph Heller's novel *God Knows*, in which the story of King David is told, by David himself, in Heller's own Jewish-American vernacular. This might lead to speculation on the relative relations of these texts to biblical narrative, to further speculation on the status of the Bible as a 'metanarrative', invariably informing the writing produced in Judaeo-Christian or western culture. Logically, this might lead to speculation that all writing is scripture, and further to speculation on the nature of the divine *logos*, the creating or creative word, to its primacy or otherwise, which might take us into the realms of post-structuralist thought.

Similar interpretive strategies might be applied to the opening stanza of Bob Dylan's 'Highway 61 Revisited':

> God said to Abraham Kill me a son
> Abe said Man you must be puttin' me on
> God said No, Abe said What?
> God said Well you can do what you like Abe
> But the next time you see me comin' you better run
> Abe said Where d'you want that killin' done
> God said Out on Highway 61.[11]

Furthermore, we may choose to note similarities here with the opening section of Søren Kierkegaard's nineteenth-century philosophical treatise, *Fear and Trembling*, which compulsively retells the Abraham and Isaac story in four different ways, each offering a different reading (it is worth noting here that the translator of the Penguin *Fear and Trembling* offers these lines from Dylan as epigraph to his introduction).[12] Kierkegaard was the founding father of that school of philosophy which we now call existentialism, which in the twentieth century we associate with the writings of Sartre and Camus, writers who were adopted in America by the 'beats' or 'hipsters' of the 1950s, American existentialists whom Norman Mailer called 'white negroes'.[13] In New York, the Greenwich Village milieu which produced Bob Dylan was informed by just such 'beat', existentialist philosophies. The opening of 'Highway 61 Revisited' could then fairly be read as Dylan's account or acknowledgement of his own philosophical origins, or as a statement of intellectual principle.

Or, a reader (or listener) might want to interpret this in a different, and more personal light. What effect might it have on our understanding to know that Dylan is himself Jewish, or that his *own* father was called Abraham? The actual road Highway 61, running south from near the Canadian border to New Orleans, ran through Dylan's hometown of Hibbing, Minnesota – it was, in other words, the road out of town. Running down through the American South, the road itself became symbolically associated with blues music: 'Highway 61 Revisited', like virtually all the songs on the Dylan album of the same title, is a variant on electric blues music – and just the year before Dylan had scandalized and (in some cases) horrified his traditional folk audience by playing at the Newport Festival backed by Mike Bloomfield and an electric blues band. On the subsequent tour, which accompanied the release of the album *Highway 61 Revisited*, his performances were frequently greeted with hostility, and with cries of 'Judas!', for his perceived selling out in abandoning 'authentic' acoustic folk music for 'popular' (and thus tainted with commercialism) electrified rock and roll. Might this contribute to our understanding of the song?

Conversely, this section of 'Highway 61 Revisited' might refer a student of literature back to 'Odysseus's Scar', the opening chapter of Erich Auerbach's influential work of literary aesthetics, *Mimesis*, in which

Auerbach argues that the Genesis narrative of Abraham and Isaac, in contradistinction to that other canonical founding text of western culture, Homer's *Odyssey*, takes place in darkness and silence, in a total absence of physical or narrative detail. *The Odyssey*, Auerbach writes, 'is narrated . . . with such a complete externalization of all the elements of the story and of their interconnections as to leave nothing in obscurity'.[14] Genesis, however, offers nothing *but* obscurity, as in the description of Abraham's journey to the place of sacrifice:

> And Abraham rose up early in the morning, and saddled his ass, and took two of his young men with him, and Isaac his son, and clave the wood for the burnt offering, and rose up, and went unto the place of which God had told him.
> Then on the third day Abraham lifted his eyes, and saw the place afar off (Genesis, 22: 3–4; King James's version).

We could argue that what Dylan is doing, and Jon Dressel in 'Let's Hear It For Goliath', is providing those details which the Old Testament does not offer – filling in the gaps, as it were – a process we call biblical exegesis, or hermeneutics, and which is one of the origins of modern literary theory, and specifically, as Paul Hamilton suggests, of *historicist* theories.[15] Thus it could be argued that both 'Highway 61 Revisited' and 'Let's Hear It For Goliath' are about exegesis, literary criticism, reading and readings. They are texts about interpreting texts. Indeed, 'Let's Hear It For Goliath' is one of a suite of poems entitled 'Searching the Scriptures'.

These may be potentially fruitful readings of these poems, but – to return us to the subject of this chapter – they are all contingent upon one important criterion: an awareness of *context*, of the cultural context which informs or produces these texts (in this instance, though not necessarily always so, biblical narratives, or Judaeo-Christian religion), which informs or produces their *meaning*. Broadly, we might say, they are contingent on an awareness of cultural *history*, and of the place of the poems in history. Fredric Jameson's study of narrative, *The Political Unconscious*, has as its opening sentence and motto 'Always historicize!';[16] that, too, is the principle behind this chapter.

One of the legacies of the writings of the historical theorist Michel Foucault, an important figure for New Historicism, is that we can no longer readily attend to cultural artefacts, such as poems, as partaking of an unchanging, 'transhistorical' order. Foucault, in *The Order of Things*, argued that historical moments or periods, which he called 'epistemes' (from the Greek word for knowledge – hence 'epistemology', the theory of knowledge), are defined not by what they have in common, but by their discontinuities or disjunctions. Simply put, epistemes are characterized by different systems of knowledge; by, as Foucault has it, their discursive regulation of what it is possible to know, what can and cannot be articulated.[17] For example, part of Foucault's book *The History of Sexuality: An Introduction* is concerned with what we understand as 'Victorian' sexual morality, and especially with the nineteenth-century taxonomy, or listing, of sexual practices: an identifying or codifying of certain types of sexual practice as illicit or deviant, in a manner which would have been meaningless to previous centuries.[18] Thus, while, in the eighteenth century, James Boswell's *London Journal* cheerfully records the commonplace sight of couples having public, open-air sex in London parks, such practices were, in the nineteenth century, deemed illicit, and therefore unspeakable. This type of thinking seriously questioned the traditional humanist view of an essentially unchanging 'order of things', and by extension also questioned meditations on art as produced by, or reflecting, an essentially stable 'human condition'. (Earlier this century, it should be noted, the American philosopher A. O. Lovejoy warned against what he called 'uniformitarianism', the belief that all people, in all places, at all times, are essentially the same. They are not.)[19]

While it may be untenable then, to talk of a generalized 'human condition' (though it is remarkable how frequently this is still done by academic literary critics), we can nevertheless discuss texts in terms of a shared cultural context, an agenda which may be very broad indeed. Imagine reading 'Let's Hear It For Goliath' or 'Highway 61 Revisited' while having absolutely no knowledge of who Goliath might be, or knowing nothing about Abraham and Isaac, let alone King David, the Philistines or Uriah. This is unlikely, though not impossible – it is possible to conceive of, say, a Buddhist reader who might have trouble with many of these names. But it *is* the case that most white, western readers would understand the poems' frame of reference, and this just goes to show how contingent our readings are on a shared cultural context, which, as has been said, informs or produces the meanings we derive from texts. This just goes to show, in other words, that there *are* metanarratives of cultural history in operation as we read, metanarratives which can be drawn on by very large interpretive communities.

This is, of course, very broad. To give a more specific example on the significance of context for reading, this is the closing section of W. B. Yeats's poem 'Easter 1916':

> We know their dream; enough
> To know they dreamed and are dead;
> And what if excess of love
> Bewildered them till they died?
> I write it out in a verse –
> MacDonagh and MacBride
> And Connolly and Pearse
> Now and in time to be,
> Wherever green is worn,
> Are changed, changed utterly:
> A terrible beauty is born.[20]

Easter 1916 is the date of the 'Easter Rising' in Dublin, the most significant date in the movement for independence in Ireland. The Rising was violently suppressed by the British Government, and many of its leaders, including Padraig Pearse and James Connolly, were executed. The Rising contributed directly to independence, with the establishment of the Irish Free State in 1922.

'Easter 1916' is now widely recognized as one of the major, canonical poems of the twentieth century, as good a candidate as any for 'timeless', 'universal' greatness. But here we need to re-ask John Barrell's questions: 'when it was written, . . . whom it addressed, . . . what was the function of any particular literary activity – writing epic poems, reading novels – at any particular period for any particular kind of reader'. The poem was clearly written at a specific historical moment, as a response to specific historical events, and with a specific audience in mind. A very specific audience. Although written in 1916, the poem was not published until 1920; between these years, it was circulated privately (and against Yeats's wishes, he claimed), to a small, sympathetic readership. Why? Clearly because this poem constituted a subversive, politically charged artefact, and would in 1916, in the immediate aftermath of the events it describes, have been considered a sufficiently dangerous text to have lost Yeats any influence he may have had in England (he had the ear of the then prime minister, Herbert Asquith). England was at war with Germany and the Rising was fought with weapons shipped by submarine from Germany to Ireland; thus any writing in support of the Rising (even the measured support Yeats's poem offers) would have been considered a *de facto* act of treason. Yeats, however, could have published the poem in Ireland or indeed America – not, in 1916, a combatant in the First World War – but chose not to. Thus the poem does not simply reflect or represent its historical moment, but it also partakes in that moment. It is, that is to say, simultaneously an aesthetic *and* a political text.

This is all, clearly, crucial to the poem. Yet imagine reading 'Easter 1916' with no knowledge at all of the significance of that date. This is a perfectly possible interpretive scenario (it might, in fact, be the dominant one). Earlier in this chapter, we referred to the status of the Bible as a metanarrative for western culture, consistently informing so many of its documents. Thus, while as products of this culture we may all be said to 'know' the Bible (though this is a half-truth – we may know about King David, Moses or the Gospels, but not necessarily about King Josiah, the teachings of the prophet Amos, or what it means to be a priest according to the order of Melchisedek – see, respectively, 2 Kings, Amos, Epistle to the Hebrews), there is no cultural imperative, certainly not outside Ireland and perhaps not even within it, that *necessitates* a knowledge of the Easter Rising. Certainly, too, valid readings of the poem could conceivably be produced without a knowledge of the specific circumstances which produced this poem (indeed, in a New Critical 'practical criticism' exercise, these are

precisely the kinds of reading which would, ideally, be produced), or even
the general ones – it *is* possible to read Yeats without attending to, without
knowing about, his status as an Irishman. But an ignorance of the context
of the poem would certainly, for a historicist, result in an *impoverishment*
of potential meanings within the poem. Although from a contrary, New
Critical, position, it should be noted that the poem's 'meaning' should not
and cannot be reduced to a kind of summary of Yeats's attitude to the
events of 1916, nevertheless a knowledge of context does provide an invalu-
able source of meaning for the poem.

This is clearly, then, once again a matter of interpretive communities, in this
case very large communities operating within the discourses or cultural
practices of religion and politics. These, of course, are discourses which are
generally figured as 'significant', that is, about which large interpretive
communities *should* be expected to know. But what of poems whose
subjects fall outside such culturally validated discourses? Of what use
would historicist poetics be then? We shall attempt to answer this question
with reference to Philip Larkin's poem 'Annus Mirabilis':

> Sexual intercourse began
> In nineteen sixty-three
> (Which was rather late for me) –
> Between the end of the *Chatterley* ban
> And the Beatles' first LP.
>
> Up till then there'd only been
> A sort of bargaining,
> A wrangle for a ring,
> A shame that started at sixteen
> And spread to everything.
>
> Then all at once the quarrel sank:
> Everyone felt the same,
> And every life became
> A brilliant breaking of the bank,
> A quite unlosable game.
>
> So life was never better than
> In nineteen sixty-three
> (Though just too late for me) –
> Between the end of the *Chatterley* ban
> And the Beatles' first LP.[21]

The first question we need to ask is about the title, 'Annus Mirabilis'.
What does it mean? What is it doing here? After all, it is clearly Latin, and
seems somewhat out of keeping with the plain-spoken 'Englishness' which
we might say is characteristic of the poem's expression (and, more gener-
ally, of Larkin). Indeed, in his book *Purity of Diction in English Verse*, the

critic Donald Davie suggests the existence of a whole 'tradition' of verse, which he clearly understands as very 'English', and which is characterized by its refusal of such Latinate ostentation or allusion, of the kinds of metaphoric complexity so beloved of the New Critics, of the overtly self-referential language which Wordsworth denounced as mere 'poetic diction', and of an academicized 'difficulty' in general.[22] This tradition includes, for example, the eighteenth-century hymns of Charles Wesley and Isaac Watts, Blake's *Songs* ('we have Hirelings in . . . the University . . . We do not want either Greek or Roman models if we are but just & true to our own Imaginations',[23] Blake wrote), and the poetry of Thomas Hardy; it is also a tradition of which Larkin himself evidently partakes.[24] It is, furthermore, a tradition which Davie associates with religious dissent, or nonconformist neo-puritanism, an important idea to keep in mind when we think of the subject-matter of 'Annus Mirabilis'. Thus, to begin with, the poem's very title stands out as an incongruity, in need of explanation.

The next thing to note here is that when the poem was first published in the February 1968 issue of the Oxford University magazine *Cover*, it was under the title, fittingly to our purposes here, of 'History'. Obviously, this suggests that Larkin, albeit ironically, viewed the poem as a historical document, a comment upon a seismic shift in societal behaviour, a 'sexual revolution' in which he himself was doomed, because of his age (Larkin, born in 1922, would have been 41 in 1963), to play no part.

We shall return to this theme shortly – but for now we will examine the question of why Larkin chose finally to call the poem 'Annus Mirabilis'. The provenance of this title can be explained by reference to what Hamilton calls 'an economy of other texts'. 'Annus Mirabilis' is the title of a poem by John Dryden: 'Annus Mirabilis, The Year of Wonders, 1666'. Dryden is amongst the most radically historical of all poets, in the sense that much of his poetry is flatly incomprehensible without reference to its specific historical moment. Dryden himself describes his 'Annus Mirabilis' as a 'historical poem', recounting the events of 1666 – the plague and the great fire of London, the second Dutch War. Dryden's poem, then, operates within a historical matrix of what we have called culturally significant discourses – politics and religion.

It is worth dwelling on the case of John Dryden for a moment, as a notorious example of a writer whose cultural context is so far back in time that it is no longer apparent to us. Dryden's 'Annus Mirabilis', for all its historical difficulty, is at least available to the reader as a poem whose concerns are recognizably historical – a poetic account of the events of a given year. But what of a poem which offers no such directly interpretable historical clues – a historical poem which we might not even recognize as such? Such a work is Dryden's 'Absalom and Achitophel', a poem which further displaces, and therefore to a modern reader further complicates, already distant historical events by presenting them in terms of a biblical allegory in which characters from the Bible are made to represent characters from seventeenth-century political history (in his own Preface to the poem, Dryden describes his role as 'only the historian').[25] One of Dryden's editors, John Conaghan, glosses the poem's cultural context thus:

> 'Absalom and Achitophel' was published in November 1681, anonymously, although there was no doubt as to Dryden's authorship. It was an immediate success, for one thing as a well-timed assertion against the tumult and hysteria of the Popish Plot. The misfortunes of Charles [II]'s reign; years of anxiety about the succession of his Catholic brother James, Duke of York, to the throne; fomentation of rumour, especially by the infamous Titus Oates in 1678; and finally the murder in mysterious circumstances of the magistrate Sir Edmund Berry Godfrey on 12 October 1678: all produced conditions of fear and panic. Trials and executions of Catholics ensued until the later part of 1679.
>
> In October 1680, still on a tide of this feeling, Parliament met in hopes of excluding James from the succession, with some support for his replacement by the Duke of Monmouth ... The move was thwarted by a dissolution, and a brief recall of Parliament in the Royalist atmosphere of Oxford in March 1681. There was a great deal of controversy subsequently, but it tended increasingly in the King's favour; and in this Dryden's poem was influential.[26]

But within the poem itself there is no clue as to a contemporary political meaning. A modern reader familiar with the Bible might conclude this to be a poetic retelling of the account of the rebellion against King David by his favoured son Absalom, with the aid of the counsellor Achitophel, as offered in 2 Samuel. To realize that the poem operates allegorically, that Jerusalem is London, Absalom King Charles II's illegitimate son James, Duke of Monmouth, and Achitophel Anthony Ashley Cooper, Earl of Shaftesbury, requires historical–contextual research. This leads to questions as to why Dryden chose an allegorical representation of these events. As we noted in Chapter 1, allegory is frequently used as a vehicle for political comment, as in William Langland's *Piers Plowman*, John Bunyan's *The Pilgrim's Progress*, or George Orwell's *Animal Farm*. Traditionally, we noted, part of the reason for this was to do with allegory's inherent interpretive *doubleness* – as a form which simultaneously says two things (about Stalinism and about pigs, for instance) it enables its author to make political points obliquely, a useful tactic when one considers that the price of political comment has at times been imprisonment or execution. In 1668 Dryden was made first Poet Laureate, a position obviously far more politically charged then than it is today; the following year he was made Historiographer Royal, that is, official historian. As such, he was deeply implicated in the (extremely turbulent) politics of his period. It was an unstable position to be in – under the Protestant Charles II, Dryden wrote 'Religio Laici, or The Layman's Faith', a vindication of Anglican

Protestantism. In 1685, Charles was succeeded to the throne by his Catholic brother, James II; Dryden converted to Catholicism in 1686 and the following year published a pro-Catholic allegory, 'The Hind and the Panther'. In 1689 the Protestant William and Mary were crowned; Dryden was removed from the Laureateship. (He was succeeded, ironically, by Thomas Shadwell, who had been viciously satirized as 'Shit' in Dryden's own 1678 poem 'MacFlecknoe'; in 1692 the post was given to Nahum Tate, now most famous for rewriting *King Lear* with a happy ending.)

A poem such as 'Absalom and Achitophel', it may be argued, is a failure because it simply has no 'relevance' for us today. Or, conversely, it may be argued that we can read it now only as a parable of man's eternal corruption, greed and lust for power – as indicative, that is, of something in 'the human condition'. The response to this would be to ask an analogous historical question: is that the way we read the poems of Wilfred Owen? As parables of man's inhumanity to man? That may be a valid conclusion, but is it really the case that Owen's work can be dissociated from its historical context, the First World War? One could further argue that the contextualization required for 'Absalom and Achitophel' is simply a more extreme version of the contextualizing we inevitably perform as readers anyway.

Philip Larkin's 'Annus Mirabilis', his 'Year of Wonders', is 1963, the year, apparently, of the 'invention' of sexual intercourse. This idea we might laugh off as an amusing poetic conceit – it is ridiculous seriously to suggest that 'sexual intercourse' was not actually practised before that year. However, bearing in mind Foucault's theories of the episteme, the radical discursive break with the past, it is possible to interpret Larkin's assertion somewhat differently. A discursive shift in the *representations* – and consequently the practices – of sexual behaviour did take place around the year 1963. Then, the conditions governing the licit – what could or could not be said or shown; what was or was not *representable* – did alter radically with the coming of what came to be known as the 'permissive society'. Thus, sexual practices as we understand them today really did come into being around then. Having no notion of the cultural–historical significance of the 1960s would lead to a genuinely impoverished response to the poem, leading a reader to infer purely from the poem's internal evidence that Larkin is simply making some manner of insupportable joke about the sudden and miraculous discovery made by humanity – copulation. This is bizarre, and yet it may well be the interpretive condition of a hypothetical reader many years in the future (assuming, amongst many other assumptions, that the future still cares for Philip Larkin – assuming, that is, according to humanist critical wisdom, that Larkin's poetry contains some abstractable 'universal' meaning, transcending its immediate context), when the precise significance of the 1960s is known only to historians.

What of 'the *Chatterley* ban' and 'the Beatles' first LP'? Simply in order to make sense of the poem we need to know that the ban on publishing or disseminating – and consequently, in theory, on reading – a novel by D. H.

Lawrence entitled *Lady Chatterley's Lover* (more texts!), a novel long proscribed by law because its representations of sexual practices led it to be labelled obscene ('Is this a book you would wish your wife or servant to read?' the jury was asked), was finally lifted in 1960 after a celebrated trial. (The novel was cleared of obscenity on 2 July; on 10 July alone 200,000 copies were sold.) This led to a more general relaxation of censorship laws in Britain, and to the publication of the works of other 'obscene' writers, such as Henry Miller. Thus the policing of sexual discourses changed dramatically in the 1960s: as Foucault would have it this decade saw a change in the discursive regulation of what it is possible to know (hence the etymology of obscene, from the Latin *ob scena*, off stage: that which it is not permissible to show). It is precisely this change which allowed Larkin to publish his most famous line of verse, 'They fuck you up, your mum and dad'.[27] This is the opening line of the poem 'This Be The Verse' (from the same collection as 'Annus Mirabilis', *High Windows*, 1974), the verse, of course, being that one can now, in 1974, say the word 'fuck' in a poem (indeed, it is a vindication of Foucauldian theory to note that, 'modern' as its inclusion may have been in 1974, back in the seventeenth century the Earl of Rochester used the word 'fuck' in his poetry all the time).

But what of the Beatles? Who might they be? This is precisely the question that a high court judge was to ask in 1965 (the alleged answer, 'A popular "beat combo", m'lud'). The Beatles were more than just a popular beat combo – they were prime agents in precisely the shift in episteme that the poem describes. And their first LP? *Please Please Me*. The semantic shift in the repetition of the word please in the title is significant, the shift from adverb – please, 'if it pleases you', to verb, 'to please', which clearly carries sexual connotations, to give sexual pleasure. As the song's full version has it: 'Please please me, oh yeah, like I please you'. The sexual meaning here would have been inconceivable or more properly unutterable before about 1963, *even in a song which had exactly the same words*.

Attempting to place the Beatles in their cultural context, and to account for their influence upon that context, Ian MacDonald offers the following account of the epistemic shift from the 1950s to the 1960s:

> Any domestic film of the period will convey the genteel, class-segregated staidness of British society at that time. The braying, upper-class voices on newsreels, the odour of unearned privilege in parliament and the courts, the tired nostalgia for the war, all conspired to breed unrest among the young. . . . Beneath the wiped and polished surface of British culture around 1960 lay a festering mass of sexual ignorance, prejudice and repression only slightly ameliorated since the 19th century. Erotic experience was mostly confined to the dutiful discontent of marriage, while women were so routinely belittled that they barely noticed it, obediently accepting demeaning fashions and

failing to demur with the prevalent male view of rape as something every female secretly wanted. In this slow-thinking world, as yet unaccelarated by television, gentle neighbourliness coexisted with half-conscious prejudice against outsiders – Jews, blacks, 'queers' – and complacently censorious ideas of what was proper and decent.[28]

This is the view of a cultural historian, and it is only proper, given the lessons of New Historicism, that we do not treat this kind of history (particularly, one might add, when it works at this level of generalization) as absolute, that we do not afford it the status of unmediated historical truth. Nevertheless, it is worth noting that this account broadly tallies with Larkin's of pre-1963 sexual conduct:

> Up till then there'd only been
> A sort of bargaining,
> A wrangle for a ring,
> A shame that started at sixteen
> And spread to everything.

Larkin clearly places himself on the wrong side of the epistemic divide ('rather late for me'): as we noted, Larkin was 41 in 1963; he was 45 when the poem was written in 1967 (the year of the so-called 'summer of love'), 52 when it was published in *High Windows*. In a letter significantly dated January 1970, Larkin writes that the 1960s rather passed him by, noting 'how little in touch I have been with the world since 1945. . . . I have registered the Beatles and the mini-skirt, but that's about all.'[29] 'Annus Mirabilis', then, casts Larkin in his familiar guise of wistful, middle-aged observer, commenting upon a climate of fun, sex and freedom in which he cannot participate. The volume's title, *High Windows*, refers to this detached, observational viewpoint, as is made clear in the poem of that title, which reiterates the thematic concerns of 'Annus Mirabilis', a poem which opens:

> When I see a couple of kids
> And guess he's fucking her and she's
> Taking pills or wearing a diaphragm,
> I know this is paradise
> Everyone old has dreamed of all their lives.[30]

The 'high windows' of the title permit observation, but are also, the poem goes on to show, imprisoning, literally coming between promised sexual licence – 'like free bloody birds' – and its actuality, 'the deep blue air'. And furthermore, this licence is only permitted to 'everyone young going down the long slide / To happiness, endlessly'. When the word 'endless' is repeated at the poem's close, with reference to the speaker's own subject-position, it signifies 'nothing . . . nowhere'.

This analysis of 'Annus Mirabilis' in terms of its cultural referents within the 1960s might, it could be argued, simply be stating the obvious. The poem's readers do not need to be informed of the meaning of the Beatles or the '*Chatterley* ban'. This would be a fair objection, but also an objection which just goes to prove that we consistently, unconsciously, historicize and contextualize whenever we read. There can be no such thing as a reading free from history, nor should there be.

Endnotes

1 Raymond Williams, *Marxism and Literature* (Oxford, 1977), p. 206.
2 Stanley Cavell, *Must We Mean What We Say?* (Cambridge, 1968), p. 269.
3 Fish, *Is There a Text in this Class?*, pp. 49–50.
4 John Barrell, *Poetry, Language and Politics* (Manchester, 1988), p. 3.
5 Paul Hamilton, *Historicism* (London, 1996), p. 3.
6 Raymond Williams, *Keywords* (London, 1976, 1988). For 'Culture', see pp. 87–93.
7 Barrell, *Poetry, Language and Politics*, p. 12.
8 H. Aram Veeser, ed., *The New Historicism* (London and New York, 1989), pp. x–xi.
9 Elizabeth Fox-Genovese, 'Literary Criticism and the Politics of New Historicism', in Veeser, *The New Historicism*, p. 216. In the same volume, Stanley Fish offers another criticism of the extremes of New Historicist thinking: 'If you are asked a question like "what happened?" and you answer "the determination of what happened will always be a function of the ideological vision of the observer; there are no unmediated historical perceptions," you will have answered a question from one practice in terms of another and your interlocutor will be justifiably annoyed.' Fish, 'Commentary: The Young and the Restless', p. 308. As usual, Fish is insisting here that the meaning of an utterance is dictated by its context.
10 Jon Dressel, 'Let's Hear It For Goliath', *Out of Wales: Fifty Poems 1973–83* (Port Talbot, 1984), pp. 60–1.
11 Bob Dylan, 'Highway 61 Revisited', *Highway 61 Revisited* (1965).
12 Søren Kierkegaard, *Fear and Trembling*, trans. Alastair Hannay (Harmondsworth, 1985), p. 7.
13 See Norman Mailer, 'The White Negro', in *Advertisements for Myself* (London, 1992).
14 Auerbach, *Mimesis*, pp. 3–23.
15 *New Princeton Encyclopedia*, p. 516, glosses hermeneutics as follows: 'Hermeneutics is the art of interpreting texts, especially via a body of rules, techniques, and a theory of literary, legal or biblical exegesis.'
16 Fredric Jameson, *The Political Unconscious: Narrative as a Socially Symbolic Act* (London, 1989), p. 9.
17 Michel Foucault, *The Order of Things: An Archaeology of Human Sciences* (London, 1989).
18 Foucault, *The History of Sexuality: An Introduction*, trans. Robert Hurley (Harmondsworth, 1981).
19 For an account of 'uniformitarianism', see Abrams, *The Mirror and the Lamp*, pp. 104–14. Abrams introduces this concept as a means of critiquing Wordsworth's ideas of the poet as 'a man speaking to men' in his influential 'Preface' to the *Lyrical Ballads*.
20 Yeats, *Selected Poetry*, p. 95.
21 Larkin, *Collected Poems*, p. 167.

22 Donald Davie, *Purity of Diction in English Verse* (London, 1952).

23 Blake, *Complete Poems*, p. 490.

24 In his essays, collected in *Required Writing* (London, 1983), Larkin outlines a consistently anti-modernist aesthetic, erecting an unholy trinity of Ezra Pound, Pablo Picasso and Charlie Parker as the destroyers of twentieth-century art. Less guardedly, in his letters he writes of Pound as the obsession of 'a pack of Cambridge cunts'. *Selected Letters of Philip Larkin, 1940–1985*, ed. Anthony Thwaite (London, 1992), p. 577.

25 *Dryden: A Selection*, p. 92.

26 *Dryden: A Selection*, p. 91.

27 Larkin, *Collected Poems*, p. 180.

28 Ian MacDonald, *Revolution in the Head: The Beatles' Records and the Sixties* (London, 1995), pp. 7–8.

29 Larkin, *Selected Letters*, p. 426. This remark is in the context of a cultural history of the period, Christopher Booker's *The Neophiliacs: A Study of the Revolution in English Life in the 50s and 60s* (London, 1969). This book, incidentally, describes the Beatles as 'evil'.

30 Larkin, *Collected Poems*, p. 165.

|8|

Public poetry

these things are important not because a

high-sounding interpretation can be put upon them but because they
  are
useful.

Marianne Moore[1]

When Shelley wrote in 1821 that 'Poets are the unacknowledged legislators of the world', he was making two potentially disparate claims.[2] In suggesting that poets are 'legislators' – that is, lawmakers – he was making a claim, albeit an unusually grand one, for the public status of poetry: that is, he was asserting that poetry, and the poet, had an important role in public life and discourse, an assertion which was itself, we shall see, far from radical. He was also, however, by making the poet–legislator 'unacknowledged', signalling a shift in ideas about the function and status of poetry, and particularly the function and status of the poet, a shift associated with Romanticism generally.

As we have asserted throughout this study, many modern readerly conceptions of poetry are heavily influenced by Romanticism. In no way is this more notable than in the shift in ideas of what a poet should be, how a poet should behave, and what relationship poets should have to a larger community. The whole notion of poetry, both its writing and its reading, as a solitary activity, and consequently of the poet as a solitary individual, set apart from others and by extension qualitatively different from the rest of humanity (able to see or feel more keenly), is to a large extent post-Romantic, as are some of our received ideas of the way poets should act. The myths of personal flamboyance or difference that have accompanied poets from Byron through to Dylan Thomas or Sylvia Plath suggest that poets are *licensed* to behave in ways which set them apart from the rest of us, a licence underwritten by notions of 'genius' as self-evidently a mark of difference. Poets have become social outsiders.

It was not always thus, nor is it always thus now: for every hairy Walt Whitman or boozy Dylan Thomas (or hairy *and* boozy John Berryman) there has been a smooth-faced, publicly retiring Wallace Stevens or Philip Larkin (though in Larkin's case, this very retirement became a kind of myth, of anti-sociability, or of a sinister normality, in keeping with the general view of the 1950s' 'Movement' poets, many of whom were civil servants!). Indeed, looking over the canon of pre-Romantic English poets, it is striking how many of them were, in different ways, social *insiders*, as politicians, courtiers or civil servants (Chaucer, Spenser, Sidney, Milton, Marvell) or as clergymen (Donne, Herbert, Swift). Certainly there is the sense – albeit at a highly generalized level – that much pre-Romantic poetry is written from *within* the society it describes, as we saw in the previous chapter with the case of John Dryden, a writer deeply implicated in his own historical moment, not least because of his status as Poet Laureate, a position which will be discussed later in this chapter. This is also true of other Augustan poets, notably Swift, Pope and Johnson, and may account for the relative unpopularity of the poetry of this period amongst students of literature. The virtues it espouses, wit and satire, presuppose a sociability or social knowingness at variance with post-Romantic conceptions of the function of poetry.

Poetry's roots in orality and community, which we examined in Chapter 5, bespeak a public function: the poet, or more properly poetry (since oral/communal verse often has no single, recognized 'author', but instead is developed and formalized by repetition and tradition, carried by many voices), articulated communal experiences, desires, histories, narratives. This public status was often formalized, with kings, courts, or noblemen employing official poets – bards – as personal remembrancers, historians or public-relations agents. Some of the earliest extant poetry from these islands is of this kind. The *Gododdin* of the bard Aneirin was written in Old Welsh in what is now Scotland at some time in the seventh century (though surviving in no manuscript older than 1100), and tells, in a series of lyrics, of a futile battle fought at Catraeth (Catterick) by a band of 300 mercenaries in the employ of the chieftain Mynyddawg Mwynfawr (Mynyddawg the Wealthy):

> Gwyr a aeth gatraeth oed fraeth eu llu.
> glasved eu hancwyn a gwenwyn vu.
> trychant trwy beiryant en cattau.
> a gwedy elwch tawelwch vu.[3]

> [The men who went to Catterick were a ready crew.
> On fresh mead they banqueted, and it was poison.
> Three hundred under orders went to battle.
> And after the rejoicing, there was silence.]

Patronage – the patronage of the nobility – was crucial to the production of poetry, and this is one of the reasons for the 'insiderliness' of so much pre-Romantic poetry. Many of the greatest poetic works in the language were written directly under patronage, for money, favour or publicity: Chaucer's *The Book of the Duchess* was written on the occasion of the death of John of Gaunt's wife; Spenser wrote *The Fairie Queene*, allegorically addressed to Queen Elizabeth I, in the hope of gaining a position of influence at court (though this never happened, in part because Spenser had been critical of Elizabeth's Irish policies); Shakespeare's History Plays are sometimes read as a vindication of the Tudor monarchy under which Shakespeare himself wrote. Certainly, *Henry VIII*, the play which treats the most recent historical events of the cycle, ends with a speech of prophecy, spoken to the king and his newborn daughter, Elizabeth, by the (Protestant) Archbishop of Canterbury, Thomas Cranmer, which images forth the future queen's greatness as divinely ordained:

> Let me speak, sir,
> For heaven now bids me; and the words I utter
> Let none think flattery, for they'll find 'em truth.
> This royal infant – heaven still move about her! –
> Though in her cradle, yet now promises
> Upon this land a thousand thousand blessings,
> Which time shall bring to ripeness. She shall be –
> But few now living can behold that goodness –
> A pattern to all princes living with her,
> And all that shall succeed.
>
> (Act 5, scene 5, 14–23)

Though poets had always written under patronage, and frequently under royal patronage (thus making them, in effect, public servants), this status was not made official in England until as late as 1668 with the establishment of the Poet Laureateship, whose first encumbent, as we saw in the previous chapter, was John Dryden – the first official poet for the nation. (The title 'laureate' comes from the laurel branch, symbolic of poetic achievement – in Ovid's *Metamorphoses*, Daphne escapes Apollo's pursuit by turning into a laurel tree: the god then decrees that the laurel branch become an emblem of honour for both poets and the victorious in battle.[4]) The politics of this post could be fraught, and were fraught for Dryden himself, who was removed from the position in 1689. A number of poets, notably Walter Scott, have declined the Laureateship. As a major part of the function of the Poet Laureate is to write commemoratively on national events, and particularly on the monarchy, its significance remains somewhat contentious – out of keeping, certainly, with post-Romantic notions of the personal nature of poetry, but also with the characteristic positioning of the poet within Romantic aesthetics (in Blake and in Shelley) as by definition socially revolutionary, and thus republican. Even (perhaps especially) in modern times, Poets Laureate are likely to come under ideological scrutiny: the current Laureate, Andrew Motion, was criticized, rightly or wrongly, in the press and by fellow-poets because of his perceived lobbying for the position – harsh interpretations made this into an act of public toadying and therefore not indicative of a real, 'sincere' poet. Integrity (an important post-Romantic notion for the poet, though meaningless for many earlier poets) was thought to have been sacrificed in the name of a pointless (because outmoded) public status.

Motion's direct predecessor, Ted Hughes, also came under criticism, though for somewhat different reasons. His 1992 collection, *Rain Charm for the Duchy and other Laureate Poems* is certainly a bizarre document. For instance, to commemorate the Queen Mother's 85th birthday, Hughes produced two poems – this is an excerpt from one, 'The Dream of the Lion':

> It was an ancient Land, the Land of the Lion.
> New to earth, each creature woke,
> Licked away to speak, and spoke
> The mother-tongue, the rough tongue of the Lion. . . .
>
> Wild Dog, Hyena, Wolf, maned as a Lion,
> Rolled on her back, and motherly smiled,
> Suckling the Lion's human child
> Under the lifted golden eye of the Lion.[5]

Part of the problem with, or the strangeness of, this poetry is that it makes very few concessions to Hughes's status as Poet Laureate: it reads uncompromisingly like a Ted Hughes poem, not like a poem written for the Queen Mother. Hughes explained his choice of imagery for the poem in these terms:

> The basis of this poem is the association of three Lions: the one in Her Majesty Queen Elizabeth the Queen Mother's maiden name [Bowes-Lyon], the one in her birth-sign, and the totem animal of Great Britain. The first and third combined inside my head long ago, during my boyhood obsession with the animal kingdom, and my boyhood fanatic patriotism, in a way that was able to stir at the surface again, in these verses, as an experience to some degree widely shared.[6]

But does the poem articulate 'an experience . . . widely shared'? This yoking together of poetry and the state through symbolism (the lion) as an articulation of community may not be one which many contemporary readers would care to endorse, on both political and aesthetic grounds. Indeed, the monarchy's lion-symbolism was criticized by Thomas Paine as long ago as 1791:

> In England, this right [citizenship] is said to reside in a *metaphor*, shown at the Tower for a shilling or sixpence apiece: So are the lions; and it would be a step nearer to reason to say that it resided in them, for any inanimate metaphor is no more than a hat or a cap. We can all see the absurdity in worshipping Aaron's molten calf or

Nebuchadnezzar's golden image; but why do men continue to practise
themselves the absurdities they despise in others?[7]

Certainly it is possible, as a consequence of Hughes's own unmistakably
powerful poetic voice, to read this poem against the grain, as undermining
the institution it purports to praise: is the Queen Mother really being
metaphorically represented as a 'Wild Dog, Hyena, Wolf . . . Suckling the
Lion's human child' (that is, the Queen) in the second stanza? One would
like to think so, and it is difficult to conceive of any circumstances under
which being likened to a hyena could be given a positive spin. Hyenas, after
all, are scavengers, and thus the image seems to tally far more closely with
traditional republican thinking (the monarchy as parasitic). Aesthetically,
Hughes's Laureate poetry might seem to many modern readers an uncom-
fortable mix of seemingly irreconcilable poetics: Hughes's usual harsh
Romanticism, a heady post-Wordsworthian mix of nature-poetry and full-
blooded animism, conflicts quite strongly with the public, celebratory
gentility expected from Laureate poetry. While this makes for fascinating
poetry, it can hardly be said to be fulfilling the traditional requirements of
the Poet Laureate.

It is no accident that the post of Laureate was instituted in 1668, at
around the time when the practice of patronage generally was beginning to
wane. Indeed, one of the reasons for the shift in the status of the poet with
Romanticism was external, to do with this decline in the habits of patron-
age. Romantic poets were writing around the time of the industrial revolu-
tion, and, as we have seen, one of the guiding ideologies of industrial
capitalism through the late eighteenth and nineteenth centuries was utili-
tarianism, whereby value was assigned according to material use, an ideol-
ogy which had little time for or understanding of poetry. In this way,
Romanticism can be understood as an aesthetic by-product of what
Raymond Williams has termed the 'Long Revolution', a gradual revolution
into modernity, beginning in the eighteenth century.[8] In 1749, Johnson's
'The Vanity of Human Wishes' contained the following lament on the
poet's (and, more generally, the writer's) current lot, in a passage whose
final line tellingly deviates from an otherwise smoothly iambic metre:

> Yet hope not life from grief or danger free,
> Nor think the doom of man reversed for thee:
> Deign on the passing world to turn thine eyes,
> And pause a while from letters, to be wise;
> There, mark what ills the scholar's life assail,
> Toil, envy, want, the patron and the jail.[9]

In his *Dictionary*, Johnson, indeed, defined 'Patron' as 'Commonly a
wretch who supports with insolence, and is paid with flattery'![10]

At about the same time, poets were rediscovering Celticism, an interest
in ancient British poetry, notably with the 'Ossian' poems of James

Macpherson, which purported to be poems from a found manuscript by a
forgotten Dark Ages Scots bard (one of the most successful literary hoaxes
of all time). Thomas Chatterton, too, wrote bogus 'authentic' ancient
British poetry, while Blake drew heavily on Celticism and Arthurianism for
his own arcane mysticism, and, in London, the Welsh poet Iolo Morganwg
(Edward Williams to his mother) reconstituted (or, more properly, fabri-
cated) the ancient druidic Order of the Bards, who claimed – and still claim
– direct descent from the ancient Celtic bards. Thomas Gray's poem, 'The
Bard' (1757), is a good example of this kind of endeavour, and especially
interesting as in many ways it sets the template for Romantic, and therefore
modern, conceptions of the figure of the poet:

> On a rock, whose haughty brow
> Frowns o'er cold Conway's foaming flood,
> Robed in the sable garb of woe,
> With haggard eyes the poet stood;
> (Loose his beard, and hoary hair
> Stream'd, like a meteor to the troubled air)
> And with a master's hand, and prophet's fire,
> Struck the deep sorrows of his lyre. . . .
>
> 'Weave the warp, and weave the woof,
> The winding-sheet of Edward's race.
> Give ample room and verge enough
> The characters of hell to trace.
> Mark the year and mark the night,
> When Severn shall re-echo with affright
> The shrieks of death, thro' Berkley's roof that ring,
> Shrieks of an agonising king!'[11]

As well as physically resembling a poetic ideal (wild-haired, bearded), the
bard here is signalled by his removal from social organization, symbolically
represented spatially, in terms of the landscape he inhabits: a high cliff over-
looking a foaming sea on the North Wales coast. Not sociable, then, but
supernatural, what Gray's bard utters is prophecy, and significantly a
prophecy vindicating the aboriginal inhabitants of Britain (the Celts),
violently disenfranchised by a colonial, hegemonic power (the Normans:
'Edward' here is King Edward I, who built a series of fortress-castles along
the North Wales coast, one of them in Conway, long understood as symbols
of oppression). The bard prophesies a future in which this unjust power is
overthrown and the true Britons return through the agency of the (Welsh)
Tudor dynasty, before hurling himself off the cliff to his death. The
precipice and 'foaming flood' here are examples of the 'sublime', which was
to become the cornerstone of Romantic aesthetics. As theorized by Edmund
Burke in his *A Philosophical Enquiry into the Origin of our Ideas of the
Sublime and Beautiful* (1757), the sublime is a profoundly anti-rationalist

aesthetic which presented spectacles (usually natural spectacles) so grand and vast as to short-circuit reason, filling the beholder with awe, astonishment or terror.[12] The sublime figures heavily in Romanticism: in the famous 'boat-stealing' episode of Book I of *The Prelude*, where the young Wordsworth, rowing on a lake, finds himself metaphorically pursued by a vast mountain; in the climax on the Jungfrau mountain in Byron's *Manfred* (another instance of a poetic 'over-reacher' throwing himself off a precipice); and notably in Romantic Gothic novels – the Pyrenean or Apennine landscapes fetishistically described by Ann Radcliffe, or the Alpine heights and seas of ice in *Frankenstein*.

So, as figured in 'The Bard', poets are socially and consequently geographically set apart, symbolically associated with wild, sublime landscapes and thus with 'authenticity' (siding with nature over culture, the supernatural or folkloric over the social), ideologically representative of the dispossessed. Now, this poetic stance should be a familiar one to many modern readers, albeit that one has to admit that it is, historically, a paradoxical one: an appropriation of a figure, the Bard, deeply implicated in a culture of poetic patronage, as a symbol of radical poetic individualism.

If this stance is familiar, it may well be so from the poetry of Wordsworth, as all of the characteristics outlined above are those which his poetry, particularly in the *Lyrical Ballads*, quite selfconsciously constructs. With this in mind, 'Tintern Abbey' is the poem in which this stance of outsiderliness is most carefully constructed – Wordsworth the solitary haunter of lonely hills, overlooking and observing, but not participating in, the ways of the world. The year 1798, when the poem was written and published, and which is incorporated into its full title ('Lines written a few miles above Tintern Abbey, on revisiting the banks of the Wye during a tour, July 13, 1798', you will remember from Chapter 1), was an extraordinarily turbulent year, even by the standards of its extraordinarily turbulent decade, with, amongst other things, a Jacobin-inspired political rising in Ireland, spearheaded by the United Irishmen under Wolfe Tone and Edward Fitzgerald. Furthermore, England was at war with France and the country was living under perpetual, and not unjustified, fear that the French would invade. (Coleridge, as well as collaborating on the *Lyrical Ballads*, produced another, highly political, volume of poetry in 1798, tellingly entitled *Fears in Solitude, Written in 1798 during the Alarms of an Invasion; to which are Added France: An Ode; and Frost at Midnight*.) The opening lines of 'Tintern Abbey', 'Five years have passed; five summers, with the length / Of five long winters!',[13] explicitly contrast 1798, the year of the poem's composition, with 1793, another highly turbulent year. This was the year of the Jacobin Congress under Maximilien Robespierre; the year of the post-Revolutionary 'Terrors' – mass guillotinings – in Paris; the year of the execution of both Louis XVI and Marie Antoinette. It was also the year in which France and England declared war, a war which was to last until Waterloo in 1815, with a brief cessation of hostilities under the Treaty of

Amiens in 1802 – which, in fact, allowed Wordsworth to visit France, a visit which occasioned many of the fiercely nationalistic sonnets posthumously collected as *Poems Dedicated to National Independence and Liberty*.

What 'Tintern Abbey' enacts (as does Coleridge's contemporary 'Frost at Midnight') is the desire, no doubt understandable, to escape from all this politics, retreating into natural isolation (again, there are parallels in Coleridge, whose 'France, an Ode' has its speaker surveying the chaos of Europe from the Alps, and concluding that political revolution is bondage, and that true freedom is to be found only in nature). 'Tintern Abbey' famously contrasts Wordsworth's radical 1793 self, young and wild, with the mature, politically quietist poet of 1798, in lines which make nature a thoroughly (conservatively) ideological construct:

> I cannot paint
> What then I was. The sounding cataract
> Haunted me like a passion: the tall rock,
> The mountain, and the deep and gloomy wood,
> Their colours and their forms, were then to me
> An appetite: a feeling and a love,
> That had no need of a remoter charm,
> By thought supplied, or any interest
> Unborrowed from the eye. – That time is past,
> And all its aching joys are now no more,
> And all its dizzy raptures. . . .
> For I have learned
> To look on nature not as in the hour
> Of thoughtless youth, but hearing oftentimes
> The still, sad music of humanity,
> Not harsh nor grating, though of ample power
> To chasten and subdue.[14]

In spite of this legacy of Romanticism, twentieth-century poetry *has* continued to carry a public tradition, and in a number of ways. Poetry has often articulated national or nationalist thinking, particularly amongst marginalized, colonized or otherwise disenfranchised peoples, offering, or even creating, potentially unifying definitions of nationhood through shared ideals, histories or mythologies. The role of Yeats in Irish national-ist politics is a good example of this, though Yeats himself was just one of a number of writers engaged in this project. As Terence Brown writes:

> It . . . [was] literary and cultural activity which, as the critic Ernest Boyd noted in 1922, had 'done more than anything else to draw the attention of the outside world to the separate national existence of Ireland.'
>
> The new literature that began to be produced in the eighties and nineties of the [nineteenth] century primarily affirmed the heroic

traditions of the Irish people, directing their attention to the mytho-
logical tales of their past, to the heroes and noble deeds of a vanished
age. When such literary antiquarianism had managed to suggest a
continuity of experience between past and present, a powerful propa-
gandist weapon had been forged.[15]

A revisionist, however, would suggest that the mythic or heroic ideals
imaged forth by such nationalist poetics are not in fact shared but imposed.
Wales had undergone a similar nationalist poetic revival in the first half of
the twentieth century, which had effectively codified both the ideological
agenda and the canon of Welsh writing, but when Dannie Abse compiled
his anthology, *Twentieth Century Anglo-Welsh Poetry* in 1997 he made his
own stance very clear: 'Those verses imbued with the most *blatant* nation-
alist valency do not find, for the most part, a place here because platform
poems of whatever orientation rarely outlast their season.'[16] There, at a
stroke, went a sizeable chunk of the century's Welsh poetry!

Through the twentieth century, though, poets have recognized that the
articulation of a unified national identity can be highly problematic. The
New Zealand poet Allen Curnow wrote a poem, 'Sestina', which contains
the following stanza:

> Gulf'd from these tall cities, twice gulf'd from Time,
> Strange even to each other these live and move
> Where Waimakakiri trowels the silted shore,
> Where the harbours and foothills feed their seasonal ships;
> Sure is the musterer's foot, safe the passage by the sea,
> But gust-crazed in gorges man unmeasured gropes.[17]

'Strange even to each other these live and move': the poem recognizes the
complexity of national identity, and also subtly recognizes the complexity
of *writing* national identity through deploying a concomitantly complex
form. The sestina is, indeed, amongst the *most* complex of poetic forms: six
six-line stanzas and an *envoi* (a shorter concluding stanza of three lines), in
which the words at the ends of the lines are the same in each stanza, though
repeated in a different (though patterned) order. This poem, then, in the
words of one critic, is one whose 'very verse form works to throw light on
the difficulties of writing the settler situation'.[18]

Brendan Kennelly's 1983 *Cromwell* recognizes similar formal and ideo-
logical complexities in writing about the matter of Ireland. Kennelly, a
fundamentally comic poet, here confronts one of the darkest chapters in his
country's history through an encounter with a major figure in Irish
demonology: Oliver Cromwell, who, in charge of the Parliamentary Army's
Irish campaign of 1649–50, oversaw a wholesale slaughter in the Irish
towns of Drogheda and Wexford in 1649. While the desire to write a
unified national narrative is present in the collection's full title, *Cromwell:
A Poem*, the complex actuality dissolves the collection into a series of

discrete fragments, largely made up of quasi-sonnets, in which the same themes and images nonetheless continually recur: 'Trouble is, sonnets are genetic epics. / Something in them wants to grow out of bounds', Kennelly has Edmund Spenser say (this poem, a sonnet, concludes ' "I'm up to my bollox in sonnets," Spenser said').[19] 'Measures', the volume's prose preface, confronts Cromwell, Ireland's monstrous Other, attempting a degree of imaginative sympathy:

> I invited the butcher into my room and began a dialogue with him, suspecting that he'd follow a strict path of self-justification. Imagine my surprise when, with an honesty unknown to myself . . . he spoke of gutted women and ashen cities, hangings and lootings, screaming soldiers and the stratagems of corrupt politicians with a cool sadness, a fluent inevitable pity. But I wasn't going to let that fool me. So, from a mountain of indignant legends, bizarre history, demented rumours and obscene folklore, I accused the butcher not merely of following the most atrocious of humanity's examples . . . but also of creating precedents of such immeasurable vileness that his name, when uttered on the lips of the unborn a thousand years hence, would ignite a rage of hate in the hearts of even the most tolerant and gentle. . . .
>
> I would remind you, returned the butcher, that you invited me here. I am the guest of your imagination, therefore have the grace to hear me out. I am not altogether responsible for the fact that you were reared to hate and fear my name.[20]

'Hearing Cromwell out' in this way requires confronting the uncomfortable fact of his contribution to modern Irish identity, rather than erecting a simplistic Self-Other binary which reinforces old mythologies: some of Cromwell's men married Irish women: 'Their children and their children's children grew / To scorn the English, love the Irish tongue.'[21]

Thus, a tradition of public poetry still flourishes, even though we tend to think of poetry as a site of primarily personal expression.

A good example of how a poem can combine overt political comment with an implicitly political form is Linton Kwesi Johnson's 'Wat about di Workin Claas?'[22] The poem is from Johnson's collection *Tings an Times* (1991), which is a commentary on the 'state of the nation' from the point of view of an Afro-Caribbean British citizen. Johnson situates his poems historically and *Tings an Times* includes poems about the Brixton riots of the 1980s, the fall of eastern European totalitarianism at the end of that decade, and on specific incidents such as the racist arson attack on party-goers at New Cross which resulted in the deaths of 14 people. A significant point about the poems of *Tings an Times* is that formally they are in the tradition of the ballad or the song commenting on public event. As we saw in Chapter 3, this tradition was part of the expression of non-literate communities and has often been deval- ued or marginalized by the invocation of institutionalized literary values.

More specifically, Johnson draws on a rich tradition of public performance of poetry and song from his Caribbean background. This tradition includes the calypso and the reggae song, which are both often improvised occasional performances, often not recorded or put into writing.

'Wat about di Workin Claas?' is made up of four stanzas, three of which have nine lines and the second stanza having eight. Typical of Johnson's work, from its opening lines the poem's language challenges the formats of standard English:

> fram Inglan to Poelan
> evry step acraas di oweshan
> di rulin claases dem is in a mess – o yes

In spite of the fracturing of the language, the poem's formal qualities are very traditional ones. It is based in fairly regular iambics, although the number of feet in each line varies from two to six (the third line quoted above is a regular iambic hexameter). Rhyme is simple and powerful although not apparently based on a prior scheme. For instance, in stanza 3 the rhymes are wes/bes/yes/day/evryday/nowaday/everywhey/day/nowaday, making a scheme of aaabbbbbb. Stanza 1, however, rhymes aabbbbbbcc and stanza 2 abaaacdd. Rhyme is important to the poem but, significantly, the lack of a scheme that each stanza obeys gives it an improvisational quality that is appropriate to the form of calypso and reggae.

Another significant dimension of the rhymes in the poem is that to hear them as full rhymes we have to hear the voice of the speaker (or singer) rather than standard English. An obvious example is the first rhyme, Poelan/oweshan. In standard English 'Poland' and 'Ocean' might be considered a half-rhyme but certainly not a full rhyme. Yet here the representation of the words to reflect the speech of a British Caribbean speaker indicates that there is a full rhyme. This is a recurring feature of the poem, again, typical of Johnson's work: you can see in stanza 3 'everwhey' (everywhere) rhymes with 'evryday'. Thematically, the poem is about remembrance, and a key phrase in the poem is concerned with what 'wi naw goh figet'. The poet claims that in the turmoil of insurrection and social change (with the Solidarity movement in Poland, for instance) the real injustices of the working class everywhere must not be forgotten. As well as the systemic injustice to the worker who pays the cost ('wi pay di caas') of supporting an unjust system, what must also be commemorated are particular incidents testifying to hatred in society: the New Cross fire particularly. The poem ends with a pun on New Cross and 'new cross' – the new injustices borne by the black worker, seen as a crucified slave:

> wi pay di caas
> wi suffah di laas
> an wi naw goh figet New Craas
> nat a raas
> wi naw goh figet new craas

The dynamic of the poem is between these larger injustices (new craas) and specific ones (New Craas); actually the next poem in the book is a commemoration of the victims of the fire.

'Wat about di Workin Claas?' is clearly political in content, if by political we understand that it thematically provides a perspective on public events, as does Wordsworth's 'London, 1802', Shelley's 'Mask of Anarchy' or Tony Harrison's *v*. It is also political in the attitude that it takes to those events, calling to our attention injustice, inequality, and, in one of the traditional roles of the poet, giving a voice to those who effectively have none. But it is important to see that the form and language of the poem also have political implications; again, as in the best poetry, there is a consonance of form and content, tenor and vehicle. For instance, the poem does not only ask us to see contemporary Britain from a particular point of view, it effectively enacts that point of view through the form of its language. In reading the poem we must, however tentatively, perhaps, start to inhabit the world-view of the poet, because the language in its pronunciations and idiomatic grammar is distinctively his language. It makes a difference to hear and say 'Poelan' rather than 'Poland' or to find that the words 'class', 'boss' and 'cost' can rhyme fully. However temporarily, we see and hear the world from the point of view of another. Since that other is part of a racial minority it is likely that the white reader is also briefly seeing her or his world from a different perspective.

Although it can look challengingly or disturbingly new on the page, 'Wat about di Workin Claas?' is a deeply traditional poem. Thematically it is entirely within a tradition of working-class radical writing and technically it brings together traditions from different sources. Its basis in performance as song is also very traditional – a tradition actually older than that of printed poetry, since Johnson writes his poem within an oral performative tradition (as well as being available as a book, *Tings an Times* exists as a record in which the poems are read to a heavy reggae beat). There is a validation of speech rhythms in the poem coexistent with a recognition of the lives of the common people which is as much part of poetry as Wordsworth's early work. Nor should the representation of a 'fractured' English in the poem be seen as something dangerously novel. Not only has non-standard English often been represented poetically, in the work of radical poets such as Robert Burns and William Barnes, but the importance of actual speech rather than standard English has often been validated less obviously. We tend to think now of Keats as a completely canonical standard English writer, but his cockney speech was derided by his contemporaries and led to his marginalization. In his poem 'Them & [uz]' Tony Harrison reminds us that in Wordsworth's speech 'matter' and 'water' were full rhymes.[23] The experience of hearing poetry was very different before the rise of standard English – find any current recording of an actor reading the poetry of Keats, Wordsworth or Hardy and you will certainly not hear their accents in the performance. Johnson avoids such misrepresentation by attempting typographically to represent authentic speech. The result is a poem and a body of work demonstrating how impressively the rich radical political traditions of canonical poetry, so often obscured, can be developed by a contemporary writer.

Endnotes

1 Marianne Moore, 'Poetry', in *Norton Anthology of Poetry*, p. 1218.
2 Shelley, 'A Defence of Poetry', in *Romanticism: An Anthology*, p. 969.
3 *Canu Aneirin* [*The Poetry of Aneirin*], ed. Ifor Williams (Cardiff, 1978), p. 3. Free translation by Darryl Jones.
4 Ovid, *Metamorphoses*, trans. Mary M. Innes (Harmondsworth, 1955), pp. 41–3.
5 Ted Hughes, *Rain Charm for the Duchy and other Laureate Poems* (London, 1992), p. 5.
6 *Rain Charm for the Duchy*, p. 53.
7 Thomas Paine, 'The Rights of Man', in *The Thomas Paine Reader*, ed. Michael Foot and Isaac Kramnick (Harmondsworth, 1987), p. 225.
8 See Raymond Williams, *The Long Revolution* (London, 1961, 1992).
9 *Norton Anthology of Poetry*, p. 600.
10 *Bloomsbury Dictionary of Quotations*, p. 200. Johnson was writing from personal experience here, following his dealings with his own patron, Lord Chesterfield, to whom he wrote: 'Is not a Patron, my Lord, one who looks with unconcern on a man struggling for life in the water, and, when he has reached ground encumbers him with help?' *The Oxford Dictionary of Quotations*, third edition (London, 1981), p. 274.
11 Thomas Gray, *The Poems of Thomas Gray, with a Selection of Letters and Essays* (London, 1912), pp. 12–13.
12 See Edmund Burke, *A Philosophical Enquiry into the Origin of our Ideas of the Sublime and Beautiful*, ed. Adam Phillips (Oxford, 1990), pp. 36–7, 53–4.
13 Wordsworth and Coleridge, *Lyrical Ballads*, p. 113.
14 *Lyrical Ballads*, pp. 115–16.
15 Terence Brown, *Ireland: A Social and Cultural History 1922–79* (Glasgow, 1981), p. 80.
16 Abse, *Twentieth Century Anglo-Welsh Poetry*, p. 15.
17 Allen Curnow, *Collected Poems, 1933–73* (Wellington, 1974), p. 105.
18 Stuart Murray, *Never a Soul at Home: New Zealand Literary Nationalism and the 1930s* (Wellington, 1998), p. 240.
19 Brendan Kennelly, *Cromwell: A Poem* (Newcastle, 1987), p. 81.
20 Kennelly, *Cromwell*, p. 15.
21 Kennelly, *Cromwell*, p. 56.
22 Linton Kwesi Johnson, *Tings an Times: Selected Poems* (Newcastle, 1991), p. 37.
23 Tony Harrison, *Selected Poems* (Harmondsworth, 1985), p. 123.

|9|

The limits of poetry

The social revolution . . . cannot draw its poetry from the past, but only from the future.

Karl Marx[1]

Ezra Pound once wrote that there was a fundamental distinction to be made between poems that could be read and those that could not. This is a useful starting-point for considering the ways in which poets have sometimes brought poetry to its limits. At times these limits represent the way in which poetry shades off into other arts. For instance, at one end of the scale, the poem may be apprehended primarily as a piece of music, to be heard and appreciated for its sound qualities. At the other end, it may be considered primarily as a visual art, seen on the page and appreciated in some measure, if not predominantly, in the way that a painting or a photograph might be. This is a very ancient way of looking at poetry; Aristotle described it, and since the first century Horace's dictum 'Ut pictura poesis' ('as is painting, so is poetry'), has been widely quoted. The poem closest to being a painting is, in Pound's sense, close to being 'unreadable' in that its verbal qualities may not depend on a sequential apprehension of meaning. Quite often poets are explicit about whether they see poetry as most like painting or most like music. For example, T. S. Eliot emphasized the musical qualities of poetry, and considered these essential to what poetry meant. In this he was following Walter Pater, who wrote that all art 'constantly aspires towards the condition of music'.[2] Eliot stated that it is the music of a poem that matters more than its paraphrasable meaning, because it was the music which gave it memorability, individuality: 'the music of poetry is not something which exists apart from its meaning'.[3] Indeed, the very meaning of the poem is in the full experience of it rather than in simply receiving the paraphrasable: 'If we are moved by a poem, it has meant something, perhaps something important, to us; if we are not moved, then it is, as poetry, meaningless.'[4] Eliot himself is not a poet who abandons the referential meanings of words for the sake of their sound quality alone, but he is certain in his identification of a musical element as crucial to our experience of and pleasure in poetry.

By contrast, other poets have written poems that accentuate the visual qualities of the printed poem. Pound's distinction between poems that we can and cannot read is a useful one in thinking about so-called 'picture poems' or 'pattern poems' because these can be divided into those which are entirely readable but have a mimetic visual element, and those which are not readable. For instance, there is a tradition of emblematic poetry, in which the poem's words are so arranged that in print they form a visual representation of the poem's subject. George Herbert has several poems like this; 'Easter Wings' and 'The Altar' are examples. In *Alice's Adventures in Wonderland* 'the mouse's tale' is printed in the shape of a tail, and poets such as Dylan Thomas and John Hollander have written poems in this tradition. In these poems the visual element is significant but, it could be said, not central to our understanding of the poem – that is, the poem is not only pictorial. The visual has a supplementary, reinforcing effect that adds to the experience of the poem; it is one factor among others. We can certainly understand 'Easter Wings' by hearing it, without seeing it on the page, even if we would be missing one of the dimensions important to its full meaning.

The exploitation of the pictorial element in poetry rather than the musical is essentially part of the shift from the poem as an oral performance towards the poem as something experienced through print. In this respect, it is telling that Jonson and Herbert were historically among the first to utilise the possibilities offered by seeing the poem on the page rather than only hearing it, because it was during the Renaissance that the balance certainly shifted towards print. Nineteenth- and twentieth-century poets have often been very much concerned with how their poems look on the page, not only in terms of the arrangement of stanzas and so on, but in the choice of typeface and paper. Sometimes the very experience of the poem is intimately, if unconsciously, bound up with our sight of it. For instance, I prefer to read the poems of Wallace Stevens in the Electra typeface that was used for the 1954 *Collected Poems*. A note on this typeface states that it 'attempts to give a feeling of fluidity, power and speed'.[5] I experience the lines opening Stevens's poem 'The Idea of Order at Key West' very differently in a typeface such as New Courier:

```
She sang beyond the genius of the sea.
The water never formed to mind or voice,
Like a body wholly body, fluttering
Its empty sleeves; and yet its mimic motion
Made constant cry, caused constantly a cry,
That was not ours although we understood,
Inhuman, of the veritable ocean.
```

And the same words in the Electra font:

> She sang beyond the genius of the sea.
> The water never formed to mind or voice,
> Like a body wholly body, fluttering
> Its empty sleeves; and yet its mimic motion
> Made constant cry, caused constantly a cry,
> That was not ours although we understood,
> Inhuman, of the veritable ocean.[6]

For me, the experience and the pleasure of reading Stevens's poetry are not just intensified by this typeface, they are intimately part of it, so that reading Stevens in another font seems unusual and even disconcerting. This is (I hope) by no means eccentric on my part; Jerome McGann for one has explored the ways in which the experience of reading poems by Emily Dickinson is altered by their appearance in print, and poets such as Blake, William Morris and Yeats were very conscious of the part played by the visual in the overall experience of the poem.[7]

Important though the visual element of some poems may be, it need not be essential to our understanding; it is certainly debatable whether we need to read Emily Dickinson's poems in manuscript in order to comprehend them. But there are poets whose emphasis on the visual has been so emphatic that the poem cannot be experienced at all without recognizing the visual as forming the essential element of the poem. Such poems go further than the pictorial; perhaps by not necessarily seeking mimetically to represent the theme of the poem, but mainly by making the visual an indispensable element. There is a thirteen-line poem by Emmett Williams with the first line 'like   attracts   like'. As the poem proceeds, the same three words are repeated but with each line the words are closer together. By line 9, the three words have begun to touch each other; by the final line, the gradually coalescing individual words are indistinguishable. Visually the poem represents an arrow. In some respects the poem is conventional: that is, it has recognizable lines, we read it from left to right and down the page, and there are recognizable words in it. To some extent it is readable, until the final five lines when the words gradually become indistinguishable. Even then the poem could be performed, say by two voices which gradually merge (just as *The Waste Land* can be performed as a poem for different voices). The poem is also conventional in having a recognizable theme; it is about the way that attraction (the arrow could represent Cupid's arrow) leads to a blurring of identities. It takes no moral stance on this theme, on whether this merging is good or bad, but it observes, even performs, the idea. The reader could certainly supply a moral: for instance, suggesting that the poem is about how attraction leads to a loss of self, a loss of individuality as one identity merges with another; or about how attraction leads to a loss of self that is positive, an enrichment of individuality through the recognition of another.

Emmett Williams's 'like   attracts   like' is not only conventional but it brings to prominence aspects of conventional poetry that are sometimes overlooked. For instance, we tend to take it for granted that we read a poem from left to right and down the page, and that repetition and parallelism are often key elements of poetry. Most importantly, though, this poem reminds us that the poem exists only in the language that the poet has created for it. We can paraphrase the meaning of Williams's poem but in so doing we are very selfconscious that we are neglecting the experience of the poem, because the experience of this poem is in fact essential to its meaning. Of course, this is true of all poems. To recall the terms of Cleanth Brooks, paraphrase is a heresy; in Eliot's terms, the meaning does not exist apart from the music. But it is easy to forget this in reading conventional poetry because there we can often abstract the meaning without being overly concerned with the medium through which that meaning is generated. Williams's poem exists only in the form he has created for it. In fact, Williams himself indicated this in a note to the poem: 'This particular poem says what it does, and does what it says.'[8] In this way it makes us selfconscious about what all poetry does; it properly exists only in the form the poet makes for it and has no meaning except in that medium.

Poems such as that of Emmett Williams have been labelled 'concrete poetry', and are sometimes seen as closer to the graphic arts than to conventional poetry. Concrete poetry is an international movement which developed after 1945, in which the visual aspect of language is emphasized. It brings the poem closer to painting and further away from music – to use Pound's terms, by often being unreadable. The fundamental axiom of concrete poetry is that the poem is an experience and that a poem enacts meaning. In these terms concrete poetry may be seen to be an extreme version of conventional poetry, if we stress once more that in all poetry the medium is the message. But in concrete poetry attention is drawn to the very materials of the poem; the words become highly visible, 'concrete'. Selfconsciously post-Saussurean, the concrete poet places great emphasis on the non-transparent nature of language and seeks to utilize the very visibility of language. One can generalize about the shared aims and ideas of the concrete poets, but one thing that is emphasized in concrete poetry is that each poem does something different and does it in a different way. In concrete poems there can be no predetermined set forms, such as the sonnet or villanelle, because part of the poet's task is to make the meaning of the poem inseparable from its form, and thus each poem creates form afresh and only for that poem. Concrete poems are, also, often fun; there is a playful element which for some critics makes concrete poetry akin to the Dadaistic. Some concrete poems are like paintings in that we do not necessarily read words in a sequential order. One of many possible examples is Ian Hamilton Finlay's 'Acrobats'. This poem is made up entirely of letters from the word 'acrobats' elegantly arranged in different ways across the page. Here are the first three lines of the poem, which has 15 lines:

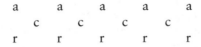

Finlay noted that he saw the poem as appropriate for a playground. The poem may seem fairly limited in the meaning that it conveys, but there is a mimetic element as the reader's eye follows the letters that make the word, thereby in a minor way performing the kind of acrobatics that the poem suggests. It is as if the eye must become an acrobat to see the acrobats. The poem has broken up the idea of reading from left to right and down the page and in so doing the eye is liberated, free to explore as it would a painting. Given this, we might raise the question whether Finlay has written a poem at all; has he brought poetry beyond the boundary at which it ceases to be poetry at all, but becomes a graphic art?

Naturally, answering this depends on how we define poetry and on how flexible that definition is. If we see poetry as purely verbal, readable in Pound's sense, then we might say that Finlay has composed something primarily non-verbal and therefore non-conventionally poetic (this is not a poem). On the other hand we could say that he has exploited a visual element that characterizes all printed poetry and that for all of its extremity the poem shares the fundamental elements of conventional poetry. It is only more extreme in kind than, say, e. e. cummings' poems; it is fundamentally similar in its techniques and effects. Furthermore, concrete poems generally make us aware of the most basic, yet most often overlooked, fact about all printed poems; that we experience them visually.

Poems which take poetry to its limits should challenge our most deeply held assumptions about poetry. Asking whether what is before us is a poem should make us become selfconscious about the ways that we read and think about poetry, to realize that although we may hesitate to write down a definition of poetry, we effectively carry a definition around with us, however unarticulated that may be. A good example of this challenge is the practice of writing 'number poems'. Although it is now generally forgotten, numerology in poetry has a long and distinguished history. Much medieval and Renaissance writing used numerological structures derived from the Bible or from the calendar, as we saw in the discussion of Donne's 'A Nocturnal upon S. Lucy's Day'. Parts of Dante's *The Divine Comedy* are organized through the significance of certain numbers, and the victory of Christ in *Paradise Lost* is placed at the poem's numerical centre.[9] In the twentieth century, however, the number poem might actually be made entirely of numbers in that the poet would arrange numbers on a page and present these as a poem. An example might look like this:

5 6 7
2 4 6
6 5 7
4 9 6
8　8

Is this a poem? We might observe that since it has rhyme and can be read so that it has rhythm it fulfils some of the requirements of formal poetry. Whether it has a subject is debatable, but if we recall the way in which the reader might generate meanings and a subject for a poem, then it cannot be said that the numbers are meaningless, since different readers will produce different meanings. For instance, I might see that the poem is about the way that in a technological society people are being represented more and more by numbers, and therefore this poem represents this fact by generating meaning in numbers rather than in words. Even if we said the poem had no 'meaning', this might not disqualify it as a poem. If we think of the ideas of Eliot and Pater concerning the music of poetry, we could say that the poem approaches the ideal of pure sound without reference; the poem might be heard and enjoyed just because of varied vowel sounds in it and not for any reductive meaning that they represent. We listen for once to the music of numbers rather than think of their referents. The divergent ways that poetry can move towards pure sound or towards graphic art can highlight conventional ways that we think about poetry and what it is.

Sometimes, the apparently new in poetry which seems to bring poetry to its limits is actually a revival of an older tradition or idiom. A good contemporary example of this would be the performance of poetry, which can be as varied as a small poetry reading or a rap concert or a gig by Benjamin Zephaniah or the experiencing of poems which exist solely as performance. Poetry readings grew in popularity from the 1950s onwards and certainly by now there are poets who are primarily live performers and whose work simply cannot exist in the stabilizing medium of print. Performance poets are often avant-garde and, again, may seem to touch the limits of what we think of as poetry, but largely they are returning poetry to its roots in song and restoring its dimension as a communal, a public, activity rather than a private one through the act of individual silent reading. The emergence of print culture and of private reading practices may have obscured the existence of this tradition, but it remains a vital one. As Peter Middleton states in a recent collection of essays on poetry and performance, even the poetry reading 'is an attempt to reintroduce features of the reading economy that have been lost'.[10]

In other developments in poetry, there has been a kind of breakdown of the conventional role between reader and writer. Concrete poetry clearly involves the reader in the act of making or discovering the poem, thereby highlighting the issues that were raised in Chapter 6 about the imaginative ownership of the poem. Some avant-garde poets have gone further than this in seeking the absolute breakdown of the distinction between poet and reader. In 1958 the poet Brion Gysin advised readers to become poets. It was quite simple:

> Cut right through the pages of any book or newsprint . . . and shuffle the text. Put them together at random and read the newly constituted message. Do it for yourself. Use any system which suggests itself to you. Take your own words or the words said to be 'the very own words' of anyone else living or dead. You'll soon see that words don't belong to anyone. Words have a vitality of their own and you or anybody can make them gush into action. . . . Who told poets they were supposed to think? Poets are meant to sing and to make words sing. Poets have no words 'of their very own'. Writers don't own their words.[11]

The language that the poet uses is not peculiar to the poet; it is part of our experience of the world and is shared by all. The poet is not a priestlike figure miraculously transforming everyday materials; the poet is more like a bricoleur or a second-hand dealer, using cast-offs. The poet can be anyone. The poet can be you. Logically, these concepts may be seen to develop from various sources. These include the twentieth-century shift in the nature of the poet from prophet to craftsman; the concern with the poet as representative rather than as estranged from the community; the breakdown of the supposed gap between vernacular and poetic language; the changing approach to language itself, in which words refer to themselves and meaning is generated through difference rather than through some mystical connection between signifier and signified. Gysin's urging to 'do it for yourself' perhaps reached its zenith (or nadir) when the Danish poet Vagn Steen published a book whose Danish title translated as *Write it Yourself*; the book was made up of blank pages.[12]

Playful though avant-garde poetry often is, we should not overlook the serious concepts that may be said to underlie it, nor imagine that it provides no perspective on what we consider more conventional poetry. This has been especially true of the development of Language poetry, sometimes designated L=A=N=G=U=A=G=E poetry.[13] The title Language poet is slightly misleading in that the term covers an actually diverse group of writers without an agreed manifesto. But the Language group, which includes Charles Bernstein, Ron Silliman, Bruce Andrews, Susan Howe and Lyn Hejinian, shares certain characteristics. Mainly American, they experiment in the poetics of language, developing post-Saussurean linguistics in emphasizing the non-transparency of the word, and are distinguished theorists in poetics as well as practising poets. Some of the poets see their poetics as rooted in the modern and post-modern poetic ideas formulated by Pound, Louis Zukofsky, William Carlos Williams and Charles Olson, while others are closer to post-structuralist thinking, notably that of Roland Barthes. In fact, Bruce Andrews approvingly quotes Barthes's statement, 'It is language which speaks, not the author', to elucidate his poetic manifesto.[14]

Typically, the Language poet eschews the idea of subject in the poem, because 'subject' deceptively suggests an unproblematic transparency which language actually lacks. Also typically, the Language poet seeks to defamiliarize language, that is, the word, the letter and syntax itself, to emphasize the way that we are positioned within language and to remind us that language is a system of organized signs, a game with its own rules, not some straightforward simulacrum of reality. Ron Silliman, for one, has sought to disengage poetics from a basis in speech, because speech is more suggestive of presence, of the relation between word and thing, than is writing. Without defamiliarization, we are prone to a form of self-deception about language's capacity to tell the truth, to engage a metaphysics of presence. Thus in a Language poem, language itself may be de-formed, twisted, lacking coherent syntax or organization. Furthermore, Language poetry tends to disturb traditional concepts of genre and of difference between poetry and prose.

Descriptions of the Language poets can make them seem playful, but along with their seriousness as enquirers into poetics, they see a serious social and political dimension to their writing. In emphasizing the non-opaque materiality of the word and the fact of language as a system, they are often engaged in making the reader sensitive to the social implications of language: for instance, in the way that language is inherently ideological. As Charles Bernstein has written:

> As persons, we are born into language and world; they exist before us and after us. Our learning language is learning the terms by which a world gets seen. Language is the means of our socialization, our means of initiation into a (our) culture. I do not suggest that there is nothing beyond, or outside of, human language, but that there is meaning only in terms of language, that the givenness of language is the givenness of the world.[15]

While Language poetry can seem to be primarily concerned with questions of aesthetics, it should be apparent from Bernstein's statement that those questions are inseparable from concerns about political economy and about how power is maintained in society. More explicitly, Ron Silliman has written that:

> By recognizing itself as the *philosophy of practice in language*, poetry can work to search out the preconditions of post-referential language within the existing social fact. This requires (1) recognition of the historic nature and structure of referentiality, (2) placing the issue of language, the repressed element, at the center of the program, and (3) placing the program into the context of conscious class struggle.[16]

For instance, Silliman argues, when we read a novel such as *Jaws*, we feel as if the words on the page were transparent, permitting an unobstructed view of a subject. This is an example of wilfully transparent, invisible language, which Silliman considers to be conceptually allied to a stage of capitalism and the 'anaesthetic transformation of the perceived tangibility of the word'.[17]

Language poetry is driven by an intense engagement with post-structuralist theory and selfconsciously requires that theory to be part of the poem. The intensely close connection between theory and poem should not permit us to class Language poetry only as a branch of critical theory. It can certainly be pointed out (and we hope this book has demonstrated it) that some form of critical or poetic theory underlies all poetry. It is more selfconsciously there for the Language poets because selfconsciousness about language and about the ideologies that drive and determine our lives is part of their rationale for writing poetry. Indeed, the very growth of selfconsciousness about being a poet and what is involved in writing poetry has been very characteristic of the twentieth century, as T. S. Eliot indicated in 1933. Another point about Language poets is that they are primarily concerned with print, and have moved away from the privileging of the spoken word as the basis for the poem, thereby dissolving a bond between the spoken and written word that has been axiomatic in much poetry.

One point which needs to be emphasized about Language poetry, however, is that as in concrete poetry no two poems are alike; this cannot be poetry reliant on set forms because its very nature requires an experimental, exploratory scrutiny of language. Nevertheless, you tend to know a Language poem when you see one. Here are the first five lines of Charles Bernstein's poem 'LIFT OFF':

> HH/ ie,s obVrsxr;atjrn dugh seineopcv i iibalfmgmMw
> er,, me"is ieigorcy_jeuvine+pee.)a/na.t" ihl"n,s
> ortnsihcldsel((pitemoBruce-oOiwvewaa39osoanfJ++,r"P
> rHIDftppnee"eantsanegcintineoep emfnemtn t'e'w'aswen
> toTT pr' –kkePPyrrr/[18]

Perhaps with 'LIFT OFF' we really have reached the limits of poetry. The poem is not made up of recognizable words. It appears to have no formal principle (such as rhyme, repetition, metre) underlying its structure; the line endings, for instance, appear arbitrary. It appears to communicate nothing to us, to contain no apparent meaning. It is not even musical or readable in the sense that a number poem is, nor even primarily visual in the way that a concrete poem is. Thus, if we think of certain principles that underlie poetry then this writing seems almost a calculated affront to them – and that of course is part of the poem's point.

It is interesting that the poem obeys a convention of poetry in possessing a title. As we saw in Chapter 4, titles can convey much to the reader in terms of expectation of the poem, and in terms of designating the piece of writing as a poem – titles may be said to perform an epistemological function in this respect. In this case, again quite conventionally, Bernstein's title does provide information that we need in order to appreciate the subsequent language. 'LIFT OFF' could suggest the launch of a rocket into space, and the jumble of letters could onomatopoeically suggest the noise of a rocket launch. The poem could be an expression of how the noise of technology disfigures language and ultimately can dehumanize communication. Another interpretation of the title, and hence of the poem, is that these letters have been lifted off something – specifically, lifted off the correction ribbon of an electric typewriter. On certain makes of typewriter this ribbon would be used to delete letters mistakenly typed on to the page. Thus the ribbon might become a record of alterations, perhaps of mistakes made or of the second thoughts of the typist or composer at the keyboard. I would suggest that there is a structuring principle behind the poem, in that each letter is a record of a deletion. So too, it should be noted, is each space, since in typewriting touching the space bar is also to make a record of something. Even space has become visible.

How far does identifying this structuring principle – to which, after all, Bernstein has alluded in the chosen title – help make 'LIFT OFF' readable as a conventional poem? Or, to put it another way, what meanings might be seen to be generated by the poem? I shall offer a few suggestions. I would begin by establishing that the principle underlying the poem, the feature or register that all of these letters and spaces share, is that they are deletions, presumably from one or more texts. That is, somewhere there exists another text or texts, lacking typographical errors, to which 'LIFT OFF' functions as a kind of discarded double. The letters and spaces of this poem represent an impurity which has made possible the purity of another text or texts. From this impurity we cannot generate the pure text nor guess at its genre; whether the text or texts were poems, letters, novels, histories and so on. This principle might generate several possible 'meanings' for the poem. For example, the poem is a reclaiming of something that is left out of final, written texts. It reminds us that for every written record of something there are exclusions, deletions. This observation might give the poem a political or social dimension, exploring the axiom, for instance, that minority groups have frequently been written out of history. If history is considered metaphorically as a text then symbolically this poem may seek to remind us of the exclusions that underlie (and even facilitate?) the historical narratives that we accept. In broader epistemological terms, the poem might be asserting the costs of kinds of communication. A letter, a history, an essay, a scientific paper, seek to communicate in an orderly and logical manner. Poetry itself has often been seen as a way of organizing reality: Robert Frost called poetry a 'momentary stay against confusion', and I. A. Richards wrote that it was 'a perfectly possible means of overcoming chaos'.[19] Such clarity and order, 'LIFT OFF' suggests, comes through denying chaos and the complicating deliberations and uncertainties from which order might arise. Here is a poem, then, which instead of the pure text that offers clarity, gives an insight into confusion, vulnerability, error – perhaps into the darkness and doubts of a mind which needs to deny these in order to function. Perhaps the poem embodies what Adrienne Rich wrote in 'The Burning of Paper Instead of Children', that 'A language is a map of our failures'. Another meaning the poem potentially generates has to do with the specific site of its composition. It is modern technology, represented by the electronic typewriter which has generated this piece of writing. Remembering this opens up another dimension of the poem; it may be concerned with how technology drives meanings, has become part of the ideology of control over language and consequently of our lives.

Naturally I am aware in suggesting these possible interpretations of the poem that I am responding creatively to it, rather than explaining what is self-evidently *there* in the text. But of course that too is one of the poem's effects, to make us selfconscious about reading poetry and, more specifically, to remind us that reading poetry should be a creative act, not simply an attempt to receive some message from the text. The poem makes me think of something that T. S. Eliot wrote in 1956 on 'The Frontiers of Criticism':

> as for the meaning of the poem as a whole, it is not exhausted by any explanation, for the meaning is what the poem means to different sensitive readers.[20]

To which it might possibly be added that unless poetry helps you become one of those sensitive readers, and unless you read creatively, you are not studying poetry at all.

Endnotes

1 Marx, 'The Eighteenth Brumaire of Louis Bonaparte' (1852), in *The Marx–Engels Reader*, ed. Robert C. Tucker (New York, 1978), p. 597; quoted in Ron Silliman, 'Disappearance of the World, Appearance of the Word', in Bruce Andrews and Charles Bernstein, eds, *The L=A=N=G=U=A=G=E Book* (Carbondale, 1984), p. 131.
2 Pater, 'The School of Giorgione', in Walter Pater, *The Renaissance* (London, 1910), p. 135.
3 Eliot, 'The Music of Poetry' (1942), in T. S. Eliot, *On Poetry and Poets* (London, 1957), p. 29.
4 Eliot, *On Poetry and Poets*, p. 30.
5 'A Note on the Type', in Wallace Stevens, *The Collected Poems of Wallace Stevens* (New York, 1981), n.p.
6 Stevens, *Collected Poems*, p. 128.
7 See Jerome McGann, *Black Riders: The Visible Language of Modernism* (Princeton, 1993).
8 Emmett Williams, ed., *An Anthology of Concrete Poetry* (New York, 1967), n.p.
9 See the entry on Numerology in *The New Princeton Encyclopedia*.
10 Peter Middleton, 'The Contemporary Poetry Reading', in Charles Bernstein, ed., *Close Listening: Poetry and the Performed Word* (New York, 1998), p. 279.

11 Brion Gysin, from *Fluxus I* (New York, 1965). Quoted in Williams, *Anthology of Concrete Poetry*, n.p. It should be noted that anyone trying to publish such a book would probably find that, legally, words do actually belong to someone else and that lawyers are happy to be hired to prove it.

12 Cited in Williams, *Anthology of Concrete Poetry*, n.p.

13 The designation L=A=N=G=U=A=G=E derives from the magazine of that title, which was edited by Bruce Andrews and Charles Bernstein and published between 1978 and 1981. L=A=N=G=U=A=G=E visually suggests the equality between letters and also seeks to defamiliarize the letter. An excellent selection of items from the magazine is available in Andrews and Bernstein, *The L=A=N=G=U=A=G=E Book*.

14 Andrews and Bernstein, *The L=A=N=G=U=A=G=E Book*, p. 54.

15 Charles Bernstein, *Content's Dream* (Los Angeles, 1986), p. 62; quoted in Sandra Kumamoto Stanley, *Louis Zukofsky and the Transformation of American Poetics* (Berkeley, 1994), p. 169.

16 Silliman, 'Disappearance of the World, Appearance of the Word', p. 131.

17 Silliman, 'Disappearance of the World', pp. 125, 127. See also Mark Scroggins, *Louis Zukofsky and the Poetry of Knowledge* (Tuscaloosa, 1998), p. 276. We might wonder whether the example of *Jaws* indicates a disdain for popular culture characteristic of the Language poets.

18 Charles Bernstein, *Poetic Justice* (New York, 1979), quoted in McGann, *Black Riders*, p. 110.

19 Frost, 'The Figure a Poem Makes', in Robert Frost, *Collected Poems, Prose and Plays* (New York, 1995), p. 777; I. A. Richards, *Science and Poetry* (London, 1935), p. 214.

20 'The Frontiers of Criticism' (1956), in Eliot, *On Poetry and Poets*, p. 113.

Further reading

For Chapter 1, students seeking specialist accounts of prosody or metrics should go to Paul Fussell, *Poetic Meter and Poetic Form* (New York, 1965, 1979); Philip Hobsbaum, *Metre, Rhythm and Verse Form* (London, 1996); Derek Attridge, *Poetic Rhythm: An Introduction* (Cambridge, 1995). For poetics in general, the magisterial *New Princeton Encyclopedia of Poetry and Poetics*, ed. Alex Preminger and T. V. F. Brogan (Princeton, 1993) is invaluable. Less detailed, but also less overwhelming and more accessible, are M. H. Abrams, *A Glossary of Literary Terms* (New York, 1957), J. A. Cuddon, *The Penguin Dictionary of Literary Terms and Literary Theory* (Harmondsworth, 1982, 1999), and Jeremy Hawthorn, *A Concise Glossary of Contemporary Literary Theory* (London, 1998).

Works on metaphor range from the lucid to the forbidding. Terence Hawkes, *Metaphor* (London, 1972) is of the first kind; brave but interested souls might wish to look at the work of Ricoeur – emphatically of the second kind – mentioned in Chapter 2. On poetic language more generally, see Winifred Nowottny, *The Language Poets Use* (London, 1962); R. T. Jones, *Studying Poetry* (London, 1986). Pound's *ABC of Reading* (London, 1991) is a must here, as it is for much of this book.

For the ideas of 'tradition' in Chapter 3, it is best to return to the originals: Eliot's *Selected Essays* (London, 1961) and Leavis's *New Bearings in English Poetry* (Harmondsworth, 1963) and *The Great Tradition* (Harmondsworth, 1962) (on fiction, but methodologically relevant). John Guillory, *Cultural Capital: The Problem of Canon-Formation* (Chicago and London, 1993) casts a sceptical eye over the whole business – too sceptical for Bloom in *The Western Canon* (London, 1995).

Balanced accounts of New Criticism are fairly rare since critics take issue with the ideological foundations of the movement, and it is most useful to go directly to the New Critics themselves. The works cited in Chapter 4 by I. A. Richards, Allen Tate, W. K. Wimsatt, Cleanth Brooks and William Empson are fundamental to understanding New Criticism, as is John Crowe Ransom's *Beating the Bushes* (New York, 1972). *Understanding*

Poetry, by Cleanth Brooks and Robert Penn Warren (New York, 1976) is a stimulating overview of poetry as well as a good example of New Criticism in practice.

For Chapters 5 and 6, the works cited by Barthes and Foucault are essential reading. More broadly, the move from New Criticism to structuralism and post-structuralism is the subject of some lucid accounts. Particularly recommended are David Robey, *Structuralism: An Introduction* (Oxford, 1973), John Sturrock, *Structuralism* (London, 1993) and Jonathan Culler, *On Deconstruction* (London, 1983). Culler's *Structuralist Poetics* (New York, 1975) is invaluable. Sean Burke's *The Death and Return of the Author* (Edinburgh, 1992) is a good account of that topic in the writings of Barthes, Foucault and Derrida. *Modern Literary Theory: A Comparative Introduction*, edited by Ann Jefferson and David Robey (London, 1992), is a readable collection of essays on topics relevant to these chapters. The works by Trilling, Peyre and Read cited in Chapter 6 are good for considering the concept of sincerity. As is obvious from that chapter, understanding of reader-response criticism should begin with Stanley Fish's *Is There a Text in this Class?* (London, 1980), while Jane Tompkins has edited a set of essays in *Reader-Response Criticism* (Baltimore, 1980).

Chapters 7 and 8 share obvious thematic concerns. For New Historicism and Cultural Materialism, see Paul Hamilton, *Historicism* (London, 1996); James Knowles, 'Marxism, New Historicism and Cultural Materialism', in Richard Bradford, ed., *Introducing Literary Studies* (Brighton, 1996), pp. 568–95. Though not directly concerned with poetry, Raymond Williams's *Culture and Society* (London, 1958) is essential reading. For an influential study of the legacy of the Romantic poetics, see Jerome J. McGann, *The Romantic Ideology: A Critical Investigation* (Chicago and London, 1983).

As noted in Chapter 9, the best introduction to Language poetry is *The L=A=N=G=U=A=G=E Book*, edited by Bruce Andrews and Charles Bernstein (Carbondale, 1984). Bernstein's writings on poetics are invariably stimulating; his collection *A Poetics* (Harvard, 1992) is especially rewarding and he has edited an important collection of essays on poetry and performance, called *Close Listening* (Oxford, 1998).

Glossary

In this glossary we explain briefly some technical and theoretical terms used in writing about poetry. It is not intended to be exhaustive either in the number of terms explained or in the explanation of them. We would strongly recommend that readers get into the habit of using reference books such as *The New Princeton Encyclopedia of Poetry and Poetics*, ed. Preminger and Brogan, *The Penguin Dictionary of Literary Terms and Literary Theory* by J. A. Cuddon and *A Concise Glossary of Contemporary Literary Theory* by Jeremy Hawthorn (London, 1998).

acrostic a poem in which a message or a name is revealed, usually through making the initial letters of each line spell it out.

aesthetics the philosophy or theory of artistic beauty.

affective fallacy term coined by W. K. Wimsatt and Monroe Beardsley to indicate the mistaken belief that the feelings a poem stimulates can play a part in critical judgement.

Alexandrine a twelve-syllable line, most closely associated with French neo-Classical prosody.

allegory a figurative device in which abstractions are personified as individual characters. Common in medieval poetry.

alliteration the repetition of consonants for certain effects. Before rhyme was used in English poetry, alliteration was the chief means of achieving musical and memorable effects, as in **alliterative verse**.

anthem a poem or song characterized by a stirring emotionalism, frequently nationalistic; originally a sacred song of praise or gladness.

apostrophe an address to an absent person, thing or place as if it were present.

assonance the repetition of similar vowel sounds for melodious emphasis; **dissonance** being the use of vowel sounds to suggest disharmony or uncertainty.

Augustan poetry in English, a poetic movement of the early eighteenth century characterized by wit, order and rationalism, and formally by the heavy use of the heroic couplet.

ballad a short narrative poem, originally a song and maintaining strong links with an oral tradition. The ballad usually deals with a single event in straightforward language. Formally it is usually made up of four-line stanzas in **ballad metre**, that is, with four stresses in the first and third lines and three in the second and fourth.

blank verse poetry written in unrhymed iambic pentameters. Famously the verse form of Milton's *Paradise Lost*.

caesura a discernible pause, usually occurring about the middle of a line of poetry, sometimes used by poets for particular effects.

calypso an improvised song or ballad, often a commentary on contemporary events. It originated in the West Indies.

canon an evaluative list of the great works of literature, usually for study at university.

closure the ending of the poem.

conceit an extended image, often ingenious or extravagant, sometimes continuing throughout an entire poem.

concrete poetry international movement which developed after 1945 and exploited the visual aspects of language. Concrete poems are often close to graphic art and may be unreadable in a conventional way.

confessional poetry poetry in which often intimate details of the poet's personal life are included in the poem. Especially associated with American poetry since the 1950s.

country house poetry a form with its origins in the seventeenth century, in which the landed estate or estate management is used to symbolize a harmonious vision of society.

couplet paired lines of verse, often rhyming.

Dada European artistic movement of the early twentieth century, characterized by nihilism, absurdity and a propensity for meaningless utterance. Also **Dadaism, Dadaistic.**

deconstruction critical approach emphasizing the text as an unstable and self-negating linguistic construct.

dialectic or **dialectics** the synthesis of different or opposing ideas in a unified whole.

dimeter a poetic line of two metrical feet.

dramatic monologue poem in which a particular persona speaks to a supposed audience.

dub poetry performance poetry which developed in Jamaica and Britain in the 1970s, involving the poet's words interacting with a heavy musical beat, usually reggae.

elegy a serious, formal poem of celebration or commemoration, usually though not always written on the occasion of a death.

enjambment a running-over of sound or meaning from one poetic line or couplet to the next.

epic a long, serious narrative poem, typically articulating a historical, national or mythological narrative.

epistemology the philosophy of knowledge.

epithalamion poem written to celebrate a marriage; the term derives from Edmund Spenser's poem with that title. A **prothalamion** celebrates a double marriage.

foot a regularized, repeated unit of stress in a poetic line; a pattern of stressed (/) and unstressed (˘) syllables. These are some of the most common metrical feet:

anapaest ˘ ˘ /
choriamb / ˘ ˘ /
cretic (or **amphimacer**) / ˘ /
dactyl / ˘ ˘
dibrach (or **pyrrhic**) ˘ ˘
iamb ˘ /
spondee / /
trochee / ˘

Formalism a critical-theoretical method which identifies form as the defining characteristic of literary discourse, and thus the proper focus for critical attention. Most closely associated with Russian critics of the early twentieth century.

found poem poem in which words not intended as poetry are presented as if they were.

free verse poetry not structured according to a set metrical pattern and usually irregular in line length.

haiku a three-line poem, usually imagistic, derived from a Japanese tradition. The first and third lines have five syllables and the second line has seven. A **tanka** has five lines with, respectively, five, seven, five, seven, seven syllables.

hermeneutics methods of textual interpretation, usually on historical principles, with their roots in Biblical exegesis. In modern theoretical terms, used to denote the art or science of interpretation.

heroic couplet rhyming couplets in iambic pentameters, characterized by internal symmetry or parallelism across the couplet and, within lines, across the caesura. Historically associated with Augustan poetry.

hexameter a poetic line of six metrical feet.

iconography the presentation of visual images to represent abstractions, often with religious or cultural significance.

image a word or words, usually used figuratively, invoking sense perceptions; **imagery** is the collective term for images, usually in the single poem.

Imagism an influential literary movement, begun in the early twentieth century, which emphasized that the image, rather than a narrative or discursive language, was central to the poem's communication of meaning.

implied author an author figure implied by or written into a text, as opposed to its actual physical author.

implied reader the typical reader presupposed or addressed by a literary text, as opposed to an actual physical reader.

intentional fallacy term coined by W. K. Wimsatt and Monroe Beardsley to indicate the mistaken belief that a poet's intentions can be invoked in critical evaluation of the poem.

internal rhyme the rhyming of words within the line of poetry.

interpretive community a group of readers with shared values or back-grounds, who are thus likely to produce similar interpretations of a given text.

Language poetry started in the 1970s in reaction to Romantic or expressive poetry. In Language poetry the non-transparent nature of language is emphasized and questions concerning language are made prominent.

limerick almost exclusively used for comic (and often indecent) verse, it is made up of five lines of varied length, rhymed aabba with a distinctive anapaestic rhythm.

long line a non-metrical poetic line of greater than usual length.

lyric literally meaning to be sung accompanied by the lyre, lyric has come to mean a short poem usually expressive of the poet's emotions.

Martian poetry a type of modern poetry which attempts to view objects as if they had no cultural or linguistic context. The name is taken from Craig Raine's poem 'A Martian Sends a Postcard Home'.

memento mori 'remember that you have to die'; an artistic trope consisting of reminders of mortality and death, common in medieval and Renaissance art.

metaphor a figure of speech whereby one thing or idea is represented by implicit comparison with another. It is distinct from simile in making a more compressed and implicit association between the things or ideas, and from metonymy in that there need be no prior association between them. In explaining metaphor I. A. Richards used the term **tenor** for the primary subject of the metaphor and **vehicle** for the secondary subject used to convey the thought.

Metaphysical poetry a type of poetry most strongly associated with the seventeenth century, characterized by formal and intellectual complexity, the heavy use of the conceit, and ideas drawn from science (including exploration) and philosophy.

metonymy figure of speech whereby a thing or an idea is represented by another thing or idea that has some association with it, as in 'the gate' being used to represent the attendance at a football match.

metre stress patterns; the pattern of stressed and unstressed syllables in verse.

metrics the theory or study of metre.

Modernism an artistic movement of the early twentieth century characterized by formal experimentation, literary allusiveness and, ideologically, a predisposition towards social conservatism and visions of cultural crisis.

narrative poem a poem that tells a story. Types of narrative poem include ballad, epic and romance.

New Criticism critical approach that originated in the 1930s, in which the poem was considered as an autonomous, self-contained object.

New Historicism a critical and theoretical standpoint that views history as inherently made up of textual representation and thus as ultimately irrecoverable to the present as objective fact.

number poetry while numerology was a key organizational feature of much pre-twentieth-century poetry, poems consisting of numbers emerged in the 1970s as part of concrete poetry and sound poetry.

objective correlative term invented by T. S. Eliot meaning the formula (such as a symbol, image or trope) created by the poet to objectify (and therefore express) emotion.

ode an extended meditative lyric, especially associated with the commemoration of public events and often ceremonial in tone and diction.

oral poetry poetry that was chanted or sung, and often improvised by the performer, usually in a non-literate society or community. Oral poetry considerably predates written poetry and still survives in a variety of ways.

ottava rima 'eighth rhyme'; an eight-line iambic stanza rhyming abababcc. In English, most famously the verse form of Byron's *Don Juan*.

parallelism the repetition of words or phrases for aesthetic effect used as the structuring principle for poetry.

paraphrase the prose representation of a poem's literal meaning, in words different from those used in the poem.

parody writing which takes the form of another piece of writing, usually for comic or satirical purposes.

pastoral a literary form offering idealized representations of country life; originally, 'pertaining to shepherds'.

pastoral elegy an elegy which figures individuals in idealized or representative terms.

pathetic fallacy the attribution of human emotions to natural phenomena or inanimate objects.

patronage the support of the poet by a wealthy benefactor, common before the development of modern publishing practices.

pattern poetry or **emblem poetry** poetry which when printed forms a pictorial representation of the subject.

pentameter a poetic line of five metrical feet.

performance poetry poetry intended primarily for public performance rather than for private reading in the medium of print. It has strong links with the oral tradition and can be improvisational.

persona the narrator or implied speaking subject of the poem, as distinct from the actual poet.

Poet Laureate the official poet of the British nation or crown, a position formalized in 1668.

poetic diction deliberately archaic, artificial or ostentatious use of language. The term is often derogatory, and as such derives from Wordsworth's critique of Thomas Gray in the Preface to the *Lyrical Ballads*.

poetics theories or philosophies of poetry.

post-structuralism a development from structuralism in which the language code is seen as inherently unstable.

prose poem a poem which although printed as prose, usually of a paragraph or so in length, exploits linguistic resources such as compression, imagery and non-literal language that are characteristic of poetry.

prosody verse theory; the study or theory of distinctly poetic elements. These include versification, scansion, metrics, rhythm, rhyme.

pure poetry poetry in which the referential element of the language is less significant than its aesthetic quality.

quatrain a four-line stanza.

rap a form of performance poetry, often improvised, similar to dub in being mixed with distinctive music having a heavy beat. It is almost invariably associated with African Americans and is often concerned with racial inequality and social conditions in urban areas.

reader-response criticism critical approach that pays special attention to the participation of the reader in constructing the meaning of the poem.

reggae West Indian music with a heavy beat, often utilized by dub poets.

rhyme the matching of the sounds of syllables at the ends of lines of verse. Since the Middle Ages rhyme has been a significant element in aiding poetry's memorability, and while it continues to have an important place in poetry, especially in popular poetry and light verse, it is by no means a distinguishing characteristic of poetry in English, and many major poets have eschewed it altogether. Louis Simpson has written that 'great poets use it, little poets depend on it'. Many poetic forms have characteristic rhyme patterns. One of the classifications of rhyme is between **feminine rhyme**, where words of two or more syllables are rhymed, and **masculine rhyme**, of one syllable (by far the commonest in English poetry). In some poems an unsettling effect is achieved by the use of **half-rhyme**, where the words do not entirely rhyme. An **eye-rhyme** occurs when the lines end with words that appear to rhyme but are pronounced differently, as in *bough* and *through*.

rhyme royal stanza of seven lines, each with seven stresses and rhymed ababbcc.

rhyme scheme A way of representing the pattern of rhyme in a poem or stanza. The first vowel sound is designated 'a' and each similar sound is also designated 'a', the second 'b' and so on. Hence the lines of

Shakespeare's Sonnet 73 end with the words *behold, hang, cold, sang, day, West, away, rest, fire, lie, expire, by, strong, long,* so its rhyme scheme is ababcdcdefefgg.

rhythm the pattern of beats or stresses in a poetic line, conveying a sense of movement or harmony.

Romanticism a literary movement of the early nineteenth century, typically characterized by self-expression and emotionalism, and sometimes by the use of informal poetic language and radical politics. More generally, taken to denote any poetry or poetics founded on self-expression.

satire poetry critical of some aspect of society or an individual, traditionally mocking 'wickedness' or 'folly', often with wit and comedy.

scansion the annotation of metre in a poetic line.

semiotics the science of signs.

sestina poem made up of six unrhymed stanzas of six lines, and normally a seventh stanza of three lines. The principle of this demanding form is that only six words are used at the end of every stanza's lines. The repeated words recur in a set order, for example, abcdef, faebdc, cfdabe, ecbfad, deacfb, bdfeca. If used, the three-line stanza, or **envoy** uses all of the six end words, three (ace) at the end of the lines and the others (bdf) within the line. The form originated in twelfth-century France. Some poets have used an even more demanding form, the **double sestina,** in which the six words are repeated over 12 stanzas.

signifier and **signified** terms used by Ferdinand de Saussure to denote the two elements that make up a sign; the word (signifier) and what the word denotes (the signified). His theories emphasized that the relation between signifier and signified is conventional and arbitrary.

simile an explicit comparison between two things or ideas, usually signalled by 'as' or 'like'.

Skeltonic verse verse made of short rhyming lines, usually dimeter, named after John Skelton (1460–1529).

sonnet literally, 'little song', a poem of fourteen iambic pentameter lines with various rhyme schemes. In the **Italian** or **Petrarchan** sonnet the poem is divided into an octet and a sestet, rhyming abba abba cde cde and the division between them is called the **turn** or **volta.** In the **English** sonnet, the first twelve lines are divided into quatrains and the turn comes immediately before a concluding couplet; the rhyme scheme is abab cdcd efef gg. A variation of the English is the **Spenserian** sonnet, rhyming abab bcbc cdcd ee.

sound poetry poetry in which the sensual apprehension of sound effects is more important than literal meaning or imagery.

sprung rhythm a form of metrics named by and commonly associated with Gerard Manley Hopkins, which allows for a metrical flexibility and deviation from standard syllabic patterns through the inclusion of extra, weakly stressed (what Hopkins called 'slack') syllables within a poetic foot.

stanza a group of poetic lines, often repeated according to a fixed pattern throughout a poem.

stress the emphasis placed on a particular syllable or syllables in a word. For instance, in the word *crimson*, the first syllable is stressed and the second unstressed. Metre is the formal patterning of stressed and unstressed syllables.

structuralism critical approach examining language as a code and how meaning is constructed.

sublime a philosophical aesthetics which transcends reason and produces awe by offering spectacles or ideas too vast or grand to be rationally comprehended.

syllabic verse or **syllabics** poetry patterned by the number of syllables in each line rather than by the rhythmical pattern of stresses.

symbol an image that represents both itself and one or more other things or concepts.

Symbolist poetry a type of poetry flourishing in France in the late nineteenth century and very influential for Modernism, emphasizing 'pure poetry' and the use of the symbol as the primary unit of poetic signification.

synecdoche figure of speech, a variation of metonymy, in which a part is made to represent the whole, as in 'hands' meaning 'workers'.

tercet a three-line stanza, generally sharing a rhyme.

terza rima a series of interlinked tercets in which the second line of each tercet rhymes with the first and third of the subsequent tercet, as in aba bcb cdc.

tetrameter a poetic line of four metrical feet.

timor mortis 'fear of death'; a poetic trope common in medieval and Renaissance poetry, often used for meditation on mortality.

trimeter a poetic line of three metrical feet.

triplet a group of three lines of verse, often rhyming.

trope figurative use of language, often recurring within the poem or genre.

typology a critical theory deriving from medieval biblical exegesis which focuses on the study of symbolic representation, and particularly on the ways in which characters or events refer to or foreshadow other characters or events.

vernacular colloquial or spoken language; originally, the indigenous or native language of a place, as opposed to the language of its colonizers or cultural élite. Thus, in medieval and Renaissance times, literature in English would have been a vernacular literature, as opposed to 'official' Latin.

verse paragraph a self-contained unit of lines of verse, usually in epic or narrative poetry.

villanelle poem comprising five tercets and one, final, quatrain, the tercets rhyming aba and the quatrain abaa. The villanelle has two one-line refrains, and they end each tercet in turn before being brought together as the final two lines of the quatrain.

zeugma 'yoking'; a figure of speech in which one verb predicates two different objects, as in 'She blew my nose and then she blew my mind' (the Rolling Stones, 'Honky Tonk Women').

Index